FURTHER MEMOIRS OF A BUSH WAR OPERATOR

LIFE IN THE RHODESIAN LIGHT INFANTRY, SELOUS SCOUTS AND BEYOND

A.J. Balaam

M.L.M. M.F.C.

Helion & Company

Helion & Company Limited
Unit 8 Amherst Business Centre
Budbrooke Road
Warwick
CV34 5WE
England
Tel. 01926 499 619
Email: info@helion.co.uk
Website: www.helion.co.uk
Twitter: @helionbooks
Visit our blog at blog.helion.co.uk

Published by Helion & Company 2020
Designed and typeset by Farr out Publications, Wokingham, Berkshire
Cover designed by Paul Hewitt, Battlefield Design (www.battlefield-design.co.uk)

ISBN 978-1-913118-58-7

British Library Cataloguing-in-Publication Data.
A catalogue record for this book is available from the British Library.

For details of other military history titles published by Helion & Company Limited
contact the above address or visit our website: http://www.helion.co.uk.

We always welcome receipt of book proposals from prospective authors.

Contents

Preface

Introduction to readers who did not read my first book ...
Bush War Operator

Like *Bush War Operator*, my second book is also a book of my memoirs. It is not my autobiography by any stretch of the imagination. Put simply, it is just a collection of incidents/memories that have stayed with me for my entire life. What made these incidents, out of the millions I have experienced, memories that stick in my mind I have no idea; the brain is a complex organ, and for some reason these stuck while others faded away.

The book is broken down into three sections:
1. My youth.
2. My Rhodesian Army career.
3. My life after the Rhodesian Army

1. My youth

I was born on 24 June 1948 in the town of Bulawayo in what was then Southern Rhodesia, the second child of 10. I spent the first years of my life on a small farm in the Matopos hills just outside Bulawayo. The only thing that grew on that farm was rocks; millions of them. My youth is about my growing up in Northern and Southern Rhodesia (now known as Zimbabwe and Zambia). This section contains stories that formed my character, preparing me in many ways for my career in the Rhodesian Army. It taught me bush craft, survival, self-reliance and a love of being by myself; but most importantly it gave me basic knowledge of the traditions and thought process of the black African.

2. My Rhodesian Army career

I joined the Rhodesian Light Infantry in 1966 at the age of 18. After several years I would move onto the Selous Scouts. In this section of the book I cover the highs and lows of my Rhodesian Army career: from the screaming and shouting of the parade ground and barrack room inspections to the stupidity of an army still learning to fight. From the bragging in the dark sleazy nightclubs of Salisbury to the brain-freezing, adrenalin-pumping fear of a fire-fight. The anger that bursts, like a ripe boil under the slightest provocation, uncaring who it soils, hurts or destroys. The stress of prolonged stints in the bush, working alone. The only communication with the outside world is your radio. These long periods of being alone left many soldiers, unable to communicate with their fellow humans, prone to extremely violent outbursts.

3. My life after the Rhodesian Army

In this section I cover various security organizations I worked for, including the debacle that was the Transkei. The inability by myself and many others like me to change from the military to civilian life. The continual struggle to find a job apart from working as a security guard. The never-ending search for the quick dollar and the adrenalin rush that combat brings; to rid your mind and brain of all you were taught in the army. There is not a terrorist hiding behind every bush, every thicket does not represent a potential ambush site and potholes do not contain anti-tank mines. And it is possible to take a ride or walk without being ambushed or blown up.

Introduction

Johannesburg, South Africa
Honey Dew, 17 July 2014

It was bitterly cold, wet, miserable and cloudy. The sun, as it fleetingly appeared between grey, sullen clouds, did little to warm up or lighten the gloomy, ice-cold day. The wind was blowing up a storm, cutting right through the two jackets and three jerseys I was wearing, at the same time sending leaves, clouds of dust and the inevitable thousands of plastic bags in all directions. The land was dry as a bone, the surrounding tress grey and lifeless, bending and twisting, as they fell prey to the power of the ravaging wind. The heavy, menacing clouds, the screaming wind, the gaunt, leafless trees and the weak, watery sun could have provided a backdrop to a *Dracula* movie; all that was missing were the ghostly castle, the smoke-breathing horses, the ornate carriage with the red velvet upholstery and the raven-haired, pale-skinned beautiful but deadly woman. But alas no, this was winter on the South African high *veld*, where temperatures can drop to below minus five and the wind is capable of cutting through steel. With trembling fingers, I finally got it right, inserted the key and opened the door. Stumbling inside on frozen, uncooperative legs, I disarmed the alarm and looked around at who knows what had happened during the night. This was darkest Africa, and bypassing an alarm was not exactly rocket science. Apart from the wind, it was just as cold inside the tin warehouse, where I was working as store man, as it was outside. The building was a fridge in winter and an oven in summer.

Clutching my large cup of hot coffee in frozen, shaking hands, I tried to get warm and think of something else, trying to shut out the cold, the howling wind and the previous night's nightmares.

Nightmares is maybe too soft a word to describe the horrors I lived through on an almost nightly basis: horrors that have gotten worse as I have grown older. My normal night's sleep was down to three or four hours of hellish nightmares, moving from bed to spare bed to couch as I tried in vain to break the sequence of scenes depicting the horrors of my service in the Selous Scouts and Rhodesian Light Infantry.

Some dreams were so real, it was as if I was still there in the Selous Scouts and had never left; they seemed to be happening in real time.

The nightmares were many and varied, but always started the same with me dressed in my long-sleeved shirt and jacket, filthy brown long trousers and balaclava, with AK47 clutched in my broken finger-nailed, filthy, shaking hands. Sweating, I was covered from head to foot in my old friend, the evil-smelling black camouflage cream. I would be struggling to get my legs moving, desperately trying to kick-start my fear-frozen brain and at the same time stop myself emitting soundless screams of fear, agony and helplessness.

The big pack on my pack, weighed down with enough food, water, radios and batteries to sink a battleship, seemed to slow all my efforts – both mental and physical – to a crawl as I struggled to escape the hellish but so-real situations I found myself in night after night .

Like a fly caught in syrup, I never seemed able to move or think fast enough. As ever, the overriding factor was fear; the fear of not being able to wake up. Even though everything seemed so realistic – the smoke, the crackling of the flames, the cries of agony, the flash from the rifle barrels – in a small, sane corner of my mind I knew it was a nightmare, a dream. But in another part of my mind I was equally convinced that if I did not wake up immediately I was going to die.

As the past and the present struggled for control of my brain, I stood there powerless, my watery eyes straining to see in the dark, almost supernatural silvery-blue light that encased everything, my nose burning from the smell of the twisting, whirling smoke. The heat of the yellow-red flames was burning my skin. There was the screaming, the pleading faces – both young and old, male and female – the shattered bleeding bodies of my enemy, my own sweating, shaking body, the unresponsive legs, the overwhelming sense of uncontrollable fear, the weapon that did not work ... I had woken up screaming, heart pounding like a drum in my ears, my body shaking like a leaf, sheets soaking wet from the acid-smelling sweat that poured off my body.

Now, three hours after my last nightmare had woken me up cold and sweaty, a hot cup of coffee in my shaking hands in an effort to keep the cold at bay, I tried to clear my mind for the long day ahead. Unfortunately, my mind, my imagination – call it what you will – longing for greater challenges, for something more exciting than selling bamboo boards and flooring, drifted back in search of something more agreeable. My memory, like that of most people, was very selective and had the ability to turn even the most dire situation into a pleasant and rewarding experience. Brushing aside my weak suggestion that I should prepare myself mentally for the long day ahead, my mind instead looked back to what it considered the good old days.

Part 1

Youth

The Farm, Livingstone, Northern Rhodesia, 1959

The eyes were big and staring, an odd white and blue, almost opal blue in colour, the ears pointed, the boiled skin and hair hanging haphazardly down their sides. A blue tongue protruded between yellow teeth. I was looking at my first boiled antelope head, impala I think, complete with skin, hair, ears, eyes and horns. My stomach heaved. Why, for the life of me, I did not know. I had eaten far worse things than a boiled antelope, and little did I know it at the time but I would eat far worse in the future.

I had been invited by my friend Snookie Van Der Merwe, who also happened to be my next-door neighbour, to spend the weekend on their farm just outside Livingstone. It was a chance not to be missed. I was fascinated by the whole family, who were Afrikaans. Like most of their nation, they loved the land and all the animals and insects that lived upon it. At the same time, they were not above doing a bit of poaching on the side. I can remember on one occasion the family purchased a glass-fibre bow and arrows. A large blanket was hung on the washing line and used as a target. The blanket was large and impossible to miss, plus hanging loose as it was there was little chance of an arrow going through it. In the following days and weeks, Snookie and I spent many hours sweating, swearing and straining, losing skin and blood as we struggled to master the bow.

It was during one of these practise sessions that Snookie casually mentioned that they were planning to smuggle the bow and arrows into the Victoria Falls Rain Forest Game Park on the off-chance they might get a chance to shoot a small duiker or bush buck. Who knows who was going to do the actual shooting. The bow was too strong for Snookie.

The family also did many strange things, or at least with my English upbringing they appeared to be strange, barbaric and even cruel. I had on one occasion at breakfast in Snookie's house seen an animal carcass hanging by its hind legs from a pole, its throat cut and a big tin basin under its head catching the blood still dripping from its throat. So recent had the slitting of the throat taken place that steam was still rising from the tin bath. (To this day I cannot remember what type of animal it was.) In later years I would go shooting with my Uncle Chappie and assist him many times in the slitting of throats of the animals he shot. I did not particularly enjoy the slitting of the still warm animal's throat, and could not understand the mad rush by all concerned, knives at the ready, as they ran towards the dead animal, lead by my uncle's dog.

It sounds so simple, to slit the animal's throat, but unless you had a super-sharp knife this simple task could turn into a sawing, stabbing, blood-flying disaster as you struggled to avoid looking into the wide, unseeing eyes of the antelope and at the same time try to cut through the thick skin around the neck to slit the throat. I asked my uncle why this was necessary, and was told if it was not done immediately the meat would absorb the blood, taste bloody and would make terrible biltong (traditional Afrikaner strips of meat). Later, when we got them back to our camp, I would see the skinning and gutting of the carcases. So why seeing the animal hanging by it back legs with its throat cut at Snookie's house stuck with me after all these years I do not know. Maybe because it was the first dead animal I had seen with its throat cut. The mind is a funny thing.

Of all the dead bodies I have seen, of soldiers and terrorists alike, the one that I remember most is not for example the body of my friend Jannie Nel, who got me to join the Selous Scouts and was later killed on our raid on Mapai, but rather my troop sergeant from Support Commando, the Rhodesian Light Infantry, Jim Kerry. Jim Kerry was shot at night, by one of his own troops, whilst on border control. The trooper concerned thought he was a rhino. Maybe it is the waste of a good soldier's life that makes it stick in my mind. I do not know, but stick in my mind it does.

Then there was the bottled guinea fowl, which because of its skin appeared to be black throughout, which I had been offered on several occasions to sample. One look at the bottle and its black contents was enough, and I had always refused. On the other end of the scale were the bottled peaches, guavas and numerous other fruits of which I could not get enough.

Getting my feeling of nausea under control, I had a closer look at my upcoming lunch. Apart from the blue-white eyes staring blindly into the distance, it didn't look too bad. Nothing to it; piece of piss. I don't know what I was worrying about. My normal Saturday lunch at home with my friend Robert consisted of Sadza and dried fish or kippers' heads, the remains of my father's breakfast. But it was dried fish with a difference – partially dried in the sun; it came complete with fresh, living, big fat white maggots. Not the odd one or two, but hundreds of them.

It was a standard routine every Saturday morning: catapult hanging round my neck, five or so marbles in my shorts' pocket to be used as ammunition, dressed in my Saturday play clothes, which consisted of a worn-out pair of school shorts, equally worn-out school shirt and no shoes. Robert, who was dressed in some of my old clothing, and I headed for the nearby black railway workers' compound, which was not only the closest source of dried fish but also produced the best dried fish I had ever tasted: not too dry, not too wet.

This was the same market-cum-compound that I stole Masis from for my fishing trips down to the Zambezi River. Stupid? Maybe, maybe not.

One must remember this was colonial Africa of the 1960s, where the white man reigned supreme. I was a white man in a white man's world. Sure they chased Robert and me when we overturned their drums of beer and stole the dregs for fishing, but we were only 10 or 12 years old and they were fully grown men, used to hard manual labour. Fit and strong, they most likely could have caught us if they had wanted to. The only problem was that once they had caught us, what were they going to do? I was royal game – to shout at me would result in the foolish perpetrator spending several days in jail, never mind being beaten half to death. To touch or hit me would guarantee a long time in jail. So why waste the time and energy and end up in trouble. Besides, the little I stole was not even worth the effort.

We were still a kilometre or two away from our destination when the first wave of flies and the smell of drying fish and rotten fish guts hit us. The stench was like a physical force; it literally tore the air out of your lungs and left you gasping. Taking a deep breath, ignoring the flies, checking I still had the half a crown I had taken from my fishing worm-selling business, with Robert by my side we pressed on, heading for the market. With the heat from the midday summer sun, the smell – a mix of coal and wood fires, rotting fish guts and brewing beer – was indescribable. The flow of black people heading to and from the market seemed never ending, all dressed in their Sunday best, some with shiny shoes and equally shiny suits, others without shoes, their feet badly cracked, wearing only tattered long trousers and tattered shirts. All were smiling, waving and greeting each other in loud, happy-sounding voices.

Some like ourselves were on their way to buy food from the market, others would be going to church and others still on their way to the many beer halls scattered around the place. From what I had heard, each beer hall had its own special mixture. Some added a bit of shoe polish for an extra kick, others claimed to add snake to get the special bite, but regardless, each hall had its own dedicated following. I often wondered what they talked about.

As we moved along the wide, extremely well-used path I felt hapily content. In no way did I feel threatened or out of place. This was me and this was what I was used to doing. I felt at home. The immediate area through which we were travelling was devoid of any large trees; they had long been cut down to supply the fires with the wood that was required for the non-stop beer-making. The odd remaining small shrub and tuft of grass did little to hold the ground together. Every little breeze sent clouds of red dust into the air, each dragging foot also adding to the red haze that seemed to hang over the area. Fighting off the never ending attacking, biting flies, trying our best to ignore the ever-increasing stench of rotting fish, we pressed on, following the path as it dipped and rose through the huge deep gullies that criss-crossed the area.

I had never heard of soil erosion, and I am sure most of the people around me had not either. If asked what caused these deep gullies, they would have answered 'rain' and left it at that.

In the distance and coming ever closer was the huge cloud of smoke that permanently hung over the market, as did the huge trees that provided shelter from the awesome heat for sellers and buyers alike.

There were hundreds of people, all pushing, all shouting, all wanting to buy or sell. All were dressed differently, some in bright reds, blues and yellows, others in the more sombre browns, greys and blacks. Some were with shoes, some without. Some had bathed, others had gone without bathing for days. It was another world, far from that of the white man. The dust was thick, red and blinding; stirred up by thousands of feet, it made breathing difficult. Packed like sardines in a tin, even if you passed out I doubt very much if your body would have managed to fall to the ground.

The heat was something else completely The air was moist from the nearby Victoria Falls, which combined with the burning African sun produced a steam bath second-to-none and the sweat poured off you in buckets. Add to this heaving, smelling mass of bodies the smell of boiling beer, dried fish, rotting fish guts and human excrement and you begin to get the feel and smell of an African marketplace .The stalls, for the want of a better word, were many. Consisting of a roughly thatched roof perched on four rickety poles, their owners sold everything you can imagine, goats, chickens and dried fish being some of the more popular. There was also the traditional medicine stall displaying dried snakeskins, baby crocodile skulls, African wild cat skins, supposedly lion bones, little packets of white man's hair and numerous bundles of herbs, to mention but a few of the items on display. All were said to have the ability to do amazing thing and cure every ailment known to mankind. The white man's hair, according to some sellers, made excellent poison, while others went with the line that to own white man's hair would bring you all the things that the white man had: houses, cars, money etc. As time went on things changed; now, to get what a white man has you need to own one of his arms!

Into this smelly, dusty, hot world of millions of flies, dark and shiny sweaty black faces, flashing white teeth and loud voices walked Robert and I. The fact that I was white and a child made no difference to the other market-goers; this was their world, and if I ventured into it I must play by their rules. I was afforded no special treatment. Pushing, kicking, fighting and screaming with the best of them, we eventually arrived at a stall selling what we considered the best dried fish in Livingstone. The 10-minute journey through the heaving mass of humanity that was the market had been long and hard. My once reasonably clean self and clothing were now covered in a thick layer of red dust. My bare feet, as usual, had taken a beating and were missing bits of skin here and there as they fell victim to the shoe wearers. My eyes watered non-stop as they tried in vain to flush out the constant film of red dust settling on them; my nose was so clogged up I had to breathe through my mouth, but my open mouth was an invitation to the million of flies to come and visit, which they duly did.

There in front of us, arranged in neat rows on what appeared to be old wooden doors, were row after row of dried fish, which seemed to move and change shape and colour under the continuous assault of countless thousands of flies. The types of fish ranged from bream to tiger fish, the colours from a deep reddish brown to very light yellow. Some pieces were still in the early stages of drying, with big fat and very alive white maggots; others, completely dried, had numerous small holes in them, homes of the once-thriving maggot community that inhabited them.

Sitting to one side in an old wooden dining room chair was the owner-cum-seller, an African lady. All I can remember about her after all these years was that she always wore red lipstick, had an amazing flashing white smile and had a soft spot for kids – both black and white. After much haggling, shaking of heads, rolling of eyes, shuffling of feet and threatening to take our business elsewhere, we settled on two dried bream. (It was always two, it was always bream and it always cost half a crown.) With our two pieces of fish wrapped in newspaper clutched in our dust-covered sweaty hands, we headed for home. We had enough fish for two Saturdays. Getting out of the market was even harder than getting in. We were now going against the flow of human traffic. I would have loved to skirt around the market and head for home, but unfortunately to the one side of the market were my old friends the beer-makers, and I did not want to tempt fate. To the other side was the railway line, which my father said if he ever saw me or heard about me walking along he would give me a hiding. (My father was a man of his word when it came to hidings.) So having little choice, we stuck to the main path and headed home. It was slow, very slow, and hard going, but eventually the stream of people thinned, as did the thick, cloying red dust. The same could not be said for the sun, which continued to beat down and we continued to sweat like pigs. Nevertheless, our progress became more rapid as we returned home. (Home to me was a big three-bedroom house; to Robert it was a one-roomed house – with a tin roof and outside toilet – which he shared with his parents. His father, whose name I cannot remember for the life of me, worked in our house as a maid. In the days of my childhood, black women were not employed to work in the houses as maids. Why? From what I can gather, one of the main reasons was the white wives were scared their husbands would stray.) Upon our arrival at home, the routine was always the same. Robert would start a fire and put two pots of water on to boil, one for the Sudza (ground maize cooked until it becomes thick, like mashed potato) and one to rid the fish of their unwelcome guests, the maggots. While this was going on I would sneak into my mom's kitchen, grab a saucer and a hand full of salt, and return to the fire with them. While waiting for the water to boil, I would go to one of the many pawpaw tress growing in the yard, collect some dry leaves and grind them up in my hands until they resembled tobacco, which I would later roll in newspaper – one for me and one for Robert – as our after-lunch cigarette. They tasted awful, made you cough violently, dried out your throat, made your eyes water and gave you a real big-time headache. But like the saying goes, 'No brain, no feeling', so every Saturday after lunch we smoked the pawpaw cigarettes, coughed violently, ended up with a dry throat, watery eyes and a terrible headache, and told each other how nice they tasted!

The smile that I am sure was on my face as I thought back to all the stupid things I did in the name of curiosity was wiped off as I heard my name called: "Andrew, what part of the head would you like?"

Livingstone, Zambia, the 1960s

The see-saw supports were made of a steel railway line, the car of tin. It was no match. The see-saw supports won hands down and ripped through the passenger-side fender and part of the door of my father's shiny new blue Zephyr 6 like a hot knife through butter. Bad times had arrived.

I had been sitting in the mango tree under which my father had parked his pride and joy, the Zephyr, trying to make a new type – any new type would do – of mango chutney.

In my hands I had an empty fruit bottle complete with lid, filled with vinegar and salt, which as far as I was concerned were the basic ingredients for a major, mind-blowing chutney. In the back pocket of my had-seen-better-days shorts I had, for want of a better word, a knife. It was one of those cheap blades that fold away into the handle and had cut my fingers many times. I was barefoot and wore no other clothing apart from my shorts. At this stage in my life, Tarzan was my hero and I would go to extremes in my attempts in to be like him: the odd scratch or cut with a bit of blood flowing always made it seem more like the real thing. Included in this world of fantasy was wearing as few clothes as possible, spending as much time as possible in trees, always hiding in the thickest parts of trees so nobody could see me (who knew where my enemies were?), eating all sorts of strange food and talking in grunts, not that I had many friends to grunt to. I was one of those lucky people – or unlucky, depending on how you looked at it – that spend the vast majority of their time alone. It was not that I did not enjoy the company of my fellow human beings, it was just that I did not talk much and took a long time to get to know people, which made people think I was a snob.

After my last business venture of selling most of the fruit of the mango trees in the yard to my Indian friend, and the horrific hiding that followed, I had decided to venture into the big business word of making chutney. If it was good enough for my Indian friend, who always seemed to have money, it was good enough for me. Success was not forthcoming. No matter how many mangoes I cut up and put into my bottle of salt and vinegar, no matter how long or hard I shook the bottle, they remained cut pieces of mango floating in a bottle of salt and vinegar.

Getting bored with shaking the bottle and eating the extremely bitter pieces of green mango produced by my failed chutney-making venture, I looked around for something else to do. Idle hands do the devils work.

Directly underneath me, shining and looking awesome, was my father's car. I had been warned not once but many times about what would happen to me if I as much as looked at the car, never mind got brave enough to touch it. What had happened in the Spanish Inquisition and the German concentration camps paled into insignificance compared to what was going to happen to me if did so. I knew where my father hid the keys; my only problem would be getting past my mother and grabbing them. My father at this stage was driving trolleys in front of the mail trains. Theses were dangerous times. The local black population was up to its eyes balls with the white population forever taking and never giving, and had decided the time was right to take back what they figured was theirs. They had started the ball rolling by blowing up the railway line; hence the trolley in front of all passenger trains. The powers-that-be must have figured rather one dead than a whole train load.

Sitting patiently in the mango tree, I had watched the washing line. I knew my mother was doing the washing of clothes and it was only a matter of time before she would come out and hang up the wet clothing. When that happened, I intended to grab the keys for the car. Every thing comes to he who waits.

Sure enough, after about 10 minutes of scratching, slapping and talking to myself – climbing and playing in mango trees without a shirt had its disadvantages, Tarzan or no Tarzan, as the mosquitoes still, bit as did the spiders and various other nasty insects – my mother appeared with a basket of wet clothing and started to hang it out. In a matter of minutes I was down the tree and back up with the car keys clutched in my dirty, sweaty, shaking hand. Once I had got my breathing under control and had rubbed spit into the skinless patches on my stomach legs and arms – the bark of a mango tress is rough and hard, and it takes its toll on skin if not treated with respect – I looked down at the car beneath me. A wave of caution-cum-fear swept over me. I had been warned about the consequences of touching the car.

Clutch in, one foot on the accelerator, turn the key, car starts. I had watched my father numerous times go through the procedure, and now as I sat in the tree it all seemed pretty simple. What little brains I had were overwhelmed by a massive wave of stupidity. So overpowering was the wave of stupidity that it even swamped my sense of fear.

My shaking hand took forever to insert the key in the driver's side door. The sweat was pouring off my body, my whole body was shaking; my sense of fear and instinct for survival were both on the comeback trail and were giving my stupidity a run for its money. Unfortunately for me, stupidity edged out fear and survival instinct, the key turned, the door opened and I stopped, my bare feet rooted to the spot. The point of no return had arrived. Up to this stage I had done nothing wrong, apart from taking keys which I knew I should not have. Keys which I could quite easily put back without my mother ever knowing I had taken them in the first place.

I stared at the dials, steering wheel and pedals, transfixed, and before I knew it I was sitting on the seat behind the steering wheel, checking if my bare feet could reach the pedals. The point of no return had now been crossed, I was in 'shit street', a long and winding road leading to pain and destruction. The key slid easily into the ignition and I turned it to start the car. After that, apart from the car jumping forward several times in rapid succession and a loud screeching noise as it struck the see-saw, I remember very little of my first and what would prove to be my most painful driving lesson.

How long I remained frozen behind the steering wheel before my mother pulled me out I do not know. Once out of the car, reality came to visit me with stunning and shocking force. On stiff unbending legs, body shaking, chest heaving and trying to fight back the tears, I walked to the front of my father's car. When I saw what I had done I could no longer hold back the tears. Sitting on the ground, I cried my heart out. I cried till I could cry no more. I might have been young, but I was not stupid. We were a large family and my father worked long and hard to support us, and I did my best with my fishing worms and fat cake business to help. What I had done was unforgivable. My mother and father never had much; everything was spent on us kids. And now I had taken the one thing they could call their own and had destroyed it. I deserved whatever came my way. As long as I live, I will never forget this one moment of complete and utter uncaring stupidity.

Part 2

My Rhodesian Army Career

Army RLI Scouts
Chimanimani Mountains Outward Bound Course, 1969

I had never been so cold in my life. I was blue from head to toe, the wind-driven spray from the nearby waterfalls and the thick, white, damp clinging mist only adding to my misery. Standing naked on the side of a freezing stream in the Chimanimani Mountains, I watched as my fellow outward bounders, chest-deep in the water of a fairly fast-flowing river, tried to make a raft using two empty 44-gallon drums, some rope and a couple of planks. Chaos reigned supreme, with legs and arms all over the place. Everybody wanted to be the boss, but nobody knew how to be the boss.

When I had been selected to go on the outward bound course, I was overcome with joy and happiness. It was like a reprieve for a condemned man. A peacetime army is a nightmare, especially for a person like me. Being a bit of a loner, I did not take kindly to the discipline and being continually told what to do. The screaming, the shouting, the drill, the 'left, right, left, right', just did not make sense, at least not to me. And the parades ... man how I hated the never ending parades. This parade, that parade, any excuse for a parade. Regimental Sergeant Major Robin Tarr hated me. Maybe hate is too strong a word; disliked me intensely is probably closer to the truth. He continually referred to me as a bag of shit with a rope tied round the middle. It got so bad that my troop sergeant used to lock me up in the Support Group Armoury every time there was a parade, partly for my protection and partly for the protection of the group, who suffered continual abuse because of my inability to move in a smart and soldier-like manner. It had taken me two recruit courses before I finally managed to become, for the want of a better word, a trained soldier.

As I stood there, the cold forgotten, concentrating on what I considered to be the vast array of stupid practices conducted by the Rhodesian Army, I was brought back to the real world by a harsh, grating voice: "And you troopie – you too special to get wet ? Get in there and help before I throw you in." Taking a deep breath, I launched myself into the freezing river below. Surprisingly, it felt a bit a bit warmer than the freezing wind-driven spray I had been standing in. Breaking water – my lips blue, my breath short and shallow – I made my way through the ice-cold, chest-deep water towards the squabbling, fighting, arguing members of my group, who had made little or no progress in trying to construct the raft ordered by our instructors from the ropes, empty drums and planks.

Pointing at one of the team members doing nothing but standing in the freezing water with his arms held above his head I screamed at the top of my voice: "And you my friend, what the fuck are you doing? Yes you, you arsehole, get your ass here and hold this fucking drum. Let's get the fucking show on the road before we all freeze to death." I was shouting as loud as I could to make sure I was heard above the thunder of the nearby waterfall, but also to try to wake the team up.

I was not in the best of moods. I had just spent the previous hour naked, sitting in a tree, trying to make a fire. All I had going for me were three matches and a couple of thin, almost dried branches. Against me I had a thick mist and a fairly strong breeze. Needless to say, the thick mist and breeze won hands-down.

I did not know any of my fellow team members – we had only formally met that morning – but I did know most were from the police, air force and army, and like me, were used to being shouted at and only responded to instructions issued in a loud bellow, followed by threats of death and various other nasty things that were likely to befall you unless you did what you were told, and quickly.

Staring at the first victim of my shouted army-style instructions, I could see the different emotions flash across his pale white face. The look of dumb indecision on whether to help his team or not was replaced by fear as my screeched instructions registered, quickly replaced by anger as he asked himself who the fuck this arsehole was shouting at him, and who did he think he was? As quick as the anger flared, it subsided and was replaced by a look of resigned obedience. Ten freezing minutes later, we finally managed to get something resembling a raft together, and had managed to ferry the instructor across the fast-flowing river without any major mishap. Thus ended day two on my outward bound course.

The following two weeks passed quickly in much the same vein, with plenty of physical exercise, road runs and map-reading exercises, and lots and lots of fish kedgeree, for breakfast, lunch and dinner.

During the third week I was lost in a dark and damp world of ceaseless drizzle, swirling mists, steep gorges, thick jungle, raging streams, unrelenting cold and ever-present hunger pangs. Standing in a small clearing, walking stick in hand, pack on my back, soaking wet and shivering with cold, I looked around.

What I hoped to see, Lord knows. Visibility was down to only a few metres. To say I was worried would have been the understatement of the year; not so much for me as for my three companions. I was tired, wet and hungry, but I came from the Rhodesian Light Infantry; I could handle what was happening and a whole lot more. Not so my fellow patrol members. Coming from Internal Affairs, they were not used to such physical exertion, weather conditions and lack of food, and already their heads were hanging, their walking speed reduced to a crawl. The thick, almost black fertile soil over which we were travelling had now turned, because of the continual rain, into a sticky goo. There were no paths – if there were, I sure as hell could not find them. Progress was painfully slow as we fought our way through the thick, jungle-like bush, detouring around massive rocks and fallen trees, wading waist-deep through fast-flowing streams as we pressed on, slipping and sliding. We were always heading for what appeared to be the high ground in an effort to get out of the valley we seemed to be in, and with a bit of luck to leave behind the thick bush, the rain and low cloud so that we could try to pinpoint our position.

Time seemed to stand still. My body became an unfeeling piece of raw bleeding meat. What my glazed eyes saw did not seem to register with my numb brain. Like a drunk person, unseeing and unfeeling, mumbling and talking to myself, I stumbled forward, tripping and falling as I went. The front of my long trousers had long since been reduced to a series of thin wet strips of flapping material, offering little or no protection against the freezing cold, continual rain, rocks, tree stumps and thick undergrowth. I had lost a large amount of skin on both my hands and legs, through continual tripping and falling. Looking down with dull glazed eyes at my raw pink hands, I registered no blood nor felt any pain; the same applied to my badly grazed and bruised legs.

A sense of helplessness, isolation and defeat enveloped me. I was supposed to be in charge of the patrol. The safety and wellbeing of its members was my responsibility. The pressure was immense and I was beginning to become a victim of my own stupidity. Instead of sitting down and coming up with a plan, I stumbled forward blindly, like a brainless beast in a horror movie in my own little dark, unthinking world of self-pity, all the while muttering to myself, and lashing out blindly at the thick undergrowth that barred my way.

Panic, anger, and defeat were beginning to take over as common sense and my brain – by now numb unthinking – were pushed aside. As I lost more and more self-control, a strange feeling of almost calm settled over my mind. It was as if I was an onlooker to the unfolding drama. I was there, but I was not there. I did not know if this feeling was a result of the lack of food and sleep, the freezing cold, over-exertion and panic, culminating in exhaustion, and the mind deciding enough was enough and taking a break.

Many years later, after the failed attack on the Presidential Palace of the President of the then Ciskei (the short-lived independent state in south-eastern South Africa), I was to experience the same strange, almost supernatural feeling of my mind – my brain if you like – being detached from my body, and myself becoming an onlooker to my own trials and tribulations.

"Get up, get up." The voice seemed to come from miles away, echoing in the empty chambers of my mind. Soft, but at the same time persistent and demanding: "get up, get up."

Slowly, consciousness returned and with it harsh reality. Struggling to breathe, I started to panic before I realised I was laying face-down in the thick black mud, held there by my pack resting on my shoulders. Rolling over onto my side, using a shaky bleeding hand, I clawed the mud out of my eyes and nose. Laying there soaking wet in the freezing rain, the front of my body – including my face – covered in thick black mud, twigs, grass and leaves, I struggled to get my breathing back to normal. The feeling of drowning and being unable to breathe was still fresh in my mind. Several seconds later, breathing now under control, I slowly opened my eyes.

Nothing ... just thick, white, swirling, morale-destroying, claustrophobic reality came rushing back. Nothing had changed. It was not a bad dream; I was still up shit creek without a paddle. Why it came as such a surprise I do not know. "What did you expect to see, arsehole, the sun?" I muttered as I slowly lowered my head onto my mud-covered chest, closed my eyes and let the air out of my lungs with a sigh. It took a few seconds of self-pity and "why me, Lord, why me?" before my brain registered what my eyes had seen. I was not surrounded by thick undergrowth, huge moss-laden trees, rocks or rotting branches. I was laying in the open on grass. Hope grew from a small flickering flame in the murky depth of my mind into a roaring blaze. Was this it? Were we finally out of the thick jungle, the rocks and the flooding streams that we had been fighting our way through for the last couple of days? Rolling back onto my stomach, I managed to get onto my hands and knees, the effort leaving me weak and breathless. Head hanging, lungs going like a set of leaking bellows light-headed and weak, I gathered my remaining strength for one last effort .This was it. I only had strength for one try; if I failed to get to my feet and stay there, I would be in real trouble. I did not think I had the strength to try again. Pushing all thoughts of failure to one side – ignoring the freezing wind, pouring rain and swirling mist, the groans and moans emitted by the trees as the wind twisted, turned and battered the huge moss and vine-covered branches, my exhausted muscles screaming, the water running from my hair into my burning eyes, seeing flashing lights and my head pounding – I fought my way to my feet like a drunk. It was touch and go for the first couple of seconds.

Screaming at the top of my voice, I encouraged myself: "Come on my man, you can do it. Come on Jim, come on, it is a piece of piss, a walk in the park. Think of the 40-mile march at the end of your recruit course, the blisters, the weight of the pack, the loss of skin on your back, the new boots that were too small, the raw bleeding feet, the lifted toe nails and the continual pain. You managed to survive all that, so you can handle this no problem. Concentrate. Pull yourself forwards. There is no room for self-pity; it is all about getting out in one piece. Survival, no matter what the price, is what it is all about."

Slowly my breathing returned to normal, the flashing lights behind my eyes disappeared, the roaring in my ears subsided and feeling returned to my battered body as my senses made a welcome return, and with them I returned to the real world. The strange, eerie, detached feeling of being an observer to my own misfortune and stupidity disappeared, replaced by a feeling of calm acceptance of my present situation and a determination, come what may, to survive.

I could feel the rain and wind against my battered and bruised ice-cold skin and, replacing the roar in my ears, the sound of the creaking, wind-battered branches. I was alive and it felt good.

Standing on the edge of what I hoped was a clearing, clutching my walking stick for dear life and fighting to keep my balance, I took a deep shuddering breath, slowly letting it out through my nose. At the same time, holding back the insane feeling of wanting to cry, I opened my eyes.

Everything seemed lighter, brighter, less oppressive. The feeling of being closed in, the doom and gloom of the proceeding days, seemed to disappear. There was no sun and the thick, swirling mist was still there, but splashes of orange and red amid its dull grey-white proved that the sun was desperately trying to show itself. Watching the trees on the other side of the clearing thrashing around in the wind as it whistled on its way to nowhere, it took a good couple of seconds for my brain to register and make sense of what my eyes were seeing and my ears were hearing.

The colours could only come from the sun, which meant the mist was breaking up and lifting, with gaps appearing for a few seconds before disappearing. Not wanting to believe what my eyes and brain were telling me, I lowered my head and closed my eyes: please God, let this be the clearing we had been searching for, the break we needed to get out of this cold dark hell we found ourselves in.

Standing with my shoulders hunched against the rain and the bone-chilling cold, I took another deep breath, slowly raised my head and opened my eyes.

My numb, exhausted brain, bleary red eyes and frozen ears had not been bullshitting me. The red-orange tinted mist, though still thick, was definitely thinning, while the rain was down to the occasional short downpour. Through the eerie mist, just a few metres in front of me, I could now see huge trees covered in vines and great hanging curtains of green-grey moss, their branches bending and heaving. Massive rocks glistening from the rain seemed to change shape as the red-orange mist engulfed them before slowly whirling away. I could hear the creaking and groaning of the branches. It was like a scene out of a *King Kong* movie: all that was missing was the giant ape.

My morale went up a few notches, having taken a pounding of late being dragged along through mud, rain, swollen rivers and thick bush.

This could be it, I thought, as I struggled to keep my emotions under control. If this was really a clearing, then the chances of paths running through it were good, and with a path came the possibility of getting our act together and completing our patrol.

I froze as I heard something. It could not be here; we were high up in the Chamanimani Mountains and I must be imagining things. Nobody could live in this bleak, freezing, wind-blown and rock-strewn hell. But regardless of what my brain was telling me, my instinct for survival was saying in even stronger terms: "Get the hell off the river-cum- path you are following and hide." But what if I had got so lost I had led us into Mozambique and straight into a bunch of locals. "Locals are fine, my friend," came back my brain, "but what if they are FRELIMO [Mozambique Liberation Front] armed to the teeth? What are you going to do? Talk them to death?" Do not panic, I told myself, you might not be the best map reader in the world, but there is no way you could have got so far off-course you would wind up in Mozambique. I might as well have been talking to the trees, for all the good it did me. Panic was in, and calm was out. It was all about finding a place to hide as quickly as possible. At this stage in my army career, I was as green as the grass and had been fed on stories about FRELIMO. These were the guys we spoke about in hushed voices in the bars, the guys kicking the shit out of the Portuguese Army, the guys who could disappear into thin air. Now it seemed there was a good possibility I was going to meet a group of them face-to-face.

In my mind, FRELIMO soldiers were a cross between Che Guevara and

King Kong: big, dark-skinned, red-eyed, afro-hairstyled, AK 47-carrying killers. People to be feared, or at least handled with care. In my present waterlogged, exhausted state, I was in no condition to handle anything. Even the smallest of problems seemed to take on gigantic proportions when fed into my half-frozen malfunctioning brain. When the word 'FRELIMO' finally registered with my brain, the wheels really fell off. My panic was replaced by full-blown fear. The fact that I was unarmed did not help at all.

With my head whipping from side to side, my eyes were searching for a place to hide; not to take cover, but to hide. To take cover indicates that you are preparing to take some sort of action against a threat you are facing. This was definitely not the case. When I say hide, I mean hide. The cold, rain. exhaustion and hunger were all forgotten; it was 'keep alive' time Dragging my battered and bruised body through the undergrowth, I managed to reach a nearby clump of mossy rocks, where I literally collapsed in a sweating, trembling heap. After much crawling about and talking to myself, I finally positioned myself so I was able to look up the path we had been stumbling along.

The barking that had sent me running to hide in the first place was getting closer, as was the shouting that accompanied it. Even my fear-frozen brain started to register that something was not right. Surely this could not be the fabled FRELIMO, the steely eyed killers who moved like ghosts through the bush, leaving no tracks and making no sound.

Shaking with cold, tired, soaking wet and hungry, I was still trying to decide what to do next when the decision was made for me. Out of the corner of my eye I noticed movement along the path behind me. For the couple of seconds it took me to figure out what was happening, panic reigned. As I would be numerous times in the future, I became a victim of my wild and uncontrollable imagination: "You are surrounded, arsehole, they have been watching you properly for days as you wandered around like a blind man, not knowing where you came from or where you were going. You walked into a trap and are in some serious trouble now; what are you going to do?" Before I could answer myself, I realised that the movement behind me was none other than the remaining three members of my group. Heads hanging, backs hunched under the weight of their packs, feet dragging, eyes staring at the soggy ground, they looked for all the world like dead men walking as they inched their way up the path I had just vacated in my search for cover from approaching FRELIMO.

I was the patrol commander. I was responsible for the safety and wellbeing of all the members of the patrol, not just mine. It sounds good, the old responsibility bit, but as I lay there watching my fellow patrol members inching their way along the path towards me, responsibility was not what I was feeling. Anger, almost hatred, flooded my emotions: "What's the matter with these arseholes; can they not hear the dogs? Do they not realise they are going to get themselves killed? F*** them, it is not my problem. If they want to walk around like they are half-dead, unhearing and unseeing, then they must suffer the consequences."

"Shut up and lay still," I muttered as I helped the last member of our patrol to remove his pack. My anger and 'F*** you Jack' approach had disappeared as quickly as it had appeared. Now all four us – our cold, hunger and exhaustion forgotten – stared red-eyed up the path, from which the barking and voices got ever louder. Nobody said a word. Like condemned men, unmoving, we stared up the path along which our fate was rapidly approaching.

First one dog and then another appeared out of the mist, barking, tails a blur of movement, one second there but the next gone as the mist lifted and then dropped. Suddenly the barking ceased and the voices grew quiet, and right on cue the sun burst through, and standing before us was a group of men surrounded by their pack of dogs. It was as if the clock had been turned back a hundred years.

Aged between 10 and maybe 60 (it is very difficult to judge the age of an old African), they appeared like a hunting party stepping out from the past. Dressed entirely in animal skins except for the odd colourful headband, barefoot, seemingly unaffected by the freezing cold and rain, they were armed with bows and arrows, spears and various knives. The entire group stood unmoving, staring at the rocks where myself and the rest of the patrol had taken cover. Even the dogs seemed to be staring at our hiding place. That they knew we were there was not in doubt; what they were going to do was. I had to make a decision. I was the patrol leader, plus I was a hairy-arsed commando from the Rhodesian Light Infantry, and the fact that the hunting party was going nowhere real soon put the ball in my court. While they were not FRELIMO, their weapons – though crude – could kill just as surely as round from an AK47. The main thing going for us was that they showed no aggression: they did not talk, did not point at our hiding place, they just stood and waited. Summoning up the last of my strength, dragging what little bit of courage I had out of my soaking wet boots and clutching on to the rocks for support, I dragged myself to my feet. No arrows pierced my body, no knives buried themselves in my chest, no spears flew into my stomach and no dogs ripped out my throat. As my morale climbed and my body stopped shaking, I spread what I considered my most friendly smile across my face, thrust a hand out in front of me and started walking towards what I now considered my saviours. The way I saw it was as they did not want to kill me, maybe they would help me. And if anybody needed help it was me. We had had been wandering around for days in the rain, cold and mist, seldom able to see more than a few metres in front of us. Whether we had been going in the right direction or walking around in circles I had no idea. We were weak and hungry, morale was low and our eyes – surrounded by circles of black from lack of sleep – were sunken into our skulls. Our flesh, cold and battered, hung like pieces of rubber around our frames, feeling neither heat, cold nor pain. We were no longer capable of logical thought, the brain starting to go into shut-down mode. It was all about survival.

As I slowly made my way forward, smiling all the time and trying my best not to trip and fall, I noticed everybody in the group tense up, their eyes scanning up and down my body, searching for what I do not know; weapons maybe? This was the border area between Rhodesia and Mozambique, a war zone and a smugglers' haven. There were no border guards or posts up here in the mountains.

One minute they were silent and staring, the next pointing and laughing. Who knows what brought about the sudden change. Maybe they noticed I was unarmed and posed no threat, or maybe they were laughing because they had never seen a worse-looking, run-down bunch of arseholes as us before. I did not know and I did not care, and nor, I am sure, did anybody else in our group. This was about survival, and standing in front of us were, as far as we were concerned, our saviours. Gradually the smiling and talking subsided, as did the pointing by the members of the hunting party, replaced by a heavy, expectant silence. I did not know what to do. I tried to get my brain working and come up with an idea, but it was a losing battle. All I could remember was seeing a movie where a group of explorers meet so-called 'savages', and to keep them happy they showered them with gifts of beads and mirrors. We had nothing to give; apart from our sleeping bags, packs and the clothes we were wearing, we were fresh out of gifts.

Coming to a stuttering halt about a metre in front of the group, with hand still thrust out in front of me, I managed a croaking "Hello". Nothing happened for what seemed a lifetime. The wind still howled through the trees, the great hanging curtains of blue-green moss still twisted and turned, the branches of the trees still moaned and groaned, the white-then-gold mist still whirled around, changing colour as it fought with the sun for control. My head drooped, my shoulders hunched, and as cold as it was I started to sweat. What little bit of hope I had that our salvation was at hand disappeared as fast as it came. "Shit, Jim," I muttered to myself, "is that the best you can do 'Hello'; you are in big time trouble and you think 'hello' is the answer?" As I stood there drowning in self-pity, it took a few seconds for me to realise what my now resurgent brain was screaming: "Somebody answered, you idiot, somebody said 'hello'. Pull yourself together, stand up, put your shoulders back. There will be plenty of time for self-pity later." Adrenalin surged through my body, my morale climbed in leaps and bounds, and the cold, pain and hunger were forgotten. Thank God for the British Empire and its spreading of the English language far and wide. Peering into the swirling mist with bloodshot eyes, hand still thrust out in front of me, my body tingling with excitement, I tried another "Hello". The replying "Hello" came almost immediately. With a huge smile on my face, on legs that were now steady I walked towards the voice. Out of the rapidly thinning mist stepped a tall, well-built young man. His shoulders were covered in a badly stitched cape of animal skins and what appeared to be canvas, both still wet and shiny from the rain, while around his waist he wore an arrangement of skins and tattered short trousers. He was barefoot, as were the rest of the group. Over one shoulder he had a quiver of arrows, and in his left hand he held a bow. He looked like Rambo ready to go to battle. Hopefully he spoke and understood English better than he dressed. If he did, he could be the key to getting out of this ice-cold, wet, morale-destroying, mist-shrouded hell hole.

His English was good and, more importantly, he knew the area like the back of his hand. My hopes soared, adrenalin surged through my body, power flowed back into my muscles, my eyes sparkled, my head cleared and my ears became microphones. This was it, my chance to get us out of the mess I had led us into. When we had left the outward bound HQ at the beginning of this so-called adventure, the chief instructor/owner, a retired policeman by the name of Bailey, had given us a list of places which we were to visit and items we were to recover to prove we had been there. Squatting down in front of our potential saviour, aches and pains forgotten, all this was forgotten. It was all about survival. After a long series of handshakes and jaw-aching smiles, I got to the point: we were lost, not a little bit lost but completely and utterly lost. I did not bore him with our long and painful journey. I took a chance and asked if he had ever heard of a person by the name of Bailey who had a farm in the area. The answer came quick and confident. He had indeed heard of him, and in fact we were not far from his farm. My heart soared, yet at the same time I cringed in shame. "My God," laughed my other half. "Here you are blaming everybody and everything except yourself for the shit you find yourself in, and it seems like you are the problem, not the team you have been running down non-stop for days." As bad as I felt for possibly having led the team around in circles for days, I still had my doubts on the "not far from his farm" claim. A white man's idea of distance is completely different to that of a black man. A white man is all about kilometres, a black man is all about the time; and he has no sense of time, hence nearby could be two days away or on the other hand literally around the corner. When I questioned him again on the distance to the farm, he thought it would take us two days due to the rough terrain we had to cover and the fact, as he politely put it, that we looked very tired. I got him to draw a map in the sand to help me understand where we were and where we had to go. In the rain it was easier said than done.

※

"One more step," I muttered to myself. "Just one more step and you will be on the top." My head was drooping, my blank eyes stared unseeing at my feet, my brain had long-since ceased to function. It was now all about willpower and determination, but I was on my last reserves of both, as were the rest of the group. The advice I had received from my hunting party had been short and sweet: "Get out of the valley, the never ending mist and away from the river and the thick, strength-sapping vegetation. Go up to where the mist is not a major problem, where the land is devoid of vegetation and the sun shines, and you can see which direction you were heading." One step forward; stop, rest, do not think, do not look around, do not break concentration. One step forward; my whole life, my existence, my reason for living was to take one step forward. One step forward, blind to what was going on around me, I blundered on, huffing and puffing, staggering around like a drunk. Warmth then seeped into my body, light battered my firmly shut eyes and voices assaulted my ears, but all this was ignored by my non-functioning brain as I concentrated on just taking one step forward. A hand pulling on my pack and a "Hey Andy, we made it!" brought me crashing back into the real world. Still bent over in a crouch, trying to take the weight of my pack off my throbbing shoulders, I opened my eyes. There were no trees, no boulders, no wet, muddy, potholed, stone-riddled path, no blinding mist and pouring rain; just brilliant sunshine, clear blue skies and rolling plateau. It felt like paradise.

I stared defiantly back into the eyes of Mr Bailey. "F you!" flashed through my mind as I stood there listening to a lecture on leadership. I cannot remember to this day if my group was first or last back to base, which actually was of no consequence: the big story was that we had not visited any of the sites we had on our list, and thus no tags to hand in. Hence the lecture. This was my introduction into being told what I should have done and how I should have done it by somebody who was not present as the situation unfolded, and therefore in my opinion he could take his advice and put it where it fitted best! Staring at the wall behind the man issuing the never ending barrage of advice and condemnation, I shook my head. For the life of me I did not understand what the problem was. If you mix the weak and the strong together, as was done on outward bound course, and the wheels come off, do not cry. People are different. Sometimes the strong get tired of carrying the weak.

As I proceeded with my career in the Rhodesian Army, I would meet many officers and NCOs who would also offer me endless advice on how to do things that they had never done themselves. The one thing I learnt above all others was that it was better to work alone. Your failures were yours, as were your successes. It was something I put into practise once I arrived in the Selous Scouts, and I worked alone whenever I could. On the other hand, I have worked with many of my fellow Selous Scouts on raids into Mozambique without a problem. We were all highly trained and of a high calibre, all professionals and cut from the same cloth. We all carried our own weight.

Zambezi Valley Support Group

Rhodesian Light infantry, 1969-70

The spinning wheels of the Ford F250 truck threw up great clouds of sand and dust as the huge V8 engine roared, but stuck in a dry sandy riverbed we were going nowhere in a hurry.

It was a hot, breezeless summer morning in the Zambezi Valley. The rains had not yet arrived, all the trees were leafless, burnt grey by the searing sun, and the remaining grass, long sucked dry, was more blackish-grey than yellow as it lay flat and listless. The river, which had not seen water in the last six months, was dry as a bone, its yellow sands reflecting the blinding heat of the sun straight up into our faces.

Wearing only our shorts and tackies, shirts abandoned, our weapons, webbing and packs on the back of the truck in an effort to keep cool, we didn't bother posting a sentry as we tried to clear the sand from around the wheels with shovels. A thankless task if ever there was one; as fast as we dug the sand from around the wheels, more replaced it. We had been at it for a while, constantly harassed by swarms of mopani flies and squadrons of dive-bombing Chewore buzzards, and were making no progress. As the morning wore on it got hotter and hotter. The sand in the dry river bed shone like a mirror. The windless sunken river bed had become a small piece of hell on earth. The smoke breaks increased and got longer, despite the bitching of the corporal in charge, whose knowledge of the English language seemed limited to two words: "arsehole" and "fuck".

Eventually, after many threats of violence and death by various means, the corporal had managed to get us fired up enough to reluctantly take our machetes and head into the thick bush growing along the dry river bed. Our plan was simple: cut down some small trees and branches and put them under the wheels of the stuck F250 truck, and all things being equal the wood would give traction to the wheels and the huge V8 motor would do the rest.

We had hacked, cut and slashed, sweated buckets and bled like stuffed pigs. The rivers of blood running down our arms and legs were many. Human skin was no match for the hooked, razor-sharp thorns of the Wag A Bikky ('Wait a bit') tree. Likewise, our blunt, misused bent pangas were no match for the rock-hard trunks of the Wag A Bikky. It was all to no avail. Even the kind words of encouragement from our hard-working, chain-smoking corporal failed to help us in our quest to gather branches to put under the wheels of the truck.

Half an hour later, crouched under what little shade we could find, with heads hanging and shoulders slumped, sweating like waterfalls and too tired to even try to defend ourselves against the hordes of flies and other nasties, we admitted defeat. Nature had won. The branches we had managed to cut were so few I felt we might as well have not bothered.

I was wrong: the corporal figured we had enough to do the job, and nobody really wanted to argue with him as the heat had taken the fight out of us. All we wanted to do was get the truck out of the river bed, get back to base, relax and get away from the screaming corporal. As I crouched there in the burning sand of the river bed next to the rear wheel of the F250, trying to push the few thorn bushes I had managed to cut under the wheel without doing further damage to my already bleeding hands, my mind drifted back to the beginning of the bush trip.

We were in the Zambezi Valley somewhere between Kayemba, a small police base on the Zambezi River, and Hell's Gate. Across the river were Zambia and Mozambique. This was my second trip into the area, and as such I was still learning the ropes. After a trip best forgotten and not talked about lasting two days, we arrived in our area. To say it was rugged would be an understatement of gigantic proportions. The two constants here were the heat and the colour grey. Everything was grey: the hills were grey, the trees were grey, the grass was grey, the rocks were grey, the mopani flies were grey, as were the choworee buzzards. The only colour other than grey was the almost white sky and sand, and the burning white sun.

The Zambezi Valley was owned and ruled by the sun. The heat was like an invisible cloak around you, draining your strength and drying out your body as you sweated in a vain attempt to cool down. Everything was distorted by the shimmering heatwaves, everything was burned and all moisture sucked out of it. Objects seemed to move, one minute close but the next disappearing into the distance. Our task, or mission if you will, while based in this little piece of grey waterless hell was to check for terrorists or signs of them passing through the area. How anybody was to pass through this hell on earth, where temperatures were often well into the 40s and where no one lived for hundreds of square miles, was beyond me. That was the thinking of the Rhodesian Army brass before the war started, and sad to say did not change much afterwards. Later in my career I was to patrol in Mozambique, south of the Zambezi River, in an area so dry and devoid of any form of human life that 44-gallon drums of water had to be brought in by helicopter. All this begs the question what I was doing there. Well believe it or not I was looking for terrorists or any sign of their passing through the area.

On our first night at our new base camp, nobody was sleeping. The heat, the attacking multitudes of bloodsucking insects, the bright moon and the strange noises coming from the surrounding thick bush made sure of that.

"That was an AK fired from the hip!" In most sections or troops in the Rhodesian Light Infantry, there was the self-proclaimed bush expert. I looked at our self-elected tracker/survival expert in disbelief. I was young and stupid, but not that young and stupid. The shot had sounded as if it was at least 4 or 5 kilometres away, and as it was a clear, quiet night maybe further. It was difficult to judge. We had not been expecting to hear a shot, and it took a few seconds for the brain to register what the ears had heard. As for the 'AK47 fired from the hip' story, I was not buying it for a second.

Sitting up on top of my barrack-room issue blanket, eyes as big as saucers, I looked around. (At this stage in the Rhodesian Army there was no lightweight sleeping equipment or decent webbing. All our webbing was genuine collector's items from the Second World War.) Forgotten were the mosquitoes, the incredible heat, the itchy legs scratched raw and bleeding, the eyes full of insect repellent, weeping, red and burning. All this was pushed to one side, replaced by a feeling of excitement, anticipation and, lurking in the background, a feeling that was to stay with me for my entire army career: fear. Not fear in the accepted sense of the word, but fear of the unknown, which my ever-active imagination always added to and distorted beyond belief. The sounds that a few seconds ago I had accepted without any problem as those of the African night now took on ominous undertones. The rustling in the grass, the crack of a twig being broken – probably caused by rats or insects on the move – now sounded like a charging elephant to my supercharged ears. The soft blue-white shadows thrown by the moon now all resembled terrorists on the move. The minutes passed with no further gunshots, no terrorists charging out of the menacing bush. Slowly, I started to relax, the loud humming in my ears subsided, my staring eyes started to blink in an effort to lubricate themselves and the itches returned, as did the realisation that my shirt was soaking wet from sweat. Looking down at my still tightly clenched hands, I realised I was not even holding my weapon. Ashamed and extremely embarrassed, I quickly looked around to see if anyone else had noticed. I need not have worried; most of my fellow soldiers' weapons were laying unattended at their feet, the same as mine. The night was long and mostly silent, apart from the constant hum of the mosquitoes; where they came from and how they survived in this heat I have no idea. Even our self-proclaimed bush and weapons expert had little or nothing to say after being told to "shut up and stop talking shit" by the corporal. Gradually the sky lightened, the stars retreated and the sun announced its arrival in an awesome display of dawn colours. Silver lit up the sky, then oranges, pinks, purples and reds, all moving and unmatched in their beauty, but all soon destroyed by their creator, the sun. The eerie silence of the night gave way to the crudely loud sounds and movements of day. The thick bush surrounding our little base camp came to life. Guinea fowl and pheasants made themselves heard, as did numerous other unseen birds This was the Africa I loved, unspoilt, no tins and bottles laying all over the place, no plastic bags hanging in the tress like Christmas decorations, no high-rise buildings, no car exhausts; just clean fresh air, peace and quiet.

The bush was thick. Thick enough to stop a main battle tank, same as the hedgerows in Normandy did during the Second World War. The trees, though small, grew very close to each other, their branches and roots intertwined and forming a solid wall. Imagine hundreds of thousands of trees growing on top of each other, all with their roots and branches entwined, and you will have an idea of what I mean when I say thick. No breeze passed through this mass of trees, which held the heat like it was made of corrugated steel. The only paths through this mass were made by rhinos as they passed on their endless quest for food and water.

Into this piece of unspoilt paradise came a patrol from Support Group of the Rhodesian Light Infantry. Two days had passed since the firing of the AK47 from the hip incident, and our corporal had decided it was time we earned our pay and did what we were supposed be doing: hunting for terrorists. We were not going to look in areas where moving on foot would be reasonably easy; we were going to look in areas where movement on foot would be extremely difficult, dangerous and stupid. Our patrol was led by our section's self-professed bush craft/tracker expert, closely followed by the corporal and the rest of us. We had left the driver in camp to keep an eye on things.

It is no easy task to find a gap in the solid wall of Jessie bush. An hour or so later, tempers were short, bodies were bleeding and clothing was torn. With the sun burning down, morale was dropping. When all seemed lost and it looked like we were doomed to failure in our quest to find an opening in the thick bush, our 'expert' came across a large pile of still-wet rhino dung. With wild abandon and a huge smile, he stuck his hand into the middle of the pile. Gathering around, we waited with baited breath to hear the outcome of his actions. What we had been taught about not bunching up and keeping a reasonable distance between each other whilst on patrol went out of the window. Then was then, now was now. The performance taking place in front of my eyes was worthy of an Oscar. Slowly, our bush craft man withdrew his hand from the pile of dung and his unblinking eyes stared straight ahead as if he was trying to look into the future – or was it the past? Raising his dung-covered hand to his nose, he took a deep breath, then painstakingly lowered it back into the dung, all the while rolling a piece of dung between his other hand's fore finger and thumb. His brow was creased in deep lines of concentration, the sweat running down the side of his face giving the impression of a man in deep thought. We watched and waited, forgetting the heat, the bleeding legs and all else, transfixed by what was happening before our eyes. In a low, almost other-worldly voice, he uttered: "Female. Dung still warm and wet. Two to three hours old." This was met with a moment's silence before the inevitable "Bull shit!" from the corporal. After several minutes of heated discussion between the corporal and our bush craft expert, it was agreed that we would follow the rhino tracks, it being assumed that the rhino would be heading back to the safety of the Jessie bush. We would enter where he or she entered: no problem.

And enter we did. This was not the world of the open savannah; this was the dark, dangerous and damp world of the Jessie bush. Visibility was down to mere metres, the heat retained by the thick bush was unbelievable and you sweated continually whether you were moving or not. The attacks by the mopani and tsetse flies were relentless, and every time we stopped the mosquitoes joined in. The only way through this maze made in hell was to follow paths made by large game like rhino. The paths twisted and turned, and were in most cases not wide enough for a man to pass along without paying for his passage in blood and flesh. It is difficult to explain what it's like to creep along paths that are extremely narrow, where your clothes and webbing are forever getting hooked on the thousands of thorns that line each side of the path. Where your only option of movement is along the path; the bush on the sides of the path are so thick even an elephant would have a problem pushing through. Because the paths twist and turn continually, you can bareley see 2 metres ahead of you, so everything is dark or in shadow. Your eyes never stayed in one place for more than a millisecond before they moved again in a continual search for danger. The screeching cicada beetles made sure you could hear nothing; not even a charging rhino. This was the world our patrol entered.

Many hours later, battered, bruised and bleeding, we gathered around what was once a water hole, but which now contained only a dark brown, soup-like liquid. That we were lost was not in doubt. What was in doubt was whether we would get out before it got dark and we would have to spend the night where we were, lost .The Rhodesian Army at this stage was not blessed by the brightest of men. Map reading was just a phrase and the compass was some strange, useless piece of equipment that was always wrong. Looking across at our corporal, crouched over what had been a nice clean map but was now torn and covered in sweat, I could not help but feel sorry for him. He was doing the best he could, but he was like a fish out of water. He was used to the routine of being in barracks. Monday to Thursday, life was not too bad, a bit of half-hearted training here and there given by an instructor less interested than you were. There was lots of shouting and screaming on the parade ground on Friday mornings as we suffered through two hours of verbal abuse heaped on us by some red-faced, bulging-eyed, spittle-spraying Regimental Sergeant Major. The corporal was given little or no time to practise the skills he was taught on his recruit course, which resulted in the position we now found ourselves in.

Looking around at my fellow soldiers, I could see by the hanging heads, the staring and lacklustre eyes, the half-hearted attempts to brush away the ever-present flies, the silently moving lips that cursed everything from the corporal to the cuts caused by the razor-sharp thorns, that whatever little bit of morale we had when we started out with had been sucked out of us. Heat exhaustion seemed just around the corner.

Nevertheless, as tired as we were, when the corporal indicated it was time to move on we all staggered to our feet, got into single file and lurched down the path, following the corporal and our bush craft expert. Time stood still. Heads hanging, eyes staring at the ground just in front of us, looking neither left nor right, ears assaulted by screeching cicada beetles, bleeding hands clutching our weapons, we blundered on like zombies, making no effort to avoid the vicious thorns or numerous branches that blocked our path.

Suddenly, I was startled out of my reverie to become a supercharged adrenalin junkie. Even through my world of heat, pain and self-pity, the word 'rhino' registered. My brain started pumping out pictures of a huge dark grey monster weighing 2 tons with beady, non-seeing red eyes, no brain and a 6ft-long curved horn with my name written all over it. With the images came a massive injection of fear and instinct for survival. My head swung from left to right as my eyes searched desperately for a break in the wall of surrounding bush. Every likely looking escape route was rapidly processed and rejected. Time was rapidly running out, my ears filled with heavy, earth-shaking thumps, sounds of breaking branches and loud snorting, but still no escape route presented itself. Then the bush heaved and the branches snapped like matchsticks, and there stood 2 tons of complete stupidity. Half-blind and relying on its sense of smell, the rhino stood there, head lowered, pawing the ground and snorting, unsure what to do next. It did not take long to make up its mind. Seconds later it filled the path, blocking out the sun, our whole world shrunk to a path and a charging, deadly rhino. It was a nightmare come true: huge, impossible to stop, its pounding the earth and angry snorting filled our ears. I was desperate. The time to think was long gone; it was do or die. In the narrow confines of the path, I was pretty sure it was going to be death that came out on top.

In one last attempt to avoid the charging rhino, I launched myself head-first into the bush surrounding the path. My heart sang, a great weight lifted off me and my leaden legs, arms and body regained their strength as fear dropped from my shoulders. I was alive and I was going to survive, to cheat the dark messenger of death. My feeling of wellbeing had no sooner arrived before it disappeared, replaced by blind, unreasoning fear. My flight had been brought to an abrupt halt as my rifle, held across my body, struck some immovable branches The force of the sudden halt knocked the air of my lungs and I hit the ground with a bone-breaking thump. Almost crying in frustration, I tried to burrow into the bush and get out of the rhino's path. "Lay still, lay still," whispered a little voice, my own. "All the noise you are making will only attract the rhino." My body as stiff as a sheet of metal, I lay dead still, expecting the worst but hoping for the best. The minutes passed with no searing pain in my stomach as the horn passed through, no crushed bones in my legs brought about by pounding hooves, no beady red eyes staring into mine, no snorting filling my ears. I started to relax and look around. Stuck in some thick bush not too far from me was Dino Newton. Somehow the heavy-barrel FN he was carrying had broken in half and had wedged into the bush, and he had ended up stuck, unable to move attached to his weapon by the sling he was using. After a few minutes of excited talk of narrow escapes, the adrenalin rush wore off and the thirst returned, as did the heat and all the other flying, blood-sucking inhabitants of the bush. Heads bowed, feet dragging, the short-lived alertness long gone, we plodded on. How many hours we spent wandering around in the hell that was the Jessie bush I do not remember. How many kilometres we covered I have no idea. If the temperature dropped I did not notice. All I knew was that the sun was bidding farewell in its usual awesome array of colours, with pinks, reds and oranges painting the sky before we finally broke free of the Jessie bush and its horrors and into the open bush again.

As luck would have it, a few metres to our front was the river on which we had established our base camp. It was getting dark before we arrived, much to the relief of our driver. That night, regardless of the mosquitoes and the other strange noises in the bush, we slept like the dead. Our corporal, a man of few words, had decided after the horrors of the Jessie bush rhino saga to cover our area of responsibility by vehicle whenever possible. It was a decision well-received by the rest of us, and even got him the odd compliment or two.

The vehicle patrols were great: no stress, no strain, and apart from the inevitable attack by tsetse flies whenever the vehicle slowed down and the odd getting stuck, things were good. Webbing was thrown on the back of the F250, as were the weapons. We just had to hold on for dear life as we sped up and down. No more sore, aching muscles, no more shredded arms and legs; only the odd sore behind from trying to sit instead of stand while on patrol! What we were supposed to see while speeding down the road I do not know. The question was never asked, so no answer was needed. The same applies to a vehicle ambush.

✂

I was brought back to reality by the screaming corporal and something else; it was the something else I had noticed out of the corner of my eye that caused my blood to run cold in fear. Shaking my head, wiping the sweat out of my eyes, I looked again. No, I was not seeing things. The heat, the screeching cicada beetles, the mopani flies, the stinging, blood-sucking Chewore buzzards and the screaming corporal had not cooked my brain or driven me mad. Charging down the river at 30-40 kilometres an hour was another 2 tons of anger, frustration, power and stupidity. "Balaam, what's the matter with you, you arsehole, are you deaf?" Not waiting for an answer, the corporal continue: "What's the matter? What are you staring at? Push those branches under the wheel and stop fucking around." He was still screaming when the rhino hit the F250. The horn sliced through the door like a hot knife through butter. The 2 tons of muscle and anger lifted the F250 out of the holes its wheels had dug and threw it effortlessly at least half a metre across the road. The deed done, the Rhino stood blowing air through its nostrils, shaking its head, pawing the sand and staring at the F250 as if saying: "Right, you had enough?" Getting no answer, and convinced it had conquered the intruder, it turned around and slowly strolled back up the dry river bed. This was my first up close and personal meeting with a rhino in the wild .Unfortunately it was not to be my last.

Centenary Farmlands, Old Mealie Field, 1970

Crack! Crack! The rounds shattered the air as they passed over my head. God, they sounded close, a lot closer than I liked. "Closer than I liked"; that sounds like I was a real hard core, tough-as-nails veteran of many contacts with the enemy. Nothing was further from the truth. I was shit scared, unable to think or act. I did not know I was in the bush, I did not know I had a weapon and I did not know I was a soldier; all I knew was that somebody was trying to kill me and somehow I had to survive. My shirt was soaking wet, my entire body covered in a strange-smelling sweat, a sweat that as time went on I would realise was the result of pure, blind, unreasoning fear. It was sweat I would experience many times in my army career, and it would stay with me throughout my life.

The mealie stalks – brown, dried-out, brittle and broken – disintegrated as the rounds struck them, showering me with small bits of stalk, leaves and dried pulp. The small depressions between the furrows of the long-since ploughed field, shallow and filled with sand, offered little or no cover, either from fire or view. Pressing my body as flat as possible, I tried to locate the area from which the firing was coming. This was a lot easier said than done. To my under-pressure brain it seemed as if I was surrounded. I could not for the life of me locate where the firing was coming from. All the training I had received on my recruit course, to listen out for the crack as the round went over my head, closely followed by the thump of where the round was fired from, went out of the window, swamped by fear and the instinct for survival.

I had done a lot of 'live' fire and movement exercises, both as a recruit and a trained soldier. Getting up and dashing forward a couple of metres before taking cover again had seemed so easy. But that was then and this was now. Trying my best to suppress the feeling of panic that was threatening to overcome me, I did the one thing that every instinct in my body said I should not do: I raised my head and tried to see what was happening.

The day had started off as most days did when in base camp in the bush. At first light the clearance patrol went out and we all stood to, armed to the teeth in our shell scrapes. Upon the return of the clearance patrol, the camp slipped into its daily routine and the previously quiet corporals found their voices. Nothing could be done without lots of shouting by certain corporals. Not all the corporals; just certain corporals. The 'certain corporals' being the ones who could not organise a piss-up in a brewery, but in an effort to cover up their lack of management skills just shouted and threatened a lot. It was shout, scream, threaten, go on a road run or do 'pokey drill' (drill while carrying your rifle). More shouting, screaming and threats, then go for a shower or wash, more shouting, screaming and threats, then go for breakfast, followed by more shouting etc., clean up the camp and more shouting before cleaning your weapons. All in all, a nice, quiet, peaceful day in a Rhodesian Army bush camp! Somewhere in between all the shouting and all the different parades (everything in the army was a parade, especially in the pre-war Rhodesian Light Infantry) we did manage to get a couple of hours' rest, during which we played cards, washed our clothes, slept or listened to the radio.

We were halfway through our truly awesome gourmet army-style breakfast – consisting of oily eggs and even more oily bully beef – when the words "Fall In!" were screamed, followed by the normal threats of death by a thousand cuts. I, like most of my fellow soldiers, ignored the screamed order, thinking to myself "what do these arseholes want now?" Whatever it was could wait until after breakfast. The thought had no sooner come when a bad-breathed, yellow-toothed, red-eyed, foul-smelling corporal pushed his ugly face into mine and screamed – spit and paint-removing fumes spreading far and wide, backed up by the sweat smell of stale gin and tonic – "Who the fuck do you think you are, Balaam?" (To me as a troopie in the Rhodesian Light Infantry, all corporals had yellow teeth, spluttered a lot and had bad breath.) How I hated that question: I knew who I was; if he had a problem remembering who I was, that was his problem and not mine. He continued: "You think you do not have to fall in? You think you are special?" The answer bubbled up to my lips, but somehow I managed to stopped myself. I wanted desperately to tell him I knew who I was and I did think I was special, but the last corporal I had said that to had put me on a charge and I got five days confined to barracks, which was unpleasant to say the least. At the same time, I was not going to take his shit. I had just come off guard duty and was tired, hungry, dirty and not happy with life in general.

"Sorry Corp," I screamed back with a mouth full of oily eggs, spraying as much as I could into his leering face. "Sorry Corp," I screamed again, trying all the while to stop myself from laughing as I watched his face turn red with anger. He was confused. He did not know what to do. After all, I had apologized. After a few seconds of indecision, he reverted to the tried and trusted screaming: "Any more shit from you and you find yourself in DB [Detention Barracks]. You hear me, you piece of shit?" After repeating the threat several times he seemed to run out of ideas, turned around and stomped off, not bothering to wait for my answer. At the entrance to the mess tent he stopped, turned and screamed – at nobody in particular – "Go and get your stuff and fall in. There has been a possible terrorist sighting."

The words "a possible terrorist sighting" caught my attention, but only fleetingly. At this early stage of the war, hardly a day passed without a reported terrorist sighting, which, depending how you looked at it, either gave the impression that there was a terrorist behind every bush or that after repeated failures to confirm such sightings the people doing the reporting needed glasses. Stuffing what I could of my breakfast into my mouth and gulping down a mouthful of nauseatingly sweet coffee, I headed for my bed space to collect my stuff, fighting back the urge to puke as the sweet coffee mixed with the oily, salty eggs and bully beef.

My 'stuff' was my FN rifle, webbing, small circulation-stopping green canvas pack and, as always, a couple of grenades hooked onto the webbing. Why the grenades in the webbing I do not know, apart from the fact that it looked good and everybody else was doing it. The honest truth is that I was always worried that some day one of the grenades would get hooked onto a branch, the pin would get pulled out and I would blow myself to smithereens, but being a dedicated follower of fashion I was willing to accept the risks to be a part of the 'in' crowd. Another truth, while we are on the subject of grenades, is that the only grenades I ever used were white phosphorous or smoke ones to guide a helicopter or an air strike or cause a fire. As time wore on and I ended up in the Selous Scouts, operating mostly alone, I used the white phosphorous grenades as an early warning devicecum-booby trap. The early warning was cool, so long as you remembered where you set them up. On one occasion I accidently set off one of my own booby traps, and if it was not for a large tree I would have ended up badly burnt.

Ten minutes later, after the normal confusion brought on by all the non-commissioned officers wanting to be boss, we were rushing, bouncing, sliding and hanging on for dear life, enveloped in a thick cloud of red dust, down a badly corrugated dirt road in our camouflaged V8 Ford F250s on our way to a possible sighting of terrorists on a nearby farm. To say we were excited when we first got the news of the sighting would be an understatement. This was it; this is what we trained for, the countless hours of weapon training, the hundreds of miles run to keep fit, the thousands of rounds fired on the range, the bloody skin-losing and bone-breaking jungle lanes, all to prepare us for this moment.

We would show them who was who in the 'zoo', who was the boss; we would teach them a lesson they would never forget. Talk is cheap. Little did we know it at the time, but it would take some while before we got around to teaching anybody a lesson. We were as green as the leaves on the trees in the surrounding bush; we had no experience, and like a chicken without a head we ran around in circles, achieving little or nothing. This would change quickly, as the easy-as-you-go peacetime army changed into a wartime army, and many of the unsuitable officers and NCOs were moved to sections in the army more suited to their talents.

At the same time, lurking in the corner of our minds was that this was the latest of many sightings that had all turned out to be lemons.

What the mood was among the would-be steely eyed killers, all looking like Rambo, in the back of the Ford F250s I did not know, as I was sitting on the passenger-side mudguard of the speeding vehicle. I had been chosen to be the human mine detector. What I was looking for I did not know, and if I saw anything that looked like a land mine through my red, weeping eyes (protective goggles were not an option – there were none, end of story) it was a mystery how I was supposed to stop the vehicle or warn the driver. Then again, the chances of me seeing anything were nil, as I spent the entire time clutching my weapon with one hand while my other was hooked under the bonnet of the bouncing vehicle as I struggled not to fall off, which would result in serious injuries if not death. When selected to be the mine detector my heart sank, my feeling of apprehension and excitement at a possible clash with terrorists replaced by one almost of fear. I had done it before on a slow-moving Land Rover as part of a training exercise, but that was a different kettle of fish to doing it on a fast-moving Ford F250.

Nevertheless, it was an honour to be chosen as a mobile mine detector, and being a follower of fashion and determined to be a member of the cool crowd, I climbed up and seated myself on the front left mudguard.

Several lifetimes and bleeding cramped fingers later, we pulled up in a huge cloud of red dust and revving engines in front of a farm gate, where we were met by what I assume was the owner of the farm property we were about to enter. As the dust settled I could not help but notice the whole area was flat, and every square inch of the red soil was covered in decaying old mealie fields. Stretching away to the horizon as far as my weeping eyes could see were thousands upon thousands of old mealie stalks. There were so many they seemed to form a solid wall, making it impossible at ground level to see more than 50 or 60 metres in front of you. In the far distance I could make out the odd large tree or two, but to our immediate front nothing; just flat old mealie fields with nothing to use as a guideline to help you keep in the right direction. Nothing of what I was seeing registered with my brain. I was new at this. In years to come I would automatically look for landmarks to help me keep direction in thick bush or wherever there was restricted vision.

Turning my attention to the troop commanders and the farmer, they were crouched around a map spread on the ground. What they were saying I could not hear above the idling V8 and V6 motors of our transport, but there was plenty of pointing at the map, followed by much gesturing towards the mealie fields. Map reading and the use of a compass in the Rhodesian Army at the beginning of the bush war was a real hit-and-miss affair, with a whole lot more misses than hits. After several more minutes of intense pointing at the map and fields, the group seemed to reach a decision. What decision they came to and what was said I have no idea, as I was just a trooper and as such was not in the 'need to know' group.

The going was slow and noisy. When I say noisy I mean a big-time noisy, the ridges between the lines of mealies causing major problems as we tried to look ahead for the terrorists and at the same time glance to our left and right and try to keep our dressing with our fellow soldiers on either side. Falling and stumbling, we moved forward. Maybe moved forward is not the right term. To my mind, 'moving forward' means doing so with a purpose, in a chosen direction and in a controlled manner. What was happening was very different. There was no direction as such, nor any purpose given to why we were doing what we were doing, and the control was non-existent. What you cannot see you cannot control.

Getting into extended order was a long and painful task as the section corporal ran up down, putting each individual of his section in the exact spot he wanted him, ensuring the gap between each of us was as per infantry school. That is the way it was at the beginning of the war; with no experience to fall back on everything was done by the book. I am sure if we had asked an instructor from the school how to handle our problem of keeping direction, they would have said to use a compass. Things would change as more experience was gained, and some of the old Second World War-era teachings would fall by the wayside.

Once everything was in so-called order, the silent signal to move forward was given. In theory we should have all moved forward at the same time. But the plans of mice and men ... From where I was standing amongst the dried mealie stalks, with burning red sandpaper eyes courtesy of my stint as the mobile mine detector, I could see nothing of our section commander or his silent signal. So I waited for my fellow soldier on my right or left to start moving before I set off. Clutching my FN in my sweaty white-knuckled hands, all thoughts of 'we will teach these terrorists a lesson they will not forget' were quickly forgotten. My whole life now revolved around keeping my dressing; to hell with it if I kept falling and stumbling like a drunk, if I could not bend my stiff, fear-gripped legs and if I struggled to breathe as my chest felt like it was in a slowly tightening vice. I did not look to my front. If there were a million terrorists laying in front of me, I would not have seen them, as I was only looking to my left and right in a vain effort to keep my dressing and spacing. Within five minutes I could no longer see anybody to edither side; all I could hear above my laboured breathing was the breaking of mealie stalks as the rest of the section crashed forward like a bunch of under-the-influence hippos!

Panic set in. I was alone and I could not see anyone else. I slowly stopped moving forward, my stiff legs coming to a shuddering halt. I did not know how my fellow soldiers were faring. Were they OK? Was I the only one panicking, the only one with stiff legs, sweaty hands and having a hard time breathing? As I stood there in the mealie field with the hot African sun beating down on my strangely cold body, trying to pull myself together, the silence was shattered by a single muffled shot. It took a few milliseconds – or so it seemed to me – for my overworked brain to get a message through to my fear-locked muscles that a shot had been fired in the immediate area to my front in a mealie field which could have a terrorist hiding behind every dried-out grey stalk. By the time I hit the ground between two of the farrows, the air was alive with rounds passing overhead. As I lay there as stiff as a board, being showered by hundreds of pieces of dried mealie stalk, not knowing what to do and with nobody to tell me, my brain eventually supplied me with one vital piece of information: the rounds were coming from many different directions. It was not from my front, my left or right, like we had been ambushed; the rounds were coming from all around. I was no master tactical genius, but I figured because of the difficulty of keeping direction and control in the mealie field, where vision was restricted to a few metres at the best of times – and even less when moving through the thick bush in files – we had veered off course, split up into small groups and started walking in circles. In due course one group walked into another and a furious fire-fight erupted. Being new to the game, as soon as the first member opened fire, the rest of us followed suit. The fact that we could see nobody was beside the point. We were working on the principle that noise kills, plus it gave us something to do. No more thinking, no more stress and tension; all that disappeared when the first shot was fired.

Slowly, the firing died down as a lone voice started shouting "Cease firing! Cease firing!" Once the firing had stopped, a strange silence descended on the area. With the silence, all the uncertainties that the firing of your weapon had eradicated returned with a vengeance. What to do? Should I stand up? Should I call out? Should I just lie here and wait to see what happens? Being a bit of a shit-scared type, I chose to wait and see. Anyhow, I needed as much time as I could to get some strength into my legs and arms and work up a bit of spit to moisten my incredibly dry mouth and lips. With a bit of luck my fear-frozen brain might then kick in. Gradually, by softly calling to each other, we regrouped. Nobody was looking at anyone; the ground seemed to hold a special reverence all of it own as we all stared at it as if our lives depended on it. There were no smiles, no slapping on the back, just a feeling of relief, touched by shame. There was relief at the fact that you were still alive. Once we had discovered we were alright, our humanity would return and we would just as quickly put our wellbeing at risk to help a fellow human. We are complicated, of that there is no doubt. Then came the relief that everybody else appeared unharmed as well.

How close we came to killing some of our own I do not know, but one thing that came through loud and clear was that our training needed upgrading, and quickly. The days of a badly trained NCO leading equally badly trained troopers was finished. As the war continued, the training improved by leaps and bounds and all the hard-learnt experience was put into practice. Unfortunately, this was not the case for the 'brown tent' brigade. There were many senior NCOs and officers in the army – I am sure this applies to most units – who because of their rank hardly, if ever, went on patrol or experienced a contact; yet somehow they seemed to have all the answers all of the time. These, then, are the members of what I call the 'brown tent' brigade.

The drive home was long and very quiet. We all carried cuts and bruises from the concrete hardness of the ground and the dry mealie stalks. Blood was everywhere; our arms and legs were a thick dust-coated red, with patches of darker red caused by the bleeding of our many scratches and cuts. Most of our faces were, like our legs and arms, a dark red, with clear white lines running from our forehead down to our chin and jaw line, caused by our own sweating. Most of us sat with hunched shoulders and heads bowed, hands clutching our weapons between our knees. Unfeeling and unseeing, we bounced up and down on the hard steel backs of the trucks. As we travelled along, some of the big stories I had told – and some equally big stories I had heard – flashed through my mind. I could not stop myself moving from one painful buttock to the next and going hot and cold in embarrassment as I realised how ridiculous they must have sounded. The curse of alcohol, a massive mouth and a minute brain! We were no longer the great terrorist killers, but rather a bunch of scared little boys, into whose frozen brains was slowly sinking the fact that being a great terrorist-killer was not all it was cracked up to be.

The end result of all our efforts, after firing thousands of rounds and sweating gallons of both blood and water, was one visiting farm worker wounded in the leg, who took much abuse and the odd slap and kick before he could convince the over-eager Security Branch that he was in fact an innocent worker from the neighbouring farm. Little did I realise it at the time, but what was already a bad bush trip was soon to become a nightmare.

Support Group, Rhodesian Light Infantry, Hyani River Bridge 1970-1971. The white wilderness

The cold, black, unblinking reptilian eyes stared back into my green ones. I had caught the small crocodiles by hand at night a couple of days ago in the Zambezi River below the Kariba Dam wall. When I had caught them I did not have a clue what to do with them. Then came orders to move to the Huyani River and a plan formed in my mind. Four inches or so long, the pair of baby crocodiles looked one step from death. It had been a long, hot, sweaty and dusty trip on some of the worst roads in the country, and travelling in a steel army cooking pot in lukewarm water bouncing around every time we hit one of the millions of potholes or humps in the mainly dirt roads was definitely not the ideal form of travel. Nevertheless, the two baby crocodiles had somehow survived and I was about to release them into, as far as I knew, the crocodile-free Huyani River. Whether the Huyani was crocodile-free or not I was not sure, but we had been based on its banks many times and had used it as a swimming pool on numerous occasions, and never once had I seen a crocodile or anything to indicate there were crocs in the river, unlike the Angwa River a hundred or so kilometres down the same road, which teemed with crocodiles.

We had been based below the Kariba Dam wall, where we had been on a training exercise, which had consisted more of swimming, braaing (grilling meat over an open fire), fishing, catching a sun tan and playing volleyball than anything else. The only military activity we engaged in was the odd bit of weapon training, the occasional visit to the jungle lane to hone our close-quarter shooting skills and the compulsory early-morning road run.

It was the middle of summer the heat was extreme, but who cared? Certainly not me, nor any of my fellow soldiers. This is what it was all about, based on the banks of the Zambezi a few kilometres down-river from the Kariba Dam wall, living a life of luxury and ease, doing as little as possible and taking as long as possible to do it. It was like the United States Marine Corp advert – 'Join the Marines. See the world and kill people'. We were not seeing the world, true, and as far as killing people went that would come later. But what the hell; you've got to start somewhere.

The millions of mosquitoes and thousands of sand fleas which inhabited the area were considered a small price to pay to be away from the parade ground, the crazy, bulging-eyed, screaming RSM and the equally hated barrack room inspections which normally led to weekends confined to barracks.

As a child living along the banks of the Zambezi in then Northern Rhodesia – now Zambia – I had a great interest in all the inhabitants of the great river, from tiger fish to hippo and anything between. One of the 'in betweens' was the crocodile. Repulsive and ugly, I was not sure if I loved or hated them. Nevertheless, I had a healthy respect for this deadly river hunter. My father, who grew up on the banks of the Zambezi and made extra cash by hunting and killing crocodiles with a spear and selling their skins – and on occasion catching them with nets for zoos – once told me a story of when he, his brother and a friend were swimming in the Zambezi, in the area where the Livingstone boating club now stands, and a croc had taken their friend. One minute he was there, the next he was gone; they saw or heard nothing. Several days and many hours of diving later, they found his body in a big hole in the river bank, jammed in the roots of a tree in what was obviously a crocodile's den.

On the evening before our departure for the Huyani River bridge to do our border control stint, we had taken a rubber dinghy and gone out to do a bit of night-time river exploring. What we were actually supposed to do on the river at night I did not then, and still do not to this day, know.

Armed with a rifle each and one torch to light the area, dressed in green army shorts and led by a drunk, shouting, 'watch-me-make-a-fool-of-myself' sergeant who had two beers clutched in one hand and his weapon in the other, we launched into the dark and dangerous world of the mighty Zambezi River. The launch was actually a disaster, but after much swearing, shouting, sweating, slipping and sliding on the soft wet river sand, we finally managed to get the dinghy free of the sand and into the water.

"Into the valley of death charged the six hundred", a line from Tennyson's poem about the Charge of the Light Brigade, popped into my mind as we – the mindless five – rushed not into a valley but a gorge. There were no cannons, true, but a growling menacing river is just as deadly, complete with a couple of hungry crocodiles for backup. While the brave 'six hundred' were led by officers drunk on glory (truly lions led by donkeys), we were the mindless five led by a beer-drunk senior NCO (no names, no pack drills) who failed to understand that it is almost impossible to stand upright in a rubber dinghy with two beers in one hand, rifle in the other, while a bunch of troopies are pushing the boat into the river with the sole intention of making you lose your balance and see your arse fall in. In the end, common sense prevailed and the sergeant – short of one beer, several inches of skin compliments of the ribbed deck flooring, hoarse from shouting "What are you laughing at?" – admitted defeat and, with drooping shoulders and hanging head, remained seated.

Seconds turned into minutes as we struggled to get the boat's motor started, all the while drifting out of our little bit of calm water between the rocks, ever-deeper into the inky, frightening darkness of the gorge and ever-closer to the roaring main Zambezi River. The normally 300-400 metre-wide river was forced between two sheer rock faces no more than 200 metres apart, resulting in a raging white-water hell of a gorge, from which issued a low, eerie moan of anger and frustration, like a beast venting its rage at being chained and denied its freedom. .

Forgotten were the millions of feasting mosquitoes and the useless drunk sergeant as we took turns pulling the rope-type starter hoping to kick the motor into life. The rubber dinghy had two oars with which we could have rowed ourselves back to the safety of the rocks. But somehow in the panic to get the motor started, the thought never entered our minds. "It is flooding. Can't you smell petrol? We'll never get it started if it is flooding," I offered, trying to be helpful. "Flooding? What the fuck do you know about boat motors? You don't even own a car, you can't even drive, so do not talk to me about flooding, you arsehole," was the answer from the coxswain. It was never good to volunteer anything in the army – even a suggestion. The answer was invariably unpleasant!

"Closer, closer, not so fast, slowly, slowly, OK let us drift in," I whispered to the coxswain as I readied myself to try and catch the small crocodile floating on top of the water a few meters in front of our dinghy. "Keep the light on his eyes," I muttered out of the side of my mouth to the torch operator, not daring to turn my head and lose sight of the small croc.

About 12 inches in length, it would be strong and incredibly quick, and could disappear under the water in an instant with a flick of its tail. My two previous attempts had ended in failure, mainly because the crocodiles I had tried to catch had been too big and strong for me to hold on to, resulting in me nearly ending up in the river minus a couple of fingers as I struggled to hold on. I had been told that to judge the length of a crocodile you needed to use the eyes as a reference. The closer together the eyes, the smaller the crocodile, and obviously the further apart the bigger, which is all good and well, but like all things practice makes perfect. For my first two efforts, the eyes were close together but not close enough.

After each failure I had had to bear the insults from my fellow soldiers. I had been taught by my father how to catch small crocodiles. It was very simple: thumb and forefinger behind the head, thumb and forefinger behind the rear legs. I had done this many times before with my feet planted firmly on the ground in quiet pools of water. Now it was different. I was trying to do the same thing laying over the side of a heaving rubber boat in a growling dangerous river with a bunch of soldiers who seemed unable to keep still and continually offered advice mixed with insults, neither of which I needed. Paying no attention to the sweat that ran down my face into my eyes, or the countless mosquitoes that attacked my exposed legs, arms and any other patch of uncovered flesh they could find, I tried to get my arm muscles to relax. Stiff, tense muscles are slow and clumsy, and slow and clumsy is not going to catch a fast-as-lightning 12-inch crocodile. "Do something!" my brain screamed. "You are going to leave it too late do something before the dinghy hits him and he disappears with a flick of his tail." It took a split-second for the message from my brain to register and get my relaxed muscles to react .The result was a pathetic half-lunge, half-dive and I nearly ended up in the river. I had been so busy trying to relax that I had forgotten what I was supposed to be doing. As usual, the normal comments flowed thick and fast: none of them nice. Even the slowly sobering-up sergeant managed to pass a comment or two, followed by the inevitable threats of all the nasty things that were going to happen to me should I continue to fail and, worse still, waste his time.

The torch pierced the inky darkness in front of the slowly moving dinghy. There were red eyes everywhere. On every bit of sand, in every little cove, no matter where you looked you saw red eyes. Looking at the spacing between the eyes, they ranged from very big to very small in size. I grey up along the Zambezi River and had dabbled in crocodile hunting as a child, but never had I seen such a concentration of red eyes. Sitting in the front of the dinghy, a cold shiver of fear ran down my back and the hairs on the back of my neck stood up. Crocodile catching suddenly lost its appeal. If I did another of my lunge/dives in my next effort to catch a small croc and ended up in the water, I would be in serious trouble.

Necessity – or is it fear? – is the mother of invention, so now as we approached victim number four I was laying on the bow of the dinghy, flat on my stomach, my legs hooked into the rope running down the sides of the boat, thus cutting down the chances of me ending up in the river.

"The sack, man; where the fuck is the sack?" I yelled, my voice high and shrill, partly from excitement and partly from fear of losing the wriggling, hissing, foot-long crocodile I had managed to grab behind the neck and two rear legs, as I had been taught. "The sack! Where the fuck is the sack?" I screamed again. I knew I could not hold onto

the baby croc for much longer, especially not laying on my stomach, half in and half out of the boat. The night was brutally hot. The sheer, at least 100ft-high rock cliffs, still hot from baking in the day's sun, slowly released their heat, and this, coupled with the lack of any breeze whatsoever, turned the gorge into a massive, energy-draining steam bath.

Out the corner of my eye, in the almost pitch-black of the night, I could see the scarcely visible blurred figures of my fellow soldiers on their hands and knees, frantically trying in the little light generated by the stars above to locate the sack we had brought along for the crocodiles we caught. A live, snapping, hissing young croc running wild in a rubber dinghy fall of shit-scared soldiers in the hot, sticky darkness of a gorge floating on the mighty Zambezi, filled with large hungry crocodiles, was something to be avoided at all costs.

I felt I was going to lose it. My forearm muscles throbbed in pain as they tried to hold on to the crocodile, while at the same time my shoulder muscles struggled to support my weight as I lay across the dingy. If my elbows slipped off the wet rounded side of the boat I was going to go head-first into the crocodile-infested river, whether my legs were hooked into the rope or not. I could feel my fingers slowly losing their grip on the wriggling young croc, and there was nothing I could do. All the hard work we had put in to get this far was going to disappear into the inky depths of the Zambezi.

Throw it in the dinghy or lose it; those were my options. After all the troubles, loss of skin on the wooden duck board bottom of the boat, and all the abuse I had accepted over the past couple of hours, there was no way on God's green earth I was going to lose this wriggling little shit. Rolling over on my side and using what little strength I hade left in my burning arms, I threw the crocodile into the dinghy amongst my fellow soldiers, who were still on their hands and knees looking for the sack. All hell then broke loose.

"Are you crazy?" I heard one fear-filled voice screech. "You stupid fucking arsehole. You are going to get us all killed!" The rubber dinghy rocked left, then right, as everybody moved like sheep from one side of the boat to the other in an effort to escape the crocodile – a crocodile they could not even see – while I clung for dear life onto the wet slippery nose of the boat, my legs thankfully still hooked into the ropes; otherwise I'm sure I would have ended up in the river. What had started out as a joke had turned into a nightmare. It seemed just a matter of time before somebody fell overboard or the dinghy capsized. "Keep still you arseholes! Keep still for fuck's sake, before you turn the boat over and we all drown!" screamed the now beerless and fast-sobering-up sergeant.

Fear of the crocodile and fear of the sergeant fought a great battle in the minds of the troopers in the dinghy. Fear of the sergeant prevailed, all movement ceased and the rocking boat stabilised. A quick search of the dinghy with the aid of the torch revealed no crocodile.

"And you, Balaam!" bellowed the sergeant. "This was your idea. You were the heavy who was going to show us arseholes how to catch crocodiles with our bare hands. How many have you caught, arsehole?" "None sarge," I replied "What the fuck do you mean 'none'? We have been out here for hours." Before I could answer he added: "You got half an hour and that is it. If you fail to catch any crocs I am going to make you regret you ever joining the army."

In the Rhodesian Light Infantry, a sergeant had incredible power and could do as he saw fit. My heart sank. I knew if he wanted to, the sergeant could make my life a living hell for as long as he felt like it. With fear in my heart, sweat pouring into my eyes and a million mosquitoes trying to eat me alive, I put my back into my crocodile-catching, and when the half an hour was up I had two 4in crocs in the bag.

The landing of the dinghy was not much better than the launching. Amid much shouting, screaming and threats of death by a thousand cuts, we finally got the boat out of the water and onto the beach. With the bag containing the two small crocodiles clutched in my hand, I headed up the path to wards my sleeping area. I needed a cardboard box of sorts to keep the two crocs in. What I was going to do with the two baby crocodiles I had no idea.

The sergeant's voice followed me up the path: "You are so lucky, Balaam. We need a new rubbish pit and I was going to let you dig it all by yourself if you had not caught those crocs!"

Mozambique, Lost Weapon, 1970/71

There was no breeze, the leaves hung limply from the trees, and the grass that had long given up hope of surviving in the heat had turned a dark brown as the last bit of moisture was sucked out by the scorching sun.

It was hot – in fact it was more than hot, it was bloody hot and strangely quiet, and as always when working in Mozambique I had the constant feeling of being watched. Battered and bruised, bleeding from hundreds of cuts and open sores, blinded by the stream of sweat pouring into our bloodshot eyes, driven insane by the massive clouds of mopani flies, we blundered forward in extended line. And 'blundered' is the correct word. Heads hanging, eyes firmly fixed on the ground, faces streaked white from the salt of drying sweat, minds blank and unthinking, we fought our way through the thick bush. Our once-clean and shiny FN assault rifles were now dirty and dusty from being used as pangas-cum-walking sticks to try to hack a path through the thick undergrowth.

We sounded like a herd of drunken buffalo on steroids. The sound of mess tins hitting against each other, and shining like neon lights at night in the bright sunshine, must have brought a smile to the lips of any FRELIMO as they watched our slow, tortuous progress.

The way forward was a minefield of thick grass, fallen-down trees and rocks. We tripped and fell often, and the more tired we got the more we tripped and fell as we fought through the undergrowth in the heat of the day. Slowly but surely the conditions started to take their toll. The bitching, cursing and swearing that followed each mishap was no longer muttered softly under one's breath, but had become loud and angry as the heat, the flies and the feeling of helplessness boiled over. We were no longer a group of highly trained soldiers hunting down terrorists; we had reverted to a bunch of ordinary men doing their best to survive in difficult conditions. Looking at the lowered heads and shuffling feet, I thought of all the bragging that had taken place three weeks previously ...

We would show those FRELIMO who was boss. We were not the poorly trained Portuguese soldiers from Portugal who knew nothing about the bush and had little or no interest in fighting for a country they did not live in. We were well-trained, knew the bush and were fighting for the country we loved and lived in. We were a difficult kettle of fish: we would show the FRELIMO the error of their ways and soon get them on the straight and narrow. It is extremely difficult to explain the excitement, anticipation and adrenalin rush of those early operations, especially in Mozambique. This is what we had spent months training for, to meet the enemy of our country, face-to-face, and destroy them. Unfortunately for us, our enemies had no intention to stand and fight, and disappeared into the bush as soon as they felt threatened. They only stood and fought when there was no other option.

It was not long before our visions of killing the enemy, earning medals and becoming famous were pushed back into the far corners of our minds as we realised war was not all it was cracked up to be. There were no beautiful women to save, no hostages to free, no welcoming crowds. Nothing – just the silence, the heat, the sweat, the pain, the thirst, the drone of ever-present mopani flies, the eerie feeling of being watched and the frustration of being led around in circles by an enemy who knew the land in which we were operating like the back of their hands. This was after all their backyard, where they hunted for food and medicines; they knew every riverbed and waterhole, every rock and tree for miles around. They used this knowledge to their advantage to lead us around in circles, and whenever we seemed to have lost their tracks, they would ambush us, just to get us back on track, then lead us through the thickest bush, through dry riverbed after dry riverbed, up and down ravine after ravine, always miles away from water and even further away from their bases and the civilian villagers that supported them. And because we were still wet behind the ears, we followed them. We had no chance of ever catching them, not loaded down as we were with rations, extra ammunition and sleeping gear, not to mention radios and spare batteries. Nevertheless, unthinkingly, sticking religiously to the tactics we had been taught, we blundered along, falling, tripping, bitching, sweating and bleeding in our slow and unwieldy extended-line formation. To anybody watching it must have appeared that we were incredibly stupid. It would it would have been so much easier to get into single file and only deploy into extended line when coming under fire. However, this was still early in the war, and the Rhodesian Army – being trained along the lines of the British Army – did not encourage independent thought or new ideas, but went heavily into the "Yours is not to reason why, yours is but to do and die" ideal. Things would change as more experience was gained and new young leaders with imagination replaced the old, as would old tactics be replaced by new and more effective ones.

Having said that, many years later I attended a senior tactical course in Gwelo at the School of Infantry and, much to my disgust and dismay, found the same old ineffective tactics were still being taught. When questioned about the value of teaching totally outdated and no longer used methods of fighting a battle to students, the answer from the instructors varied from "I know it does not work, but hey, that what is says in the book and that is what we are teaching" to "you think it is bad here, you should try the South African Army; they are still teaching 'Fix bayonets and charge' as a means to close with the enemy". As I have said before, 'Lions led by donkeys'!

What the FRELIMO thought of our efforts to capture them I do not know, but I am pretty sure they spent a good many hours laughing themselves stupid as they watched our clumsy, futile attempts to track them down. Not that I could blame them. I can imagine what we must have looked like: torn clothing, mouths wide and gaping as we struggled to draw the super-heated air into our oxygen-starved lungs, heads hanging, eyes fixed firmly on the ground in front of us as we tried to stop ourselves from tripping and falling, with heat and the extremely rough terrain and thirst starting to take its toll and exhaustion setting in. With the exhaustion came the lack of coordination or the ability to think clearly and logically; blundering herd of buffalo syndrome set in.

※

It seemed to me that we had been walking around in circles for the last couple of hours, getting ready to disappear up our own arse, as the army saying goes. First the sun was directly in front of us, then on the left, next the right, as we tried in vain to catch up with our fleet-footed enemies. We were not following tracks; there were no tracks to follow. We were following a long-disused path, almost completely overgrown and in places which had disappeared. Why follow a path that had no tracks and had not been used for years, you may well ask yourself? The answer was simple: because the FRELIMO wanted us to. Every time we appeared to get lost and wandered off the path, we were guided back in the right direction by the sound of the chopping of wood, shots or loud voices.

Stops were many and ranged in time from 10 to 30 minutes. The reasons for these stops were two-fold, the first being we were lost and/or tired. It seemed to me we were always lost and always tired. The second reason was for the patrol commander to consult his map, pinpoint our position and send it back to our HQ. The consulting of the map was an event to behold: the brains trust of the patrol, their faces wrinkled with responsibility, bearing a look of prisoners doomed to be hung at first light, gathered around the map.

It was during one such stop that an incident occurred that makes me remember this wandering around Africa with my finger up my you-know-where, without a clue where I was, where I was going and what I was supposed to do when I arrived, more than most beetle-crushing boots on the ground. My stomach had been giving me trouble. Why, I was not sure, but the chances are it was the water we had been drinking. The word 'water' conjures up visions of ice cubes, waterfalls, cooling spray, crystal-clear fast-running streams and deep blue pools. In reality, the water we had been drinking was completely the opposite, coming instead from stagnant, evil-smelling pools.

The day had been normal: the normal bitching and complaining, the normal tripping and blundering onwards, the normal heat, the normal mopani flies, the normal thirst, the normal "where are we?" and the normal stops. It was during one of these "where are we? – let's get out the maps and check" stops. As I sat there, my back against a mopani tree, rifle in hand, watching the brains trust drag their weary bodies toward the patrol commander to begin another long and painful exercise to try to establish where we were, that my stomach tensed and sharp pains and loud rumbling noises followed. I knew the time had arrived. Leaning my rifle up against the tree, I took off my pack, grabbed some toilet paper and headed into the bush. I forgot all about my rifle, the FRELIMO, the heat, the thirst, the flies, even where I was. It was all about my stomach.

Then shots rang out, echoing through the thick grey bush and disappearing down the river we had been following. I froze. There was a moment of utter silence: nothing moved, no more shots, nothing, just fear-laden silence. Even the screeching cicada beetles missed a beat. Then sounds again battered my ears. Puffs of dust appeared magically in the ground mere metres in front of me as bullets went on their journey to deal out death. Leaves floated down from the branches above me, patches of white appeared on the nearby trees as bullets struck, penetrated and went on their way, showering the area with scraps of bark. Stomach forgotten, brain in top gear, I hit the ground behind my intended toilet, a large tree. A split-second later, looking down at my empty hands, I knew I was in deep shit: my weapon was still leaning against the tree where I left it, 20 metres from where I was laying. As I lay there, head pushed into the ground as far as it would go, eyes firmly shut, my body was stiff as a board, sweating partly from fear and partly from having to make a decision on what to do about my rifle. This was not going to be easy. Bullets were flying all over the place – some high, some low; some from behind me, some from my front; others from my left, yet others from my right. We were new at this. This was not the open field where we practised our formations and coming under fire, where we were always facing the same direction, always in a straight line. This was the real thing, in the thick bush of Mozambique, where there was no straight lines. Every time we stopped during training, you moved to what you considered a safe place, sat down, relaxed and waited for the order to move on. If you came under fire while resting, you took cover and fired in the direction you were facing. But now there were no arcs of fire, and only firing when you had a target went out of the door. It was all about survival, and the golden rule seemed to be the more noise you made, the better your chances of survival.

As leaves and twigs fell like rain, tree trunks shuddered and shed bark under the relentless assault of the bullets, and a small cloud of red-grey dust was starting to rise as the numerous rounds struck the ground. Add to this darkening world the buzzing, screaming ricochets and it seemed as if chaos reigned supreme. Laying there, feeling naked and vulnerable, with bullets flying all over the place, shaking with fear while trying to look to my front, left and right all at the same time, my brain in full survival mode, it was not hard to make a decision. There was no way on God's green earth that I was going to move anywhere.

As quickly as it started, the firing ceased, replaced by silence – thick with dust and the smell of cordite – and fear. Twenty minutes later, my rifle firmly and lovingly clutched in my hands, a smile on my face, morale the highest it had been for days, with aches, pains, torn clothes and battered legs and arms forgotten, I bulldozed my way forward through the thick bush, following who knows what, going who knows where, to do who knows what. I was just happy to be alive.

Mavuradona Mountains Support Group, RLI, 1970

His shiny black face was distorted by pain, great rivers of sweat running down his deeply lined forehead into his wide, staring, blank, unblinking eyes. Out of his partially open mouth ran a stream of spittle and a continuous low moan of indescribable pain. He was a black man, middle-aged and strongly built, dressed in a ragged old pair of khaki shorts held up round around his waist by a piece of rope. His white shirt had seen better days, the front of it now sopping wet from the sweat running off his forehead and the spittle from his distorted mouth. Shoeless, his swollen feet were the size of rugby balls from the beatings they had received.

Even the white, badly cracked hardened skin under his feet, which must have been several inches thick from countless years of not wearing shoes and travelling over the harsh rocky terrain that was the Mavuradona, was no protection against the persistent beating by a harmless-looking tree branch against the soles.

His crime? Being in the wrong place at the wrong time; end of story. The fact that he was black did not help.

The bulk of the mountains was imposing as they rose out of the flat savannah, steep and criss-crossed by hundreds of small ravines, forming a formidable obstacle for any terrorists crossing from Zambia. These were the Mavuradona mountains, or as they were known by the Rhodesian Security Forces, the Train.

It was midsummer, with no breeze, and the rocks we were climbing over were hot enough to fry an egg and rough enough to remove huge patches of skin off our arms, legs and any other part of our bodies unfortunate enough to come into contact with them. The sun was a molten ball of fire in the blue, cloudless sky. Up, down; up, down. We had covered maybe a kilometre in the last hour.

Things had started off badly. What had looked on the map like a doable cross-grain patrol (a patrol against the run of the land), difficult but doable nevertheless, had turned out to be an assault course, designed in hell by the devil himself to destroy morale, kill and maim. The steep sides were covered with hundreds of massive boulders, some the size of a house, the gaps between them filled with smaller rocks and the thickest undergrowth imaginable. To add the final touch to this hell, there were hundreds of small, boulder-filled rivers. No man – terrorist or otherwise – in his right mind would use this as a route into the country. There was no water, no food, no friendly locals to lend a hand; only hardship, pain and sorrow.

What were we doing halfway up, or down depending how you looked at it, the Mavuradona Mountains conducting a cross grain patrol was beyond me. Why not patrol along the base of the range looking for tracks, and if tracks were located, follow them to wherever they led? If they go up the mountain, so be it. To stumble around halfway up the mountain, through extremely difficult terrain, loaded down like pack mules, was stupid as far as I was concerned, but then again nobody gave two shits about what I thought.

So here we were, on the whim of some so-called terrorist tactics expert, stumbling around, fighting our way through some of the toughest countryside I had ever encountered. We were not a patrol; we were four individuals, each in their own little swearing, bitching, sweating, bleeding hell of heat and mopani flies, with burning, cutting, bruising rocks and tearing, ripping undergrowth, each doing their best to move forward.

Due to the extremely difficult terrain we had started out in single file, but within half an hour, after arguing amongst ourselves about which was the best route through the mass of rocks and thick bush facing us, this formation had disintegrated into four separate patrols. There was no control, no formation, no plan. The reason for the patrol, the looking for tracks or signs of terrorists passing through the area, was long-forgotten, not that we had any idea what to look for in the first place This was still early in the war, and very few of us had any knowledge of tracking. I would have found it difficult to tell the difference between baboon and human spoor; as it turned out later, I was not the only one.

As we fought our way through this almost impenetrable mass of rocks and bush, it had now become a matter of survival. Terrorists? What terrorists? F*** the terrorists! Caution was thrown to the wind as we blundered forward. If you wanted to know the whereabouts of the other members of the patrol, you merely had to stop and within seconds the sounds of rifles and mess tins hitting against rocks would be heard, accompanied by a flow of abusive words second-to-none. Verbal communication was reduced to climbing onto the biggest rock you could find and shouting at the top of your voice. Today, when I think how unprofessional we were, I cringe. But that was then, and we were angry at having to patrol an area that we figured no person in their right mind would travel through. To make matters worse, it was an idea dreamed up by an individual who had spent the last 10 years sitting in headquarters, whose only knowledge pertaining to the bush and patrolling halfway up mountains was obtained via the odd bit of Sunday gardening.

Four long, tortuous, energy-sapping, foul-mouthed days later we dragged our weary, battle-scared bodies through the last barrier of rocks and undergrowth, and collapsed on the side of the main road between Mukumbura and Mount Darwin. It had been a bitterly hard four days.

※

Back against a tree, cigarette hanging out of my foul-tasting dry mouth in an effort to keep the mopani flies at bay, rifle resting on my pack that I had taken off and had thrown on the ground in disgust, webbing belt undone, legs stretched out in front of me, I tried to relax.

The heat was incredible. It was midday under a blazing sun, not a breeze, no chirping birds, nothing. It was as if every living creature had taken cover in the nearest bit of shade and was saving what little energy they had in an effort to survive the terrific heat. The one exception to the rule was my old friends the 'orchestra of death', the cicada beetles. Even though several years had passed since my disastrous changing patrol formations in the burning heat of the Zambezi Valley, every time I heard their high-pitched screech my hair stood on end, the memories came flooding back and I realised again how close I had come to death.

Shaking my head, brushing aside the uncomfortable feeling of not being invincible, I tried to concentrate on the present and the shit I was in. As normal in the burning heat of an African summer, everything revolved around the availability of water. The hell we had been travelling through for the last four days was not ideal terrain to find water. We had managed to locate water – no, locate is not the right word, giving the impression that we knew how to search for water, what to look for in the way of vegetation and animals to indicate its presence. This is untrue, so I think 'fell over' or 'stumbled across' are better words to describe our finding of several water sources. In the main they were pools hidden between the maze of rocks, out of the direct rays of the sun. They were clean, cool and drinkable, but unfortunately not enough to quench four very thirsty individuals. Thirst became our constant companion, and combined with the scorching heat it dictated our movements. We tried to move early morning and late afternoon, thus avoiding the worst of the African sun.

God, what I would not have done for a drink of water. I was not fussy: clean, from a tap, with ice tinkling against the frosted sides of the glass, or a combination of elephant piss and lukewarm, foul-smelling, algae-filled brown water would do equally well. Pulling the cigarette out of my dry mouth, at the same time a removing a whole lot of skin off my lips, I looked around at my companions. What a sight: exhaustion was etched into each and every face, mine included. We looked like old men. Our dark brown faces, cut and bruised from countless contacts with the thick undergrowth and huge boulders; our eyes red, sunk deep into their sockets, underlined by half-moons of black; white streaks of dried salt running from hairline to jaw, adding a striped, almost clown-like look to the exhausted faces. Our legs and arms were one mass of dried blood and scratches; some deep, some shallow, some septic, some not. We looked like escapees from a lunatic asylum: the dried blood and scratches, the battered faces, the black-rimmed eyes, and the hair – unwashed for days – having taken on the look of thatch.

Nobody said a word. We looked at each other, shook our heads and looked away, each in their own little world. Here we were, only halfway through our patrol and we were already on our last legs.

Squish-quash-squish ... the water rolled around in my bloated stomach as I tried to keep my balance and at the same time watch the bush on either side of the ploughed mealie field we were crossing. I had drunk too much water too quickly, with the result that I now felt nauseous and was struggling not to puke. On the 'up' side I was no longer thirsty and I had two full water bottles on my web belt. A little later, still somewhat nauseous but feeling much better, morale having climbed a notch or two but sweating like a pig – much to the delight of the millions of mopani flies – I did my best to keep my position in our extended line formation. Things had taken a turn for the better, depending on how you looked at it.

We were no longer fighting our way through the deadly maze of boulders and thick bush along the sides of the waterless Mavuradona Mountains, courtesy of what looked like barefoot human footprints. While resting on the side of the main dirt road running between Mount Darwin and Mukumbura, having just completed four days of hell on earth trying to cross grain patrol the Mavuradona Mountains, feeling more dead than alive, I had received a message over the radio. Terrorist tracks had been found by a sister call sign not too far from my location, and I had been instructed to join them – my sister call sign that is. Map reading then being a mystical art form still trying to be learnt by the Rhodesian Security Forces, the joining up took several hours of screaming, shouting and finger-pointing.

It was a case of run, trip, stumble, curse, mouth wide open – trying to feed your staving lungs – ears filled with the sound of your laboured breathing and pounding head, eyes red and burning, looking straight ahead but seeing nothing. All the while the baboons barked. If a herd of elephants had charged across our front, I doubt we would have seen or heard them, as our whole life depended on keeping our dressing. And all the while the baboons still barked. Keeping our dressing was easier said than done, as the tracks that the two trackers of the patrol we had joined were following weaved in and out of patches of thick bush and small clumps of rocks. One minute we were heading north, the next west, then south and then east. The bush got thicker, the rocks more numerous and the tracking more difficult. And those baboons kept on barking.

Rests were many, and eventually the tracks were lost. Our headquarters told us to remain where we were; they would fly in a tracking team. During our wait, a black man was seen walking down a path towards us. We forgot all the aches and pains, the flies, the heat, the anger and frustrations of the past hours; here was our chance to capture a terrorist. That he might be an innocent local going about his everyday business did not enter our minds. He was black, we were following terrorists' tracks, all terrorists were black, so he must be a terrorist. The fact that he was unarmed and his clothing looked nothing like how the terrorists dressed was immaterial. All the while the baboons still barked.

The questions were quick and fast, the answers slow and unsure, the beating slow and never ending. And still the baboons barked.

The sun burned down, the sweat blinding the eyes and setting scratches on fire. The questions continued, the answers replaced by a low moan of pain as the beating continued. All the while the baboons barked.

The trackers arrived. There was a shake of the head, a whine of the turbine and the trackers were gone. The dust settled, and shame arrived and settled on our shoulders like a suffocating cloak. All the while the baboons we had been tracking still barked!

Taking one last look at the painful, twisted, hate-filled face, the eyes that would never forget or forgive, the swollen feet, that would never walk properly again, doing my best to ignore the low moan of pain coming from his mouth, I turned and shuffled away. My back was bent, shoulders drooping like an old man, looking for a dark place to hide my shame and try to understand and make sense of what happened. All the while those damned baboons barked.

Mozambique, South of the Zambezi River, 1971

There was nothing: not a footprint, not an old fireplace, no axe marks on the surrounding trees, no old blackened tin that could be used for cooking, no old clothing. Nothing. Not a single sweet thing to indicate that this was or could have been a terrorist camp. In fact nothing to indicate anything other than that we might be the first people to stumble through this section of hellish desert in the last 50 years.

Exhausted, my spirit down in my rotting green Portuguese parachutist boots, slumped against a stump of a long-dead mopani tree with a cigarette stuck in my dry mouth, I tried to get my sluggish, overheated brain working. What little bit of moisture I had left in my body was draining away in the continual flow of sweat in a valiant but doomed attempt to cool down.

Legs stretched out in front of me, ignoring my pounding head and the smell of rotten meat rising from my feet enclosed in the rotting Portuguese parachutist boots – I could not believe how quickly they had started falling apart – my rifle was across my thighs and my combat cap pulled low over my burning eyes in an attempt to protect then from both the sun and ever-present, indestructible mopani flies.

I looked around aimlessly, but my overheated brain was not registering what my eyes were seeing. Every movement of my head brought flashes of white light behind my eyes. I was exhausted, as were the rest of our four-man patrol. I had been looking at basically the same landscape for the past three weeks: billiard table-flat, stunted mopani tree, waterless, burning hot, morale-destroying desert.

It was early morning and the sky was on fire, changing colour from a deep indigo blue to orange, pink, gold and yellow, with slashes of fiery red. A new day was dawning in the waterless wastes of Mozambique, south of the Zambezi River. With my back resting against a tree, a burning cigarette in hand to ward off the early-rising flies, I admired the beautiful sunrise, trying to put aside all thoughts of the upcoming day and relax.

The past week or two had been hard, constantly on the move, searching for ZANLA terrorist camps that we were told were at such-and-such a grid reference, but never were. How in God's name the numerous terrorists we were told were living in the area survived in their camps in this waterless waste was beyond me. Where they were supposed to get food in this sparsely populated, searing hot desert was a mystery. In the two weeks we had been searching the area, the only tracks we had come across belonged to parties of two or three people, most likely fishermen. Of the large groups of terrorists we were searching for, there was no sign.

It was all taking its toll: the lack of sleep, the heat, the mopani flies by day, the night assault by the multitude of biting insects, including mosquitoes, combined with the pressure of continually being told of large ZANLA terrorist camps in our area which we were to locate and attack with our four-man patrol. Spirits were low, nerves were shot and tempers short. The bitching went on non-stop, most of which was directed at the members of our headquarters staff – or "cupboard kakas" as they were otherwise known – based at the one-horse border post village of Mukumbura. I was young and full of myself My whole world revolved around me: me this, me that. But as the war progressed, I was to realise – somewhat belatedly – that the people who in my arrogance I called "cupboard kakas" were just as important to the war effort as I was.

The silence was awesome: no screeching birds to welcome the slowly rising sun, no breeze, no sound from the surrounding bush. It was as if the entire area – its inhabitants both wild and civilized – were in awe of the nearby flooding Zambezi River. As my eyes, took in the beauty of the slowly rising sun and its magical array of colours, my ears tuned into the deep, pulsating, menacing roar of the Zambezi. Having spent most of youth in the small town of Livingstone in Zambia – then known as Northern Rhodesia – I had enjoyed many happy, carefree hours on its banks and in its cool, fast flowing clear waters: swimming, fishing and occasionally hunting for small crocodiles. I knew the Zambezi River and all its moods well.

I had witnessed the beauty of the African sunset reflected on its waters, and had seen vast herds of animals drinking its life-giving waters. I had also seen its almost supernatural power when in flood. Its roaring, heaving, twisting, brown-frothed waters ripped up massive trees and tossed them around as if they were nothing more than matchsticks. It tore up tar roads and low-level bridges with ease, totally destroying fishing villages too close to its raging waters. Even the Livingstone boat club was not immune. Standing on the wall in front of the club's little harbour, I had watched in awe as, like a hungry monster, it devoured everything in its path. Boats, their anchor chains snapped by the wall of water, disappeared over the nearby Victoria Falls. Other craft, their chains too strong to break, were sucked under and destroyed. Even hippos were not safe, their great bulk treated with disdain as every rainy season saw several of them hurled over the Falls by the raging river.

It had been a long, very hot night. Based on a small hill 2 or 3 kilometres from the flooding Zambezi, sleep had been impossible. The hill had been taken over by numerous biting insects and countless mosquitoes. I had passed the night fighting a losing battle against wave after wave of attacking mosquitoes, and the continuous assault by stinging insects that inhabited our base camp. I, and the rest of the four-man patrol, used everything at our disposal to try to keep the assault at bay, rubbing urine mixed with our oily, useless, army-issue insect repellent onto our arms, legs, faces and ears, but all to no avail. In the end we reverted to the tried-and-trusted method of scratching, slapping, bitching and complaining.

The early morning sun had turned into a supercharged ball of fire, so bright it was impossible to look at directly. Sticking the filter of my long-dead cigarette under the roots of the tree I had been leaning against, I stood up and looked around. Lord knows why. What greeted my eyes was the same scenery that had greeted them for the past two weeks – mile after mile of flat, waterless, burning countryside, broken only by the odd isolated hill and thousands of stunted mopani trees.

I was to return to this area of Mozambique, south of the Zambezi River and north the Rhodesian border, a couple of years later, when it was so dry that water in 44-gallon drums were placed in strategic positions by helicopter for use by Rhodesian security force patrols. This begs the question: if there was no water, what the hell were we doing patrolling the area? To the man on the ground it was simple: no water means no locals, and no locals means no terrorists. But trying to explain this fundamental truth to somebody who had never worked in the waterless wasteland that was Mozambique south of the Zambezi was like trying to explain colours to a blind man.

Absently lighting another cigarette to keep the early-rising mopani flies at bay, I thought about the new task I had been given by my headquarters. Due to my failure to locate the thousands of terrorists and the hundreds of camps that they were using, which according to the powers-that-be were under my nose, it had been decided that instead of wandering around aimlessly in the waterless hinterland, I was now to concentrate along the banks of the flooding Zambezi, checking isolated pieces of high ground – islands if you will – in the massive flood plains for any hiding terrorists. Who in the fuck was going to cross the raging, flooded Zambezi River, and what were they going to cross it in? But the war was in its early stages, and the headquarters was always right! As the war progressed, the various headquarters would realise the error of their ways, leaving most of the decisions to be made by the man on the ground.

I was dressed in green shorts, short-sleeved camouflaged shirt and brown face veil tied around the top of my head to keep the sweat out of my eyes. Around my waist was my standard-issue green web belt and four FN magazine pouches complete with fully loaded 20-round magazines. I no longer used my kidney pouches, now being the proud owner of a big pack bought with my own money. To top off my uniform, my pride and joy was heavily greased, Portuguese green canvas parachutist boots. With a 30kg pack on my back, FN rifle clutched in my dirty, broken finger-nailed hands, grenades hanging from the straps of my webbing, skin colour varying between white and black – with a bit of red thrown in – I must have been a sight to behold. Dressed like a professional, but as it turned out acting like an arsehole! In the big pack was everything but the kitchen sink – spare ammunitions, five days' rations, sleeping gear and cooking gear.

It was hot – heat fatigue hot – it was the end of November and the Zambezi was in flood, turning the flood plains and surrounding land into one massive swamp, alive with hippos, crocodiles, snakes and all sorts of biting, stinging critters. Even more dangerous were the deep holes, hidden logs and in particular – the one that had nearly cost me my life as a child, and that was going to try and take my life again – the small tributaries flowing into the Zambezi itself.

Hidden under what appeared to be the motionless dirty water of the flood plain, these tributaries were death traps. Not only were they deep, but each came with a strong current created by the raging Zambezi as it rushed past, sucking the water out. All of these potential death traps were impossible to see because of the debris-strewn dirty water, glaring sun and mangled, energy-sapping yellow grass, and only made their presence known when you either tripped over or disappeared down one of them.

Then my foot became trapped. I was going to die unless I pulled myself together, of that I was convinced. And with the conviction came panic. Caught in one of the submerged tributaries of the raging Zambezi, my boot trapped in what felt like a tangle of submerged tree roots, I struggled in vain to get my foot free. My body held taut by the unseen current, my foot was anchored in the roots. I was loaded down with the big pack on my back, a pack which at the beginning of my ordeal had provided a degree of buoyancy, but had now filled up with water and become a death trap. Rifle in one hand, using the other to try and keep my head above water and get some oxygen into my lungs, I knew I was fighting a losing battle. Dumping the pack would have been the obvious solution to my problem, the decision taken by any clear-thinking person. But I had left it too late. In an effort to keep my pack – second only in importance to my Portuguese parachutists boots – I had put my life in great danger. The clear-thinking stage was long gone; I no longer had the strength to remove my pack even if the thought crossed my mind.

Taking great mouthfuls of water, struggling to get my foot free from the tree roots, a grey mist seemed to blanket my brain, while strange thoughts passed through my mind: "Thank God you are not carrying the radio or the maps; both would be wet and useless ... If you had been wearing your normal vellies you could have easily got your foot loose." Time was running out, but something deep inside of me refused to call it a day. "Stop flapping around like beached whale, arsehole," my brain screamed. "You've got about 30 seconds before you lose consciousness and drown. Jesus wept, pull it together, relax man, relax. Think man, think. The other guys, even if they managed to see you through the glare of the sun, are not going to be able to get to you in time to help you. You are going to have to help yourself if you want to get out alive. All you have got to do is relieve the pressure on your trapped foot for a split second so you can hopefully pull and twist your foot free of the tree roots. Think man, think!"

Two hours earlier, soaking wet, nerves shot from never knowing what was under my feet, and living in constant fear of disappearing down a bottomless pit and drowning, being attacked by a crocodile or swept away by the raging Zambezi, I had decided that discretion was the better part of valour and taken a decision to move closer to land. Taking the decision was easy enough. I was shit-scared of the flooding Zambezi River. I could hardly drag my eyes from it. Drowning was not on my 'things still to do' list.

The actual moving closer to land was easier said than done. Turning my back on its twisting, heaving brown waters, I headed for the nearest land about a kilometre or so away. It was like operating in a vacuum. The roar of the river was unchanging, blocking out the sound of everything else, while the blinding white light reflecting off the water restricted you vision to a metre or two directly to your front. Instead of one four-man patrol working together to get to the nearest dry ground, we had become four one-man patrols. Each man picking his own route, we headed for dry land. The conditions – the thick grass, logs, holes and submerged tributaries – reduced progress to a crawl. The masses of mopani flies and stinging Chewore buzzards only added to our misery.

Rifles resting on our shoulders, sweating even though we were waist-deep in water, the heat reflecting back off the surface was like a live beast, battering and pounding you, robbing you of your strength, your will power and your ability to think logically, turning you into a robot with only one thought: get to dry land no matter what. Heads bowed, caps pulled down to shield our eyes from the glare of the sun, we pressed on. I felt alone, isolated and vulnerable in my own little world, a cocoon created by the roar of the river and the glaring white sun. There was no reason to feel as I did; the rest of the patrol were all around. Yet we were together but isolated, united but divided.

Every now and again, unbidden thoughts came to me: "What are you going to do if a group of the thousands of terrorists that were supposed to be operating in the area opened fire on you?" The answer – supplied by my devil-may-care, 'I am bullet-proof', positive side – was always the same: "Fuck them! We will handle it if it happens." Before my imagination could take off with all its ifs and buts, the soothing voice continued: "Relax Jim. You have been wandering around this God-forsaken area for weeks now, like a dog with no home, and what have you found?" "Nothing," I answered. "Exactly, so relax and be cool. It's all under control, my friend, let's get out of this swamp and onto dry ground and then take it from there," continued the voice. After hearing what I wanted to hear – even if it came from an unusual source! – I did what most people would do. I relaxed and, feeling more confident, pushed on.

Uncaring and unhearing, we waded, tripped and stumbled our way forward. Great flocks of birds took to the air as we approached, but where there should have been screeching and the sound of beating wings, there was nothing; just the all-encompassing roar of the river.

＊

Now, slowly being dragged under the water by the weight of my pack and the current of the small river in the massive flood plain, I wondered if I would not have been better off island-hopping, moving from one small island to the next.

It was now or never. In a last desperate effort to take the pressure off my trapped foot, I grabbed my weapon by the butt and thrust the barrel down towards what I hoped was a bit of firm ground, at the same time forcing my upper body clear of the water. For a split-second – and a split-second only – my rifle barrel hit something solid before slipping down through the mud. But it was enough to take the pressure off my foot and for me to twist it free.

A coughing, spluttering, stomach muscle-wrenching, lung-burning minute or so later, armpit-deep in water, puking under control but shaking like a leaf, I looked around. The roar of the river was still overpowering, the glaring sun still blinding, reflecting off the floodwaters. The same slow-motion pantomime was still being played out by the rest of the patrol, each in their own little cocoon, heads bowed, rifles over their shoulders, backs hunched under the weight of their packs, eyes staring unseeingly as they fought their way through the obstacle course that was the flood plain. Nobody had even seen the difficulties I had experienced, and my disappearance would only have been noticed much later, once dry ground was reached.

Two days later, after being resupplied by helicopter, we were still searching the banks of the flooded Zambezi for the super-swimmer terrorists when we received information over the radio of a terrorist camp in our area a mere 15km or so away. We were to attack/reconnoitre it at first light the next day. When I asked how many terrorists I could expect to find in the camp, I was told the numbers were unknown, but the camp was large and had chickens and dogs running around in it. Chickens and dogs! It must be a huge camp, and they expected four of us to attack it. When I enquired where the intelligence had come from, I was told the Portuguese Army. My heart sank; another bullshit story! If it was there and so large, why did the Portuguese not attack it? I did not bother asking. I just told my

HQ I would let them know when I was in the area of the camp. Even at this early stage of the war, I had heard stories of the unwillingness of Portuguese territorial troops to engage FRELIMO troops in combat, and that whilst on patrol they would warn the FRELIMO of their presence by talking loudly, banging mess tins and firing off shots. Like I say, just stories, but where there is smoke there is fire.

After a quick look at our map, we headed for a small group of hills we could see in the far distance. According to the map, these were about a kilometre short of where the camp was supposed to be, and thus an ideal place from where to check out the area. Three hours later, tired, back rubbed raw from my big new pack and my Portuguese parachute boots disintegrating around my feet, we stopped for a rest. We automatically adopted all-round defence, nobody saying anything; we were too tired to talk. The last three hours had been anything but easy. The heat, the flies and the buzzards had made things very difficult, to say the least. As I pulled out the map for another look, I could hear the matches flaring as the other members of the party lit cigarettes in a vain attempt to keep the mopani flies at bay.

The sky slowly lightened, the inky black giving way to a colourful African sunrise. We had spent an uncomfortable night halfway up the hill that we figured overlooked the terrorists' camp (complete with its dogs and chickens). The amount of noise we had made as we slipped, fell, bled, and cursed our way up the hill was frightening. If there was a FRELIMO camp nearby they should have heard us; if not the people, then at least the dogs. But there was nothing: no shouts, no barking, no tracers piercing the darkness and streaking towards us. Just an eerie silence, broken only by the distant roar of the Zambezi. The night was long, the insects relentless in their attack. With daylight came increased tension, a sense of excitement tinged by fear. Would we hear dogs barking or roosters crowing around the camp? As it became lighter, I used my binoculars to search the area where the camp was supposed to be, but there was nothing; just countless stunted Mopani trees struggling to survive. The small stream beds that I could see were as dry as a bone. There were no paths; nothing to indicate movement of either animal or humans. I was convinced there were no terrorists or terrorist camps for miles around. This was Mozambique, south of the Zambezi River, where there was no water and the only living things were the flies and buzzards. The big problem was trying to convince my HQ. So half an hour later, in extended line, we stumbled down the side of the hill we had spent the night on in search of the camp our HQ insisted was there.

Many hours later, after failing to find any sign of a terrorist camp, we were instructed to head back to the flooded Zambezi and look for signs of river crossings, presumably by Olympic swimmers and rowers who seemed to have joined the terrorists! This, then, was going to be the story of this bush trip: patrol the Zambezi looking for a crossing point, leave the Zambezi and attack a nearby non-existent terrorist camp, then go back and patrol the Zambezi again. It is very difficult to explain the anger and frustration I felt when being ordered all over the place and told what to do by officers who had never been on patrol or had their arses shot off, but whose sole bush 'experience' revolved about the bar in the mess tent.

Mozambique, North of the Zambezi River. Support Group, RLI 1970-71

It was a wet, cool, overcast morning. "Thank God for little mercies," I thought to myself as I fought back the urge to vomit and pass out. On my hands and knees, I gathered my strength for an attempt to stand. I was having extreme difficulty in getting my eyes to focus. All I could see was bursting flashes of white light; everything else was a blur. I knew from past experience that flashing lights in front of the eyes meant that passing out was just around the corner. To recover from my self-inflicted misery I needed food and plenty of rest, neither of which were available.

I had spent the previous evening getting acquainted with our Portuguese hosts, the local fire water and – my personal favourite – the small brown cigarette with its sweet brown wrapper. I remember little of what happened, other than puking my heart out watched by a group of laughing, sneering, unsympathetic fellow Rhodesian and Portuguese soldiers. Why I did this to myself I did not know. After each episode I always promised myself "never again", but needless to say, every time an opportunity arrived to have a couple of drinks I always found a reason why it would be to my advantage to indulge.

We were at a dirt air strip somewhere in Mozambique. Exactly where, I do not know. I was only a lance corporal and nobody told me much. I was not on the need-to-know list. All I knew for sure was that we were north of the Zambezi River and we were there at the request of the Mozambique Army. Lurching unsteadily to my feet, grabbing onto a tent pole to steady myself, putting a smile on my face and giving the thumbs-up to my watching, smiling friends – most of whom had varying looks of pity on their faces as they watched me try to sort myself out – I must have looked a sight. I was still fully clothed, with green army shorts, camouflage shirt and jacket, and Portuguese army boots which I had managed to exchange my Rhodesian Army black tackies for. Half of what I was wearing was coated in red mud, damp, crinkled from being slept in, and had in places what appeared to be pieces of the previous night's dinner. The combination of the smell of Firewater (the alcoholic drink the Portuguese soldiers had fed me the previous night), puke and body odour was enough to get me heaving. And heave was all I could do as my stomach was empty. My dinner – complete with all the booze I had drunk – was spread far and wide about me, with a good deal of it on my blanket, ground sheet and myself. Being the life of the party definitely had its down side!

Trying my best not to fall over, I squatted next to my pack and dug around trying to locate my towel, soap, toothbrush and toothpaste. I couldn't concentrate, my mind wandered, my head pounded, the sweat poured off me by the bucket-load and the urge to puke was overwhelming. It was a mission to stay upright and not pass out, never mind trying to locate what I needed for a shower. Many lifetimes later, with shaking grimy hands, I had located what I needed, including my one and only change of clothing. Standing up slowly and carefully, ignoring the flashes of light behind my eyes, the pounding head and the laughter from my watching friends, I stepped gingerly – trying to keep my balance – over my pack and rifle, lying on the side of what I called my bed. The latter was nothing more than a damp, muddy, puke-covered grey army blanket, underneath which was my green army ground sheet, also full of mud and other strange-looking things. As I headed for the showers, I knew I should not leave my weapon behind, but I also knew that if I tried to bend down and pick it up I would most probably pass out. Slipping and sliding, feeling very sorry for myself, I made my way along the muddy path towards the nearby toilets and showers. It had been raining the previous night and the ground was wet and slippery, so what should have been a simple walk became a long, lonely journey. I had great difficulty putting one foot in front of the other, and continually veered off the narrow path. Once off the cleared path and into the thick undergrowth that bordered it, I found it very hard to get back on course. The fact that I was still half-drunk did not help, and it took some very stern words to myself to get back on the path and stay there.

※

Slish-slosh, slish-slosh, as well as "fuck this" and "fuck that", muttered just below hearing level of the corporal leading the patrol, were the only sounds to break the damp, oppressive silence. The going was very slow. The weight of the big packs on our backs – containing extra ammunition, rations and radio batteries – caused our feet to sink ankle-deep into the thick mud. The mist was heavy, with visibility down to only 30 or 40 metres. In single file, we followed the narrow, rain-soaked path as it twisted and turned through the thick undergrowth, massive trees and moss-stained rocks. It was cool, with the odd drop of rain and a slight breeze blowing, twisting and turning the mist into ghostly shapes, thick one minute, thin the next, white then grey, trees and rocks eerily appearing and disappearing. Visibility was reduced to 2 to 3 metres on occasion; ideal weather for walking, but also ideal for getting your arse shot off!

The clearing slowly appeared through the swirling mist, surrounded by thickly wooded hills. Massive cave-filled rocks created a natural killing ground for anyone positioned there. The sucking, squelching sound made by our feet as they fought their way through the mud sounded like minor volcanic eruptions. I knew we were going to be ambushed; it was just a matter of where and when.

The sound of the shots echoed around the clearing, making it impossible to tell from which direction they had come. The 'crack and thump' method of locating where the shots came from that we had been taught as recruits was useless in these conditions. The trees, rain and mist absorbed the sound of the gunfire, individual shots merging into one roaring sound, making it impossible to locate the source.

We had been on the move for weeks, trying to disrupt the ZANLA supply lines of men and equipment into Rhodesia, as well as trying to teach the FRELIMO that to help terrorists destined for Rhodesia was not a good idea. Who was teaching what to who was open to debate. I was dead tired, as were the rest of the patrol, now playing a deadly game of cat and mouse with the FRELIMO: you chase us, we chase you; you ambush us, we ambush you. We had entered the 'you ambush us' phase.

Lying behind the small clump of rocks I had taken cover behind, bleary-eyed, head throbbing and hands shaking, I tried to bring my breathing under control. Dressed in shorts, t-shirt and tackies, I had covered the exposed white of my skin as best I could with black camouflage cream, which in the weather we were operating in was a waste of time; the mud could do the job with a whole lot less hassle, but hey, I did as I was told. One thing was for sure: I had definitely seen better days. My feet were rotten, the smell escaping through my torn and equally rotten tackies was overwhelming, and the torn and battered remains of my t-shirt and shorts were slowly disintegrating under the continual assault of sun and rain. I was on my last legs, as were the rest of the patrol. Our bodies were run down, and we had not had a decent hot meal in weeks. Every scratch turned septic, becoming a weeping, rotten patch of flesh. There was no way on earth that you could keep it dry and clean, not in the conditions we were working in, and the continual use of black camouflage cream did not help. The best you could do was piss on it and hope for the best!

The sound of the shots gradually subsided, replaced by a deadly silence, broken only by the sound of dripping water from the tree leaves onto rocks below. My body tensed up as I prepared myself to carry out whatever order the corporal shouted. The seconds ticked by, turning into minutes, but still nothing. I could not believe it. No get into extended line and prepare to advance? No skirmishing? No sounding like a burst geyser as you struggled to dart forward two or three paces and then take cover, all the while trying to keep the muzzle of your weapon out of the thick mud? As the time passed I started to relax, and as my body warmed the mud I even nodded off, sores, aches and pains forgotten

We had not been sleeping well of late. By 'we' I mean the guys from the Rhodesian Light Infantry and the unit we were attached to, who operated differently to what I was used to. In the Rhodesian Light Infantry, the 360-degree circle or all-round defence was the way we were taught. If there were more than four of us, that was the method we used. If less than four, we would walk until it got dark, stop, and sleep where we stopped with no guard. We worked on the basis that anybody watching would not be able to see where we stopped or if we changed direction once it got dark. But in the unit we were attached to we slept in a circle, shoulder-to-shoulder, feet touching to form a smaller circle. It seemed crazy to me, laying in a clearing inches deep in red mud, in the pouring rain for all to see with our feet touching. When I asked why we adopted this tactic, I was told it was easier, and quicker to wake up the entire patrol if danger threatened. So night after night in the pouring rain we slept in this formation. Did I say slept? There was no way you could sleep laying flat on your back, soaking wet, freezing cold, all the while trying to make sure one foot touched the person to your left and your other foot the person to your right. Every morning at first light we would abandon our sleeping formation, put up our ground sheets for shelter from the rain and try to prepare breakfast. Here once again there was a difference in tactics. In the Rhodesian Light Infantry we liked to pitch our ground sheets as low as possible in the thick undergrowth, making them harder to see and at the same time stopping the wind from blowing the rain in. The unit we were attached to preferred to pitch their ground sheets straight and flat at eye-level, claiming that the ground sheet was harder to see as it only presented a thin green line to the enemy, unlike our V-shaped pitched ground sheets. Each unto their own, I suppose.

"Let's go, everybody up, let's get moving!" The message slowly filtered through from the front. Using my rifle butt for support, I literally clawed myself upright like a zombie rising from a swamp of mud. Standing in the swirling mist, covered from head to toe in thick red mud, I was shivering from the cold that seemed to have penetrated deep into my bones, my head dropping in exhaustion from the lack of sleep. It was not that there was no time to sleep; there was plenty. We would normally stop just before it got dark – we had no choice as you cannot follow tracks in the dark – prepare a meal, eat and then bed down. It was the stupid tactics of lying in a circle, feet touching, that was robbing us of our sleep and turning us into the patrol of the walking dead.

Shifting the weight of my body from one foot to the other, I waited for the order to move forward. In the days that followed, the weather cleared up, our morale improved, our sleeping habits remained the same and the contacts with the FRELIMO became more regular, but always from a distance; not too far, just close enough to make us deploy from single file into extended line and keep us on the brink of exhaustion. It is difficult to explain the state of mind of people operating in such conditions. There was the constant rain, the fear of ambush, knowing that the nearest help was many hours away – so the last thing you needed was to get injured – and the thick, green, menacing jungle which reminded me of the *Tarzan* movies I had seen as a child. All played a part, but the most deadly of them all was the lack of sleep. After long periods without sleep, you lose your ability to think clearly, to react on instinct. If you come under fire you deploy, you run forward, you have weapon in your hand, but you do not know you have a weapon in your hand. I am convinced that if on one of our skirmishes we had with the FRELIMO I had come across a terrorist on my way forward, it would have taken me several seconds to realise where I was, what I was doing, the fact that I had a weapon and that the man in front of me was my enemy and I was supposed to kill him with the weapon I forgot I had. Such is the power of exhaustion.

In the days that followed we found many small transit terrorist camps, all deserted long before we came across them and yielding little of interest. We continued our game of cat and mouse with the FRELIMO. At one stage I can remember them using dogs to try to hunt us down, or was it to attract us to them and get us out of the area we were in? I do not know. All I can remember is running up and down streams, scrambling up steep river banks, falling often, my pounding heart sounding like a drum in my ears and drowning out all other sounds, and trying to keep in visual contact with the man in front of me. And yes, I was scared; this was the real thing, not the movies. Even today, at night, I dream of the running, the falling, the pounding heart, the struggle of keeping up with the man in front of me, and forever in the distance the sound of barking dogs.

I do know how we got out of the area we were operating in. Did we walk? Did helicopters pull us out? Your guess is as good as mine. I was so exhausted I was basically brain dead; I could not remember then, and I do not remember now.

This was what the war was about at the beginning, the blind leading the blind. It was all about putting boots on the ground. The fact that there was no plan did not seem to matter much. All the different coloured pins sticking in the map back at HQ looked good and gave the impression that everything was under control and working according to plan. The truth was far different: we blundered around like a herd of drunken elephants, forever told where to go and what to do by an HQ who had no idea of what was happening on the ground. There was no fire force; the nearest help was many hours away, providing the radio you carried was capable of contacting HQ. The fear of being shot ever-present. You felt all alone, deserted. The only constants were the heat, the mopani flies, the continual FRELIMO ambushes and the never ending stream of orders and advice issued by a bunch of non-combatant officers.

There was no Selous Scouts to find the terrorists, no fire force to destroy them. If you wanted to find and destroy the terrorists you had to do so yourself, which was a whole lot easier said than done. In the years to come, the Rhodesian Light Infantry would no longer patrol the thick jungle of Mozambique north of the Zambezi or the bleak, waterless flatlands of Mozambique south of the river. They would be used only as a fire force, a role at which they excelled. I have done both the patrolling and fire force roles. The patrolling in the hell hole of Mozambique was by far the most stressful. You had nothing good going for you: no 'casevac', no air support and very little in the way of communications. When you did have a contact and finally got through to your HQ, sometimes hours later, all you got was a whole lot of useless advice. I am not saying being called out as a fire force six or seven times a day – sometimes more – to a probable contact is easy or a stress-free occupation. At the same time, not all callouts led to a contact, and a lot of the time only one stick of the fire force would actually get involved in a fire fight. On a fire force callout, you also had access to immediate air support and, more importantly, instant 'casevac'.

The First Land Mine of the War in Rhodesia, 1972, Operation Hurricane, Centenary (Farm Lands)

Support Commando of the Rhodesian Light Infantry hit a land mine in Mukumbora, a small village on the border between the then Rhodesia and Mozambique. They were on their way to visit the Portuguese Army unit on the other side of the river, which was the boundary, when they hit the mine. The mine was deemed to be in the Portuguese half of the river and laid by FRELIMO, and was therefore a Mozambique land mine.

My head pounded, my mind was blank, my eyes dry and staring, my mind frozen, my brain still struggling to accept what had happened in the last couple of hours. I was more of a robot than a human being. I looked down unseeingly at my raw, bleeding hands and knees. Little rivers of bright red blood ran down dust-covered legs from the many wounds inflicted by the curved thorns of the 'Wait a bit' thorn bush, many of the thorns still embedded in my flesh. I felt nothing. I had spent the last couple of hours tripping and falling, unknowing and uncaring, as I tried to keep my position in the extended line our patrol had adopted. I was doing a typical mind-in-neutral walk.

Staring unblinkingly at the ground to my front, ignoring the sweat that was causing my eyes to burn and turn red, hands clutching my FN as if my life depended upon it, I hunched over trying to get some blood into my throbbing arms. Breathing like a boiler with a hole in it, neither looking to my left or right, I blundered on. I would not have seen a terrorist if he was 5 feet in front of me, and if I had it would take many seconds for my brain to acknowledge the fact. Slowly, my brain would have told me: "He must be a terrorist because he has got an AK and is wearing terrorist webbing, just like you saw in the pictures back at camp. He is the enemy; you must do something." By then I would most likely have been dead while still trying to figure out what to do. This might sound a highly exaggerated description of my mental and physical condition; it is not, believe me. The combination of shock and exhaustion can do strange things.

The country side we were moving through was beautiful. The water in the small streams was crystal clear, glittering white, silver and blue under the clear African sky. The grass, short and green, was soft underfoot; the rocky outcrops – large and small – awesome in their beauty; the trees many and varied. It was a picture of peace and quiet, as beautiful as only nature can be. My eyes saw all this, but did not register it.

It seemed as if we had been walking forever. My once-clean green army shorts were stained and torn, as was my camouflage shirt. My webbing consisted of four magazine pouches, shoulders straps, belt, two kidney pouches and two water bottles, complete with pouches. The straps of the webbing had two steel rings, from which I decided to hang a high-explosive and smoke grenade. Why the grenades? Who knows ... it looked good. Maybe I had seen too many war movies.

On the back of the Ford F250, standing on the tailboard, everything had seemed to fit comfortably – the belt was tight, but not too tight, the kidney pouches fitted nicely into the small of my back, as did the straps with the two grenades.

That was then, this was now. The weight of the kidney pouches containing five days' rations and extra ammunition, flanked on either side by a full water bottle, with my waterproof groundsheet and blanket tied underneath, had forced the belt up in front until the buckle was riding on my rib cage, making breathing difficult and painful. My front was bad enough; my back was even worse. The kidney pouches with the rations and extra ammunition, sleeping gear underneath, was now hanging down level with my knees. Every step I took, the kidney pouches and bedroll would hit me in the back of my knees, causing me to stumble and on occasion fall, resulting in raw and bleeding knees, elbows and hands. We had been stumbling, falling and getting up over and over for many hours now. Were we on tracks? Who knows, but by the fast pace we were moving and the continual change of direction, I would say not.

At the beginning of the follow-up the pace was very slow, with much looking at the map and long conversations on the radio, the trackers staring intently at the ground and having numerous get-togethers. To say progress had been slow would have been an understatement, but this was at the beginning of the war and none of our trackers had much on-the-job experience; hence the continual checking and double-checking, followed by a meetings between the tracking team and our section commander.

What was discussed, I do not know. What I did know, and I am sure everybody in the patrol knew, was at the rate we were progressing there was no way on earth we were ever going to catch up with, never mind capture or kill, the terrorists whose tracks we were following. The ground we were moving across was for the most part fairly open, short-grassed and lightly wooded; the only down-side the numerous outcrops of rocks, a scattering of trees and extremely thick undergrowth, ideal for ambushes. Whenever the tracks headed towards one of these outcrops, the advance, slow as it was, would come to a grinding halt. Then there would be a long discussion between the tracking team and the section commander. The result would always be the same: from about 30 metres short of the rocky outcrop we would start skirmishing forward. It was slow and exhausting. Fully laden as we were with rations and all the other odds and sods, a short 5-metre dash forward and then dive to take cover, repeated every few seconds until the rocky outcrop was reached and cleared, was torture in the extreme. The dashes forward got shorter, while the time spent lying on the ground got longer. Webbing started falling to pieces, grenades started to fall off, rations started to fall out of kidney pouches, blanket rolls unrolled and belts dropped to knee-level, complete with magazine pouches and magazines, so every time you hit the ground you nearly castrated yourself with your spare magazines.

Why we put ourselves through this hell I do not know. If we had come under fire and needed to close with the enemy, fine, I could understand. But it made no sense just to do it because that is what you were taught by people who knew less than you. Several years later, while moving into an ambush position in the hot, unforgiving Zambezi Valley, our troop commander, a senior NCO, in his wisdom – and calling on his vast experience in such matters – decided to practice patrol formations on our way there. We practiced while he walked along the path. The end result was that we very nearly died of thirst, an incident covered in my first book.

So while did our best to tire and make as big an arse of ourselves as we could, the terrorists went on their merry way. The 30 metres could take anything up to half-an-hour to cover. Towards the end we did not even bother to take cover; we just stood where we were, hunched over, staring at our feet, using our rifles as a support in an effort to keep from falling to the ground. Covered in sweat, grass and sand, minus large areas of skin on our knees and elbows, chests heaving and mouths open as we fought to get air into oxygen-starved lungs, we stumbled forward.

The clearing of the outcrops was a sight to behold. By the time reached our target we were so exhausted we had no strength left to fight though the thick undergrowth, never mind climb the boulders to see if any terrorists were present. We did what most tired people do – take the easiest route, which in this case was skirting around the base of the rocky outcrop not, that I heard any complaints from the section commander or the tracking team, both of whom were just as exhausted as we were. After each such clearing the rest got longer, our spirits lower and the urge to close in on and kill the terrorists waned and almost totally disappeared as each of us, in our own little word of fear, tiredness and pain, concentrated on our own survival.

I am not saying we did not care about the death of our fellow soldiers at the hands of the terrorists and were no longer determined to make them pay. But we were doing what we had to do; the human body and mind can only take so much abuse before it starts to shut down and the instinct for survival kicks in.

✂

The beauty of the setting sun was breathtaking. The murmur of the breeze as it moved through the trees, bringing the leaves to life, was like music to my ears. Nature's delights were such a contrast to the ugly, tragic invents that had happened under the same, equally beautiful, morning rising sun.

Sitting with my back against a tree, feeling though my sweat-drenched shirt the roughness of the bark, the solid strength of the trunk, seemed to give me strength. It sent a message to me my brain: relax, you are alive and well, a whole lot worse for wear but nevertheless alive and kicking. Laying my rifle on top of my discarded webbing and small pack, I tried to pull myself together. I was tired, hungry and feeling sorry for myself.

I knew I should eat something, even it was just a couple of dog biscuits, a tin of bully beef and maybe a cup of very sweet tea. The problem was that I was so tired mentally, as well as physically, that every movement seemed like climbing Everest with a 100lb pack on my back and no oxygen mask. It is difficult to explain the mental and physical state I was in. I was there, but I was not there; I was tired, but I was not tired. It was if there were two of me, one looking down at the other. Everything seemed otherworldly, slow, silent and strangely peaceful, all shrouded in a golden light. Is this the writing of a madman? A man whose mind could not handle the harshness of reality, and took refuge in the world of fantasy? I don't know; you be the judge.

My mouth was dry. It had been dry the whole day, and no matter how much water I drank it remained dry. Five metres away was water; all I had to do was grab my water bottles, walk five paces, fill up and return five paces, and I would have water. Yet the mental and physical strain to complete the 'water run' was beyond me, so I stayed there, a blob of unthinking, unfeeling meat.

We had spent the day skirmishing, falling, sliding and blundering through one steep-sided river after another, always in extended line, always so slow, clumsy and energy-draining. It was all done with little or no control, and was all so unnecessary.

I let the beauty of the sunset, the almost complete silence – broken only by the chirping of the birds and the occasional low-pitched human voice – sooth my aching body and bring peace to my troubled mind as I thought back to the beginning of the day.

※

The morning had started a bit earlier than expected. The voices of the NCOs issuing the normal run of threats seemed more strident and urgent than usual. Through the chaos of trying to get everything ready in the darkness came a chilling message that there had been an attack on one of the farms in the area. As usual, details were non-existent. Being kept in the dark and fed on shit was standard Rhodesian Army policy at the beginning of the war, and remained unchanged throughout its duration.

I struggled in the dark with my fellow soldiers to roll up my blankets in my so-called waterproof ground sheet, check my blood-stopping small green canvas pack had all my requirements food and ammunition-wise, with the overflow put into my kidney pouches. I always struggled with my webbing: nothing seemed to fit, and everything seemed to fall off or dig in where it shouldn't. (RSM Robin Tarr referred to me as a bag of shit with a rope tied around my middle!) In the end I used army socks to carry what I needed, and tied the socks to my webbing at what I considered the best places. Needless to say, this method was doomed to failure. The socks got caught in every bush I walked past, never mind the noise the contents made as one sock smashed against another. Most of my fellow soldiers managed to get their webbing working and looking neat and professional.

I was a nervous wreck courtesy of my vivid, uncontrollable imagination which brought unwanted images to my mind. Shiny black faces, 'dead' eyes – red from the continual use of dagga – filled with hate, flashing white teeth and drooling mouths. Bayoneted bodies and burning farms. Bright flames, with great bursts of embers every time a beam in the roof collapsed, lighting up the farm outbuilding and nearby bush and casting frightening shadows. Black smoke, rising in an endless column, disappearing, swallowed up by the dark night. Mutilated livestock moaning pitifully, dragging their hamstrung rear legs. All these images flashed through my mind as I got my equipment ready so that by the time I fell in I was already covered in sweat and my hands had a slight tremor. Was it fear, excitement or just the instinct for survival kicking in? Maybe a touch of all three.

Several hours later, with the sun beating down on us under a clear blue sky, we were no closer to finding the farm that had been attacked than we were when we left our base camp. Map reading was not a strong point in the Rhodesian Army, and to most NCOs – junior or senior – the map merely represented a nightmare of meaningless black lines.

To overcome this deficiency we spent a lot of time riding up and down, talking on the radio; what was being said I would have loved to know .Our OC at this stage was Captain Ron Reid Daly. After each radio conversation there was much looking at the map, and on occasion even reverting to the compass to try to figure out where we were and where we wanted to go. Standing on the tailboard of the Ford F250, watching our inefficiencies and lack of experience come to the fore, all I could think was thank God the farm attack had already taken place and the farmer wasn't waiting for us to appear over the horizon like the 7th Cavalry and save the day.

Eventually, after much deliberation, raised voices, waving arms and claims that the map was wrong, it was decided to try a well-used track that we had driven past many times in our quest to find the road leading to the farm that had been attacked. I had been travelling in the second truck of our two-vehicle follow-up force, hence I was covered from head to toe in thick dust – my rifle, my webbing and all my other equipment – as were my fellow soldiers. We all had red, itchy eyes, which led to rubbing and resulted in even redder and more itchy eyes. During our wanderings – or should I say bouncing up and down trying to find the correct turning to lead us to the farm that had been attacked – the bitching and moaning from my fellow soldiers was something to behold. Nobody was spared. The drivers were sworn at constantly for going too fast, not avoiding potholes, going too slow, being too close to the vehicle in front ... the list was endless. Then there was the NCOs: "arsehole", "thick as pig shit" and various other comments referring to different body parts and wild animals!

Now that a decision had been made, the bitching stopped, morale climbed a few notches and there was even a little laughter, nervous though it was. While we were riding up and down, going nowhere fast, we had felt safe. The meeting with the enemy had been delayed, hence all the bitching, which was to cover up the fear and uncertainty we were all feeling. However, now that we were once again on course to meet the enemy, the fear and uncertainty returned and all conversation dried up as we retreated into our own little worlds.

While some of us were standing on the tailboards of the Ford F250, as was the custom in Support Group, others were in the back of the vehicle. All were holding onto the railing with one hand, with rifle in the other. Dressed in our green army physical training shorts and camouflaged shirt, with *veldt skoens* or tackies on our feet, webbing adorning our chests, packs on our backs, face veils around our foreheads Rambo-style, we bounced down the dusty, potholed dirt road, laughing and smiling, giving each other the thumps-up like a bunch of kids off on a picnic. Appearances can be so deceiving.

Through the thick, swirling dust thrown up by the Ford F250 in front of us – why we had travel one vehicle on top of the other I did not know – I could see its brake lights flicker red on and off as it slowed down to turn down the side road that was going to lead us to the farm. My hands automatically tightened their grip on the canopy railing and my rifle, while my legs tensed to ride the turn the vehicle was about to make.

As the trucks slowed down to take the corner, the dust thinned and barely 10 metres in front of me I could see my fellow soldiers standing on the tailboard of the first Ford F250.

The Rhodesian Light Infantry had many strange traditions, one of them being that the smaller you were, the more weight they made you carry. In later years I was to carry the MAG machine gun for many miles across rivers and mountains, not because I was small in stature but because I had a big mouth which I had great difficulty controlling. Standing on the left edge of the tailboard of the vehicle in front of us was Corporal Titch Moore, an ex-British Royal Marine. As the name suggests, he was small in stature, but being an ex-marine he was a good soldier, hard as nails, complete with a dry British sense of humour. A signaller by profession, he had a large TR48 radio strapped on his back. How he got the rest of his webbing to fit around his small frame and carry the weight was beyond me. But he all ways looked neat and tidy, was a true professional and a pleasure to talk to and work with.

The ground then rippled, shuddered and heaved before erupting in an ear splitting roar, a sight and sound that would be permanently burnt into my brain. The rear of the first F250 truck in front of s disintegrated, the unfortunate occupants standing on the tailboard sent flying into the air. I stood there motionless, thoughtless, my brain unable to absorb the messages of horror and destruction my eyes were sending to it. After a split-second that lasted a lifetime, my brain started functioning and had to accept the grim reality. Then the shock set in; the type of shock that robs your mind of reason and your body of motion. Who brought us back to reality and got us moving I do not know. Neither could I tell you who served with me on the follow-up mission, who the NCO in charge was or how the dead and injured were taken from the scene. All I can remember of the truck hitting the TMH46 land mine is the different colours as it exploded, the huge black dust cloud, the heaving of the ground and the huge hole it caused. Whether there was more than one land mine involved I did not know, and never tried to find out. The smell of gunpowder accompanied the sweet, cloying odour of burnt blood. I remember the bodies flying through the air, that of Titch Moore laying crumpled and lifeless at the base of a tree, and the sound of the explosion echoing across the open bush. I do not know how many of my fellow soldiers were killed, how many were injured or what injuries they suffered. I do not recall hearing any calls or cries of pain, although I am sure there were many. I cannot remember talking to anybody or receiving instructions from anybody. Why the huge blank I have no idea. Maybe it was too much, too soon, for a mind that thought war was like in the movies to accept.

※

"Balaam, hey Balaam, what's the matter with you? Wake up – we are all fucked!" The rough voice of the corporal pulled me back to reality. The aches and pains returned, as did the feeling of hopelessness, of doing too little and being too late. Tomorrow was another day. Clutching my rifle, I lay down and tried to sleep. Little did I know at the time, but although this had been my first meeting with the TMH46 land mine, it was not to be my last. Later on in my career in Support Group, I guided trucks coming to pick us up over a land mine, and later still I was to use the same land mines against the FRELIMO. Both these incidents are covered in my first book.

Support Group, RLI, Mount Darwin, 1972–73
RPG 7 Rocket Attack, 8 January 1973
It was winter and extremely cold, the bitter, biting wind cutting through my uniform. My body was shaking uncontrollably, my nose running and eyes watering, the extra civilian clothing I was wearing under my uniform having little or no effect on the freezing cold. The wind moaned and groaned its way along the dirt road, creating great clouds of sandy dust and dry leaves. The large trees bordering the road, powerless against its strength, swayed and bent as they struggled to survive, adding their own woeful sound to that of the wind.

The crescent moon, giving only a watery yellow light in the menacing night, appeared and disappeared behind the wind-driven clouds, creating strange shapes and shadows. It was a horrific scene where every sound and shape took on a menacing persona. Everything screamed "Terrorist!", be it sound or shape. Being still very new at this, I saw a terrorist behind every bush and death around every corner.

The beams from the spotlight mounted on the side of the Ferret armoured car cut weakly through the thick cloud of dust and leaves. The dust thrown up by the slow-moving Ferret in front of us did not help. While pissed off at having to travel through the dust, sand and leaves created by the wind and the Ferret scout car in front of me, at the same time I was relieved – not that I would ever admit it to anyone – believing that if there was a terrorist running around with an RPG-7, hopefully he would try to take out the first Ferret and not me.

Tired, freezing cold, swearing and cursing, nerves stretched to breaking point, fingers raw from continual contact with the crude and abrasive welding and the .303 Browning mounted in the turret of the Ferret, of which I was in command, I struggled to keep awake. Even the thought of being attacked failed to generate any energy in my run-down body and frozen brain. In desperation I resorted to lighting a cigarette and letting it burn my fingers in my efforts to keep awake. The burning of the fingers was an old trick I had learnt on guard duty at the Rhodesian Light Infantry barracks. You were not allowed to smoke on guard duty; if you got caught you normally got a day or two confined to barracks, whereas sleeping got you a free holiday to detention barracks. A couple of burnt fingers were nothing compared to the damage I would do to myself if I dozed off and my head hit one of the sharp steel edges of the scout car turret.

Slowly creeping along the potholed dirt roads, the searchlight on the Ferret penetrating no more than 20 metres through the darkness, cigarette burning my fingers, I wondered what we were trying to achieve. The horse had long bolted, and here we were trying to shut the stable door. True, the town of Mount Darwin whose streets we were now patrolling had suffered an attack by terrorists using RPG-7 rocket launchers and various small arms. Several buildings and a road bridge had suffered minor damage, but as far as I knew nobody had been killed or seriously injured. The frightening thing about this whole debacle was that the attack had taken place approximately three weeks earlier.

My wandering thoughts were bought back to the present by a slight change in the tempo of the Ferret's engine. "Oh no, not again; not another burst pipe!" screamed my brain, immediately followed by a surge of uncontrollable anger with a healthy dose of hate. Those feelings disappeared almost as fast as they arrived, replaced by an equally strong fear and uncertainty as the engine died and the

Ferret ground to a halt. Above the howling wind I could hear the hissing of escaping steam. Not bothering to turn to look at the engine compartment behind me, all my anger, frustration and hatred of the stupid things the army did came boiling up to the surface. Tilting my head back, I screamed at the dark, menacing sky. No words issued from my mouth; rather it was an animalistic cry of pain and anger. Head hanging, body shaking with cold and anger, watching the other Ferret's tail lights disappear into the night, I stretched out my hand ad picked up the radio hand set and reported my plight to HQ. Did I expect immediate help? Not me. Procedure was procedure. There was no way on earth that a tow vehicle would be sent out on such a night. It was never going to happen. There was more chance of hell freezing over. The recovery team were probably all still getting pissed in the police bar.

✂

We had arrived in Mount Darwin about three weeks before and had, because of the lateness of the hour, camped in the grounds surrounding the municipal offices. That night the terrorists attacked the town using RPG-7 rocket launchers and various small arms. I had been sleeping on the hard tar of the parking area under a civilian petrol tanker. I had chosen the tanker for the simple reason that it shielded my eyes from the street lights, and would thus allow me to have a good night's sleep. Where my fellow soldiers were sleeping I had no idea. It was a case pick a spot you liked, open your bed roll and sleep. This was still early in the war; towns were thought to be immune from terrorist attack, and thus all-round defence and guard duty, fields of fire and other such nonsense that was practiced in the bush were thrown out for the night. We were, after all, in a town and terrorists did not attack towns. The thought that sleeping under a petrol tanker might not be safe never entered my mind. The war had really not got going at this stage, as I have previously mentioned, and most of us fought the war in our minds and with our mouths in and around the pubs and nightclubs of Salisbury.

I am not sure what time I was awakened by a brilliant flash of light followed by an explosion that rattled and shook the petrol tanker I was sleeping under. A silence in which you could have heard a pin drop from a hundred metres followed. Laying there as stiff as a board, muscles locked, eyes staring up at the undercarriage of the tanker, I tried to get my brain out of frozen fear mode into survival mode. Twenty fear-frozen lifetimes later, or so it seemed to me, another explosion ripped through the still-quiet night, followed almost immediately by a blinding flash of light and a further huge explosion. For a split-second silence reigned as the explosion echoed its way through the buildings and was swallowed up by the night ... then all hell broke loose.

The strange feeling of impending doom was shattered by a single shot. Who fired the shot I do not know, but everyone with a weapon took it as a personal invitation to join in. Muzzle flashes and tracers lit up the skies, followed by the screeching of bullets ricocheting off the ground and vehicles. The tracers seemed to be coming straight for you, while the sound of the bullets and shuddering thud of the machine gun pounded your head and ears into submission. Everything seemed brighter, louder, more frightening as adrenalin surged through your body.

I lay where I was, petrified, weapon tightly clutched in my hands. How long I lay there before my brain and senses started to function I do not know, but eventually the sounds of the battle raging around me registered. The strange whining noises and solid thuds my subconscious had been hearing now made sense; they were bullets hitting the petrol truck I was laying under, some solidly, hence the thud, some glancing blows, hence the strange whining noise. The solving of the strange noises I had been hearing did nothing for my morale and only heightened my feeling of impending doom.

The hair on my neck and arms stood on end, and my body started shaking as taut muscles protested. Summoning every last ounce of courage I possessed, ignoring the vile sweat pouring off my body, I forced my head free of the tar surface that it had attached itself to and looked around through bloodshot eyes. What I saw was not for the faint-hearted – or the shit-scared. Being a member of both sects, I pushed my face back into the tar and closed my eyes, hoping everything would go away. Imprinted on my mind were the flashes of weapons being fired, my ears were full of double-taps and the shudder of machine guns. "Do something!" my instinct for survival told me. "You're going to be burnt alive if this tanker gets hit and explodes." It was wasting its time: fire or no fire, being burnt alive or not, my fearful brain would not answer.

This was the real deal, where you could lose your life if you made the wrong move. You might only be shot accidently, but you would still be dead. The glib answers of a drunk holding up a bar in Salisbury had no place here; all the bravado and the devil-may-care smile disappeared in an instant, brushed aside by fear. Slowly and painfully, my brain fought free of its shackles and started to function, and my training came to the fore. Top of my list of things to do was to keep alive. To achieve this I knew I had to move from where I was and get behind some decent cover. A tanker that was possibly full of fuel was definitely not decent cover. However, knowing what to do and doing it are two different things. Back and neck muscles staining in protest, I lifted my head, expecting to shot any second. I looked around. Behind me was open roadway, the area from which most of the firing was coming from, all of it seeming to head straight for me. I was scared to death, but at the same time angry as all the fire heading my way was from my fellow soldiers. So much for firing only when you have a target visual! To my front was pitch-black darkness, and possibly a group of terrorists. While I lay under truck wrestling with the problem of what to do next, my brain kicked up a gear and listened to what my ears were telling it: the firing had stopped and been replaced by loud, questioning voices. The relief was instantaneous. I was alive! My spirits shot up and even the anger I briefly felt towards my fellow soldiers who were shooting the hell out of me disappeared. Being of a cautious nature and an adherent of the saying "believe nothing of what you hear and half of what you see", I slowly lifted my face and poked it around the front tyre of the petrol truck. How I had ended up laying between the front tyres of the truck I have no idea. As my eyes adjusted to the light, I realised that the wild, random firing had indeed ceased. No more tracer heading straight for me, no more shuddering of the machine gun, no more cracks as the rounds passed over my head. They were replaced by an almost embarrassed silence, broken only by the occasional high-pitched laugh and loud, enquiring voice.

Dragging myself from between the wheels of the truck, I attempted to stand up and alert my trigger-happy comrades to my presence. I failed on both counts: my legs were like rubber and were not interested in standing up, and as for my voice the croak that emitted from my mouth was not worth the effort. Sitting flat on my bum, weapon between my legs, eyes wide and firmly fixed on my nearby comrades, I took deep breaths and tried to get some moisture moving around my mouth so if challenged I could at least answer. I need not have bothered. Nobody noticed when I finally joined the milling ranks. Everyone was too busy telling anybody who would listen their version of what had happened. As I stood waiting for the screaming and shouting to begin, as it surely would, I took stock of myself. Apart from a couple of patches of bleeding flesh on my elbows and knees – the result of my love affair with the tarmac! – I was, all things considered, in pretty good order. I had all my equipment, nothing was damaged or missing, and I was ready to go.

In the following hours, days and weeks, things became hectic and confusing, chaos seeming to reign supreme. Eventually, after all the screaming, shouting and threats, some semblance of order prevailed. The Ferret armoured cars arrived from Salisbury. Maybe 'arrived' is too strong and misleading a word. 'Crawled in' would better describe their arrival. How long the scout cars had stood unused, apart from a short trip here and there, was anybody's guess. To think they were roadworthy and could make the trip from Salisbury to Mount Darwin was stupidity of the highest order. All one had to do was open the engine cover and look inside: there was red, blue and yellow paint everywhere. Gallons of different coloured paint was used to cover all the pipes of the engine. Be they rubber or steel, they were all painted. The purpose of painting the same pipes time and again, layer upon layer, was always a mystery to me. I am no mechanic, and know very little about motors, but I do know a steel pipe covered in inches of dry paint does not cool down like it should, and rubber encased in paint hardens, perishes and bursts under pressure. My knowledge of a Ferret armoured car's capabilities are non-existent, but the little I did know was picked up during our many pipe-painting sessions. Regardless of this, the army being the army, it decided to send the Ferrets to Mount Darwin under their own steam. I must admit I had got it wrong, and most of them did arrive in one piece under their own steam.

In the days that followed I was appointed as a driving instructor of a vehicle I knew nothing about and had never driven in my life. The test to be become a driving instructor was simple. A line of four or so tins were set up in a straight line, and your task was to drive zig-zag style through the tins without hitting them. If you succeeded you became a driving instructor. Rules of the road, road safety and other such rubbish were deemed a waste of time.

Once the required number of drivers was met, I was moved on to vehicle escort duties. Escort duties meant driving a Ferret armoured car as fast as you could along a terrible dirt road, in front if you were lucky – but at the back if you were not – of a column of army trucks and any other vehicles that cared to join in from Mount Darwin to Mukumbura, a small Rhodesian border post on the frontier with Mozambique. What the distance between Mount Darwin and the border post was I have no idea, but if I remember correctly it was a trip of about four to five hours down to the border post and five to six hours back again. Coming back was mainly uphill, hence the time difference.

All that sticks in my mind about my short career as a Ferret driver on escort duty is the dust, the cold, the bursting water pipes, the blown gearboxes, the dodging of potholes, the headaches, the burning, watering eyes, the cramp from sitting hunched up over the steering wheel and – top of the list – our instruction that if we were ambushed we were to drive our Ferret armoured car, Browning machine gun blazing, straight into the ambushers. As the saying goes, 'some mothers have them, then the army gets them'. I was quite happy to give up the long runs and return to town patrols.

※

The radio crackled into life and brought my thoughts back to the present with a heartfelt "for f's sake!" as my frozen hand shot out to pick up the receiver. The answer was what I expected: help would come in the morning. In the meantime we were to stay where we were and guard our crippled Ferret.

To try to describe how cold I was sitting in the steel turret of the Ferret would be impossible. The raging wind made short work of the clothing I was wearing. In the Rhodesian Army we had one type of combat uniform: thin. It felt like I was naked standing under a cold shower with a fan blowing an ice-cold breeze onto me. In a desperate effort to overcome the cold, my mind searched desperately for a solution. Like a cornered rat, it darted from one possible answer to the next. Every possible remedy my brain could come up with was blocked by the same brain with a reason why it would not work. Then tiredness, exhaustion, lack of willpower – call it what you will – overcame me and my mind slipped back into the past. Back to my last pay parade, which had happened about three weeks previously on this very same bush trip, the bush trip on which I was now convinced I was going to die of cold.

I have always though there was something degrading, almost dehumanising, about a Rhodesian Army pay parade. It made you feel like a programmed object, like nothing, just a number. Nevertheless, I had lined up, with pay book in hand, like everybody else, ready to do the halt, the salute, the number, rank and name, the pay checked and found to be correct sir. "Ah, Mister mature," commented Captain Ron Reid Daly, looking down at my signature after I had signed for my pay. Unmoving, I stood with my pay in my hand, staring back into his pale blue eyes. What his problem was with me I do not know, but then again I never asked. This clash of wills – or maybe mutual dislike – between the two of us had started back on my recruit course, when the then Lieutenant Reid Daly was my training officer, and would continue throughout my army career. After what seemed forever, I managed to mutter "Pay checked and found to be correct, sir", turned and marched away.

Even in my half-frozen state, the anger about the pay parade surged up and brought me back to reality. Muttering to myself about "arseholes", I sent my numb hand on a search through my combat jacket looking for a cigarette I did not have.

Giving up in disgust, I stuck my head out of the turret and looked around. The wind still howled, it was still freezing cold, and the leaves and dust still whirled, turned and danced to an unheard song. The only difference was that the sky was lighting up . No sunrise to write home about – no vivid reds, oranges and pinks, just a watery yellow slowly lightening the sky. And with the lightening of the sky the devils of the night fled, replaced by rapidly climbing spirits and a muttered "I hope those useless recovery arseholes are on their way".

Salisbury, 1977

Like a lanced boil, all the anger, frustration, uncertainty, self-pity and hate came pouring out. Common sense, decency, compassion and respect for your fellow human being, especially a comrade-in-arms, was replaced in one blinding second.

Sitting in the front row of the wooden benches in the court room, I felt bad; uncomfortable and ashamed. Dressed in a suit jacket two sizes too big, trousers two sizes too small, green army-issue socks on my *veldshoen*-encased feet, tie tied awkwardly round my throat, long hair neatly brushed, beard trimmed, eyes downcast, staring at the shiny red cement floor of the courtroom, I listened to the young policeman – he could not have been older than 19, and of slight build – trying to explain to the court exactly what had happened.

He was speaking slowly, and not too clearly. That he was still in pain was obvious. Every word came out slowly, painfully and with great difficulty. The cause of his pain was his still-not-completely-healed jaw which had been broken in many places in his encounter with me and several of my Selous Scouts friends. During his entire testimony he never took his anger-filled eyes off myself and my two co-accused friends. Unable to meet his accusing gaze, my eyes dropped to the shiny red floor of the courtroom and my thoughts raced back.

I had been on a seven-day break from the bush and had started the evening off before hitting town – as I had started numerous other evenings – drinking half a bottle of brandy. Why, I do not know. I just sat there in the couch in the lounge of the house I was sharing with my friend Paul Kruger, listening to but not hearing the radio, and drank half a bottle of brandy. Did it make me feel good? Did it make me happy? Did it make me sad? Did it make me feel aggressive? Did it make me help me relax ? Truth be known, it did nothing: I felt no happier, no sadder, no more relaxed or more aggressive than I normally felt. I guess I just drunk it because I drunk it.

The night continued with a visit to a *Chibuku* beer party accompanied by my friend Jim Lafferty. *Chibuku* beer was the native Zimbabwean beer, made of maize and several other types of grain, all brewed together to produce a thick white, somewhat coarse liquid which I found quite nauseating. Nevertheless, I managed to squeeze down a glass or two mixed with Coco-Cola before my stomach revolted – not that I blamed it – and I ended up rushing outside and puking up the whole lot on to the lawn. Lights flashed in front of my eyes, hot flushes attacked my body and sweat poured off me in buckets, the thick puke threatening to block my air supply as it gushed out through my nose. My stomach muscles twisted and heaved, my vision blurred, as I staggered around desperately trying to get my balance and not fall into my own puke. The life of a big-time drinker is fraught with dangers. Gradually the world stopped spinning, my eyes stopped watering, my legs strengthened and my drunken waltz steadied to a weaving, sideways shuffle. A minute or two later I managed to actually stand still. The word 'stand' implies I was upright, but nothing could be further from the truth. Bent over at the waist, mouth open, breathing like I had just completed a marathon, I tried to suck in air through my mouth, my nostrils being blocked by a thick mixture of *Chibuku* beer, neat brandy and a dash of coke. For a while it was touch-and-go as to whether I would die from lack of oxygen or drown in my own puke, which threatened to gush out every time I tried to take a breath to feed my burning lungs. Being a survivor of many and varied puking episodes, I managed to control the almost overwhelming urge to vomit and sneak in a couple of mouthfuls of oxygen.

As my breathing returned to normal, I straightened up and took stock. As usual, my on-looking friends offered sarcastic advice amid much laughter, both of which I chose to ignore. Not because I wanted to, it was just that I was afraid that if I opened my mouth to answer I would start puking again. Putting on an air of "all is well, I can handle it", I did a quick inspection of my clothes and shoes. I knew exactly what I was going to see. My maize meal washed velies, my pride and joy, were covered in a dark brown layer of puke. My denims, from the knees down, were covered in the same, as was the front of my shirt. I could handle the shoes, the denim legs and the shirt front being covered in puke; a hosepipe, a bit of watering down and some vigorous rubbing, and all would be well. The fact that my breath smelled like I had a decaying body in my stomach bothered me not in the least. The way I saw it, a couple of beers would sort that out. When you are drunk, you are drunk, brains and common-sense having long departed. After much searching, my eyes finally located a tap. It took a while for my confused brain to register that my eyes were looking at a tap, and a further couple of minutes to realise why my eyes were looking at the tap. I casually strolled across to the tap, which unfortunately did not have a hosepipe attached, to begin my clean-up. I say 'casually strolled across', well at least in my mind I did. In reality I probably lurched towards the area of the tap, my feet making squelching noises in my puke- filled velies. The washing-up was not easy. The velies and trouser legs, which should have been simple, were the opposite. They took time, as I found it difficult to stand still, especially on one foot. It was one step forward, one step to the left, one step to the right and one step to the rear. Every time I came to what my mind told me was close enough to the gushing tap, I would stick out a leg in the hope as I staggered past that some water would start the cleaning of my shoes and trouser legs. After several failed attempts, I realised I would have to get up-close and personal with the tap. Blocking out the laughter ringing in my ears, ignoring the hot flushes that seemed to have taken root in my face and neck, I fought back the slowly mounting anger and frustration and tried to concentrate on the task at hand. Concentration was a non-starter. Being drunk, to try and do two things at the same time was impossible. In a last-ditch effort, I managed to grab the tap as I two-stepped past it. On my knees, head hanging, breathing like this was the first oxygen I had drawn into my lungs in the last half an hour, hands clasping the tap in a death grip, I tried to relax and clear my mind of the mammoth task ahead, ridding myself of the puke covering my clothing and shoes. Anything that requires concentration and co-ordination is impossible for a drunk. And drunk I was.

Time stood still as I battled to get one leg under the tap in an effort to kill two birds with one stone, cleaning one velie and one trouser leg at the same time. Magic! As far as my alcohol-soaked brain was concerned, it was definitely the way to go. The only problem was to convince my hands to give up their death-like grip on the tap. Eventually my hands forgot why they were holding onto the tap and released their grip. Sitting flat on my behind in the mud, I proceeded to clean myself up. One velie, then the other; one velie, then the other. How many times I washed them out, and how many times I rinsed my trouser legs and shirt front, I had no idea. One thing I did know was that wallowing around in an ever-increasing mudbath was not the way to go if I was serious about cleaning up. I was fighting a losing battle. It was splish, splash, stumble, fall, as I fought to keep my balance and what dignity I had left. I was, after all, a hairy bummed Selous Scout, and to be affected in this way by a couple of *Chibuku* beers and half a bottle of brandy was a disgrace.

A couple of minutes later, sobering up rapidly and dying of embarrassment, all the while trying to act cool and in control, I decided it was time to move on.

Gathering what little I had left of my pride and dignity, I squish-squashed my way – amid much laughter and crude comments – towards the nearby road and darkness; darkness that would hide me from my friends and their harsh, but true, comments. That I looked a sight, I had no doubt. Soaking-wet long hair plastered to my skull, scraggy beard pointing in all directions, wet clothes plastered to my body, the *Chibuku* that had adorned my clothes was now gone, only to be replaced by large patches of red mud. Add to this my squishy velies, themselves now a dark red, the runny red eyes and the never ending snorting as I cleared my throat and nose of the last remnants of my encounter with the beer, I was definitely somebody I would hate to meet in a dark alley.

I was on my way to grace Le Coc Dor nightclub with my presence. The scenic route I took was long, hard and filled with many hazards, but by sheer determination I conquered them all and arrived at the bottom of the dark, narrow steps leading up to the Round Bar, my favourite drinking spot. If truth be known, any place I happened to be drinking in was my favourite drinking spot! I huffed, I puffed, I slipped, I crawled. Bright lights flashed in front of my eyes every time I hit my head on the wall, and the loud music rushing down the stairs was like a physical force pushing me backwards, causing my already throbbing head to feel like it was going to burst, all the while struggling not to puke up what remained of the *Chibuku*. To say I was having difficulties would be putting it mildly. I had climbed up these self same stairs that now seemed Rhodesia's answer to Mount Everest many times without any problems; the only difference was that then I was sober, now I was drunk.

I was tough, I was lean and I was mean – Rambo had nothing on me. I could handle anything that came my way, no problem, anything that is except the stairs leading up to the Round Bar. Ten lifetimes later, having suffered verbal abuse on an unprecedented scale, I stumbled out of the 'dark hole of Salisbury' onto the brightly lit pavement. I was back to where I started, at the bottom of the steps leading to the Round Bar. Bent over, sweating like a pig, head pounding, and swinging from side to side as my eyes struggled to focus on something – anything – to try to get some form of stability to my upside-down world. I tried to make sense of where I was and what I was doing. It was a non-starter. Then, like a light in a dark, demon-filled night, a parking meter floated into view. It was my salvation; all I had to do was grab the parking meter and then all my problems would disappear and the world would make sense again.

Slowly, like I was stalking a highly strung antelope in the bush, I approached the parking meter. One step forward, one step to the left, two steps to the right, half a step back. Things were going from bad to worse: I could not stop weaving. In one last throw of the dice, I launched myself towards the parking meter; it was all or nothing. If I missed, I would land on the bonnet of the car parked behind the meter. Time stood still, my whole world revolving around getting my hands on the parking meter. It was my lifeline, my way out of the situation I found myself in. Such is the mind of a drunk: directionless and confused.

Flashing lights, pounding head, watery eyes, legs doing their own thing, co-ordination non-existent, brain locked into getting to the parking meter, I floated – or so it seemed to me – towards my salvation. Somehow I managed to get a hand to it, and like a shipwrecked sailor hauling his body on to a deserted island, I pulled my body towards the parking meter. Head resting on the top of the meter, eyes firmly closed, arms in octopus mode wrapped around the pole supporting the meter, breathing like this was the last oxygen on earth that I was cramming into my lungs, I tried to calm myself.

"Hi Andy – you OK?" Like a drowning man, my mind latched onto the question. Confusion, self-pity, anger at myself; all dropped away. The question was a lifeline and became the centre of my existence; my sole reason for living. My brain stepped up a notch from pickled stone dead and floating in alcohol, to just floating in alcohol. Lifting my head and not letting go of the parking meter was a feat of concentration. The world swirled, lights flashed, my heart pounded as though it was about to burst and my watery eyes struggled to bring the smiling face towering above me into focus. Then the mist lifted, my eyes focused, my brain fought free of the clutches of the demon alcohol and started to register what my eyes were seeing. Standing above me was my friend Joe Bressler, ex-SAS, and next to him was another friend, Mervin Gallias, ex-Support Commando – now both Selous Scouts. Both were also awesome soldiers and took shit from no one. If you wanted trouble these two were the right guys to give it to you. On the other hand, if you were in trouble they were also the right guys to get you out of it. And I was in trouble.

I was drunk, to say the least. Regardless of my earlier clean-up efforts and short-lived feeling of wellbeing, I was still drunk. Nevertheless, I was now amongst friends, which raised my spirits tremendously. My eyes seemed able to focus, and the pounding in my head came down to a steady thump. The pavement, however, had a will of its own, seeming to twist, turn and do whatever it liked, as did the whirling, upside-down world around me.

I latched onto my two friends like a leech. Salvation was at hand: they would make sure I got home in one piece. Where we were going, I do not know. I moved from parking meter to parking meter, all the while trying to give the impression that all was well. But although my clothing was now basically dry after my efforts to clean up, what the rest of me looked like is anyone's guess. Leading the way was Joe Bressler, leapfrogging over the parking meters as he came to them. Joe and Mervin had had a couple of drinks, I am sure, but compared to me they were sober.

It is difficult to explain the anger, frustration and hate you carry around, hidden just below the surface but forever boiling, ready to erupt in a split-second. We were doing nobody any harm. Maybe leaping over parking meters was breaking the law – I do not know – but it wasn't hurting anybody. Suddenly, out of nowhere, a small police van with a canopy on the back, brakes screeching and lights flashing, came to halt next to the pavement just in front of us. Drunk I might have been, but I knew as sure as the sun would rise tomorrow that whoever got out of that police car was treading on very dangerous ground. If he said one word out of place he would regret it for a long time to come. Out of the front of the van jumped a very young and frail-looking white policeman, complete with weapon – a pistol of sorts, in a holster attached to the belt around his waist – while out of the back of the van jumped a black policeman complete with a barking, lunging Alsatian.

It was a mismatch from the start. There was no way on earth that one young white policeman, armed though he was, and one black policeman with a dog were going to handle the three of us. The policemen were doomed to failure. They were casualties waiting to go to hospital, and the dog was dead meat. The anger, aggression and hate we carried with us was directed against anyone, or anything, that threatened us. We had spent weeks or even months at a time in the bush, living like animals, unwashed, nerves stretched to breaking point, eating and drinking whatever was available as we fought to survive and stay sane. Add to this boiling cauldron of anger and aggression a string of commands and instructions – nine times out of 10 issued by people who had not the faintest clue on the subject they were issuing orders or instructions about; instructions you have to obey no matter how ludicrous – and you have a volcano ready to explode for the slightest of reasons.

Adrenalin surged through my body, my legs strengthened and straightened, the moving pavement steadied, my eyes focused, my headache disappeared, my breathing slowed and my brain kicked into survival mode. We did not move, we did not talk to each other; we just stood there and waited. The blaring music from the nightclub above us disappeared, the street lights seemed brighter, the air smelt cleaner and the cars moving up and down the road seemed to float on soundless engines. The 'slightest of reasons' required for the volcano to explode struggled out of the police van, joined by the dog handler with his wildly straining-at-the-leash charge.

It was finished before it even started; it did not last more than 60 seconds. The barking dog – so full of life – was now a cooling lump of meat laying on the pavement, his handler disappearing into the night and safety. The frail young policeman, his face and uniform covered in blood, was lying across the front seat of his van, radio microphone in his hand, screaming for help from his HQ. His jaw was shattered, hanging at a strange angle, and he was having great difficulty speaking, even in shaping his mouth so the words would come out correctly. I felt nothing. No anger, no happiness, no hate, no fear – nothing. Just a great sweeping tiredness.

"Will the accused please stand." The words jolted me back to reality. Still staring at the red polished floor, head hanging, I rose to hear the verdict of the court. To this day I do not remember what the outcome was, but I knew there was no way anything serious would happen to us. They needed us in the bush, the war was raging on and we were good at our jobs. If one dog had to die and one policeman had to suffer a miscarriage of justice, then so be it. It was, after all, for the good of the country.
Cherededzi, 1977

Selous Scouts Bouncing Bomb

It was a hot, quiet, still night. Loaded like a pack mule, crouched down on the side of the path I had been following, an AK47 assault rifle was clutched tightly in my trembling, sweaty, camouflage glove-encased hands. Why the gloves? Mainly for protection: climbing thickly wooded, boulder-strewn hills at night was no easy task, and my hands took a pounding, either from grabbing onto trees and rocks to stop myself from falling or from breaking falls which I could not prevent. I stared intently though bloodshot eyes into the surrounding darkness, ears straining to pick up the slightest sound. My foul-tasting mouth was dry and my tongue, thick with plaque from teeth that had not been cleaned in weeks, darted in and out in a vain attempt to keep my chapped lips wet. Cleaning teeth with salt was fine, but it also made you thirsty so unless I had plenty of water available I did not bother. Water was a problem in the area where I was presently working, so I did not bother.

My body tense like a coiled spring, my heart pounded and – worst of all – my imagination started to run wild. The 'what ifs' flew thick and fast. The trickle of sweat running down my back turned into a river as my imagination took hold. Every shadow looked like a terrorist, each noise my straining ears heard sounded like an AK47 safety catch being flicked.

It was the middle of summer and the rainy season, and the dark cloudy night was typical for that time of year: hot, sticky, with little or no breeze. The watery yellow moonlight would normally have been enough for me to see what was happening around me. However, because of the clouds the little moonlight we had was more of a hindrance than a help as it continually disappeared and reappeared. It did not allow my eyes to adjust properly to the light, and scared the shit out of me by turning what I knew to be trees and bushes into terrorists.

With a shaky hand I tried to stem the river of sweat and black camouflage that was pouring out of my balaclava into my eyes. My back was a throbbing mass of muscles and raw, burning skin, partly from the weight of my big pack which somehow – no matter what I tried to do to prevent it – always managed to remove the skin from my shoulders, but also from the tension of the moment. To make matters worse, the blood was no longer flowing freely into my legs and they were starting to cramp up. Time seemed to stand still. I had no idea how long I had been crouching by the side of the path, but one thing I did know was that if I did not move in the next couple of minutes, I would fall over as I lost all feeling in my legs.

Planting my AK47, butt first, firmly between my feet, ignoring the burning eyes and throbbing back, I took a deep breath and, holding onto my rifle-cum-walking stick for dear life, I attempted to stand up. It was touch and go for the first couple of seconds as I fought to keep control of my spaghetti-like legs. Bent over at the waist due to the weight of my pack, I knew if I fell it was going to be face-first, and the chances were that I would do myself some grievous harm, losing teeth or even an eye as my face smashed into the rock-strewn ground. Like a drunken ballerina on steroids wearing size 10 army boots, I lurched and staggered around, all the while trying desperately not to make any noise, lose my weapon or – more importantly – smash my face into the ground. Backwards, forwards, to the left, to the right, round and round in circles I went in a desperate effort to keep my balance and stand up at the same time. Failure seemed imminent. I was breathing like a 60-year-old halfway up the stairs in the Empire State Building. I was starting to lose control of the situation; my legs were starting to buckle again.

Suddenly, bright lights flashed in front of my eyes as my head slammed into something hard and unmoving. Still bent over under the weight of my pack, I dropped my weapon and instinctively grabbed hold of the object I had walked into. The sound of my weapon hitting the rocky ground seemed loud – unbelievably loud – echoing away into the still night. "For God's sake," screeched my fear-frozen brain, "why do you not put up a neon sign with an arrow pointing to where you are? You have been doing this for years and you still can't get it right."

With the fear came the adrenalin rush. One second I was clinging desperately to what turned out to be a large tree, struggling to stand up; the next I was standing up against the tree. My heart pounded, sounding like a bongo drum in my ears, as the adrenalin surged through my veins, and with it came instant strength. The pack suddenly weighed nothing, my fucked-out legs became pillars of steel, my bloodshot eyes became night vision binoculars and my ears could pick up the sound of a pin dropping on a carpet from a hundred metres. Such is the power of fear and the instinct for survival. Standing unmoving next to my saviour – the tree – my body was braced for the impact of incoming bullets, which my wild imagination assured me were on their way and which is what I deserved after the dropping my weapon and making enough noise to wake the dead.

Barely breathing, my hands clenching and unclenching, frozen still, my body now covered in the cold, rancid foul selling sweat of fear, I stared into the ever changing shadows. As the seconds passed I started to relax: no bullets, no shouting from the nearby villages, no strange noises from the surrounding bush, none of the eery moonlight-covered bushes suddenly turning into a charging terrorist. As the seconds turned into minutes, the sweating eased, the muscles in my back unwound, the tension left my legs and, concentrating hard, I managed to get my hands to relax. I was alive. I had a throbbing, bleeding head from my connection with the tree to add to my woes, but nevertheless I was alive.

My spirits started to rise, my brain started functioning and I realised I had been lucky that the noise of the fallen weapon – and subsequent dancing routine – had not alerted the numerous dogs in the area to my presence. Eyes still scanning my surroundings for any movement, ears straining to pick up the slightest out-of-place sound, I slowly lowered myself back into a crouch. I had to recover my weapon as quickly as possible. If things suddenly turned nasty, loaded down as I was, I was not going to be able to run myself out of trouble; I would have to try to fight my way out. To do that, I needed my AK47. The sound of my pack sliding down over the rough bark of the tree, as I lowered myself down, seemed awfully loud. I hesitated. Would this tiny noise, which sounded like a drum roll to my adrenalin-charged ears, be the straw that broke the camel's back and pin point my position to anybody listening?

As always when under pressure, I started talking to myself. In these instances I had two names: Andy and Jim. Who knows why; it just happened!

My mind latched onto this strange set of circumstances and used them to basically create a 'fall guy' for Andy. His name was Jim. In times of stress, Andy always seemed to disappear and hand over the mess to Jim, and then from a distance heap scorn and abuse on poor, panicking Jim, trying at the same time to lay to rest all the demons that were troubling him when he had handed over the situation to Jim. It is strange, weird, even frightening, but it worked and had got me out of a lot of tight situations.

So in this instance Andy said: "For F's sake get a grip of yourself Jim, there's nothing happening, there are no terrorists attacking you. You have not even seen one, you have heard no shots, so what is with the prima donna story? You are supposed to be rugged, devil-may-care, hairy assed commando. Pull yourself together, find your weapons and let's get the F out of here before all the terrorists in the area are attracted by all the noise you made and shoot the shit out of us."

Taking a deep breath, pushing my throbbing, bleeding head, and other aches and pains, to the back of my mind, trying desperately to control the jerky movements of my head and eyes – left, right, centre, left, right, centre, like a wind-up toy with a broken spring, looking everywhere but seeing nothing – I continued lowering myself downwards.

"For F's sake, it has got to be around here somewhere. Slow down; you will find it, so do not panic. It is here somewhere; it hasn't grown legs and walked away." Down on my hands and knees, talking to myself, back bent to breaking point under the weight of my pack, head pounding, eyes burning, I tried to locate my weapon. What should have been a simple task was rapidly turning into mission impossible. Like a chicken without a head, I crawled around, this way then that, all the while feeling with one hand in the grass and amongst the rocks. My other hand at this stage was busy stopping my backpack sliding forward and slamming my face into the ground. Panic reigned, all logical thought going out of the window. Instead of taking the pack off and searching, slowly and carefully, I scurried around on all fours like some demented baboon. If there were any terrorists watching, I did not need a weapon to defend myself: they would have died laughing!

As the seconds passed, my search became more and more frantic. Rolling my head from side to side like a wounded buffalo, mumbling and bitching to myself, I was almost crying in frustration as I attempted to locate my weapon amongst the grass and rocks. Slowly, from the dark and misty world of my brain, a simple message got through: "What the F-ing hell do you think you are doing?" Like a punctured tyre, all the anger frustration and panic left my body as I cringed in embarrassment. My body and face went hot and then cold; if I had not been wearing camouflage cream my face would have shone like a beacon.

Sitting on my arse, leaning against my big pack, head hunched between my shoulders, I forced myself to relax. Slowly the tension left my body, my muscles started to unknot and my senses returned .I was no longer a mindless, panicking animal; I had become a thinking, breathing – but shit-scared – human being again. With the thinking and breathing came the throbbing head, the aching back, the sore eyes, the shaking hands and the cold sweat of fear.

That there were terrorists in the immediate area was not in doubt: one of my pseudo-groups had spent the last couple of days trying to arrange a 'meeting' with gthem. Whatever happened to me now was my own fault. If I got ambushed, so be it; maybe I would learn something from this self-inflicted disaster. Slipping my arms through the straps of my pack, all aches and pains forgotten, I slowly got myself up into a crouch. Every nerve in my body was stretched to breaking point, my whole body was covered in a cold sweat, my legs trembled, my ears strained to pick up the slightest sound and my eyes sought out the slightest movement which could indicate the presence of anyone. The seconds, then minutes, ticked slowly by, but there were no strange sounds, no suspicious movements. Everything appeared normal.

I could hear the dogs barking in a not-too-distant village. Barking dogs always made me nervous when on operations, especially at night. It meant there was somebody else moving around out there in the darkness. I assumed the dogs were barking at terrorists. The locals did not usually walk around at night: they had learnt from experience or word of mouth about security force ambushes. On the plus side, the barking was not spreading from village to village, so whatever they were barking at was not moving. My breathing slowed down, the panic receded, the brain kicked in, the imagination disappeared and reality returned, as did strength to my legs and arms. I located myAK47, and as my shaking hands clutched it to my chest, a feeling of happiness swept though my body, all the recent doubts and demons evaporating as my shattered confidence returned. Big pack returned to my protesting back, lost AK47 in my hands again, I continued with my journey.

Barely two hours later, I started my assault on the hill which was to be my home for as long as need be. A walk in the park it was definitely not. Swearing, tripping, falling and bitching, with every step forward the Jesse bush took a piece of skin off my legs, arms or face. Clad in long black pants, long-sleeved shirt, my lucky green padded jacket, balaclava and AK chest webbing, carrying an AK47 which seemed to catch and hook in every bush, I struggled up the steep hill. My clothing and weapon were hindrance enough, but added to these was my big 40kg pack crammed with radios and spare batteries, food, as much water as I could carry and of course my lucky blanket. A walk that should have taken a leisurely three or four hours in the daylight, turned into a six orseven- hour test of endurance in the hot, mosquito-filled night.

How I wished I could move more during daylight hours. Not only would I be able to see where I was going, but I would be able to cover ground so much quicker. But as I was working in a so-called tribal trust land, movement had to be done at night. I was working alone, as I preferred, and if I had stumbled into a local villager during daylight hours, especially at close range, and I was seen to be a white man, I would not have many options open to me. I could either let them go and blow weeks of hard work, putting myself and my pseudo-operators in danger – not a likely choice – or 'eliminate' or capture the local. Being alone, weighed down by all my equipment and clothing, the thought of trying to capture a local who recognised me for what I was and keep them captive did not even enter my mind. This was a frozen area (out of bounds to security forces other than the Selous Scouts) and in it my decisions were final: I was the judge, jury and executioner. There was no leave to appeal, no second chances. What I said went, end of story. I answered to nobody but myself and my conscience. So rather than put myself in an unwanted position of judge and jury, I moved whenever possible at night.

As the sky slowly lightened, I stopped my noisy assault up the hill for a rest and to determine how long I still had to go before I reached the summit. Why I bothered, I do not know, as whereever I looked all I saw were huge boulders and thick undergrowth, with nothing to indicate how far I was from the top. The bush was so thick that even the goats had failed to make paths through the undergrowth in their never ending quest for food. With no help by way of a path or game trail, I would have to revert to the blundering, swearing, tripping, falling and bleeding method. But should I stay where I was for a while and set up my radio, in case my call signs needed help, or maybe the fire force? Mornings and afternoons were the busiest times as far as the fire force where concerned, plus I had the added worry of a possible terrorist meeting one of my call signs. If I stayed where I was, would I have communications with my far-flung call signs? Sitting on my arse halfway up the hill, I doubted very much if I would. Putting my fate and those of my call signs into the hands of the gods of war, I continued my fighting my way up the hill. It had been hard work so far, but now the going was even tougher as the A63 radio I had taken out of my pack and put on my chest hindered my vision and restricted the movement of my arms, so the falls became more frequent. The rising sun also meant the day once again became incredibly hot.

The radio by my side crackled into life. I was so tired after the beating I had taken climbing up the hill to my present position that all I could do was stare at it in confusion as I tried to figure out where I was, what I was supposed to be doing and where the radio fitted into all that. Eventually everything fell into place. Stretching out a shaking hand to pick up the receiver, I hoped it would be good news.

"Eeche," the silky smooth voice of Corporal Clemence floated over the airwaves. "There is a group of eight to 10 terrorists who want to meet with us." My hair stood on end, my body started to shake with excitement, as a cold shiver of anticipation, mixed with fear, ran down my spine. My already parched mouth, tasting like a urinal mouth, went even drier . All the aches and pains, all the bitches of the previous weeks, disappeared. Who cared about the nauseating smell of rotting camouflage cream, the stinky feet, the putrid sores, the millions of ants by day and the equally large swarms of mosquitoes by night, the sanity-destroying mopani flies? Not me.

The adrenalin started to flow. My brain raced ahead: pictures of fame and fortune flashed through my mind. If this was the resident group that wanted to meet with Corporal Clemence, and we managed to capture the whole group without the locals knowing, the sky was the limit. We could clean out the whole sector without too many problems. It all depended on whether, after we had captured the resident group, we could turn a couple of key members of the group into working with us. If we could, we could capture every new group that moved through the area. The plans of mice and men! Forever lurking in the background was the dreaded IF.

"When do they want to meet?" I whispered into the receiver. "They sent us a letter requesting a meeting," came the reply. "We replied asking them when. We are still awaiting an answer." The area we were operating in was very much in support of the terrorists, and we had had found the going very difficult. The locals, very sympathetic to the terrorist cause, were very suspicious of any new faces and our groups had struggled to get food and water, never mind be accepted as the real deal. In many cases, if the resident group was not sure if terrorists passing through their areas were the real thing or not, they would instruct the locals to feed the in-transit group and at the same time find out as much about the group as they could. The letter Corporal Clemence had received asking for a meeting could be a genuine indication that they had been accepted. On the other hand, it could mean they had not been accepted and were being set up to be ambushed. The answer lay in the letter. If they were willing to come to us, fine; we were home and dry. If they wanted us to come to them, then maybe we were not accepted and were about to have the shit shot out of us. Yet as the resident group, they had the right to demand that the meeting took place in their camp or any other place of their choosing. There were so many 'ifs' and 'buts'. All would be revealed in the letter.

The sun was by now beating down, with my thirst growing by the second, and I fought the temptation to gulp my last drop of warm, dirty water as I swept the villages below me looking for the closest water supply. Working alone had its disadvantages: if you wanted water, you had to go get it. The mopani flies continued to try ad drive me crazy, getting in my ears, up my nose and even diving into my eyes. I cannot adequately explain the anger and frustration that surged through me as I sat crouched in a small cave waiting to hear back from Corporal Clemence. It was not directed at any particular person or thing, but at the world in general with all its stupidity.

The heat was unrelenting. To touch the rocks with your hands was asking to be burned. I was so tired I sat in the cave with my pack still on, while at my feet lay the A63 radio with my AK47 on top of it. My eyes burned non-stop, day and night. My jacket – indeed all my clothing – was soaked by sweat. The stench from my clothing, unwashed body and rotting camouflage cream was enough to floor an elephant. My shoes were covered in small black ants – thousands of them. Those same ants would swarm all over my body at night while I tried to sleep: up my nose, in my ears, up my trouser legs and jacket and shirt sleeves. It had happened to me before. After one of my moonlight travels, I had ended up on a hill previously used as a relay station or maybe an observation post. It had been dark when I finally reached the summit, and as was my custom I looked around for a place to sleep which also offered a bit of cover from incoming bullets or mortar bombs. Nearby had been a small outcrop of rocks which seemed to meet my requirements. Selecting the flattest piece of ground I took off my big pack, unrolled my ground sheet and lay down with AK47 clutched in my hands and radio switched on near my head. Several hours later I had woken up screaming. I was covered from my head to toe in ants. It felt like my skin was alive, moving of its own accord. My nose and ears were blocked and it felt like I was suffocating. I could not breathe or see. It felt like I was being enveloped by a moving mass, a flowing monster. I panicked, screaming and shouting as I tried to get my clothes and shoes off. How long it took to undress and rid myself of the thousands of ants I have no idea. In the early morning light of the following day, I could see the deep scratch marks I had inflicted on myself in my efforts to get my clothes off. In the days that followed, I used all my army-issue mosquito repellent to eventually kill the last of the ants in my ears.

Back to the here and now, all around me were empty food tins – from bully beef to baked beans – hence the ants. The hill I had chosen had also been used as a relay station. The ants no longer bothered me when it got dark, as I would gather all my equipment and move to a sleeping place well away from where I had spent the day. You could never tell who had seen you and, if anyone had, what plans they were hatching. It would only cool down in the early hours of the following morning, many hours hence, so to pass the time while waiting to hear about the meeting from Corporal Clemence I returned to searching the area with my binoculars looking for the closest water source. I had very little left, and would have to go down to get some tonight like it not, tired or not. But where ever I looked all I could see was burning red sand. The paths – some of them as wide as a single-lane tarmac road – lay dead under the shimmering heatwaves, their surfaces occasionally brought to life by tiny dust devils. The few trees that had not been cut down for firewood hung their heads as if waiting to join the already dead mealie stalks in the unploughed fields. Huts, red in colour with grass roofs long turned grey-black by the harsh African conditions, stretched to the horizon. All was still, all was dead, all was red, with no movement of animal or man, bird or insect. I was struggling to find a water source of any kind, never mind one close to me.

I knew there had to be water somewhere, and with the amount of huts spread out in front of me it had to be a large and steady supply. Lowering the binoculars, I leant back on my pack and closed my eyes. I needed to rest my eyes: I was starting to see things that I knew were not there. It had been a long night, and a bit of a rest would do me the world of good. Several hours later, I woke up with a fright. Panic set in, my head swivelling left and right, my hands instinctively shooting out to grab my AK47. Still half-asleep, it took a split-second for me to realise where I was. How I had managed to sleep at all in the heat, bugged by ants and mopani flies, was a miracle in its own right, but to sleep for three or fours hours was something else again. A whole barrage of thoughts struck me as I looked around with big eyes, heart pounding, AK47 clutched in my hands. "You've been stupid; you could have got your head shot off," I muttered to myself. I had a couple of rules when working by myself: never sleep in daylight hours, and never sleep in a place you have spent any time in. I had broken both! As my breathing returned to normal, the tension left my body and my muscles relaxed, I started dealing with the barrage of questions that had built up since opening my eyes. First and foremost, had Clemence called while I was having my beauty sleep? If he had, I could only hope that the situation he was reporting was not serious. A close second was the fact that before I had dozed off I had not managed to locate a water source – and no water equals no life.

Grabbing the binoculars, radio and my weapon, I moved closer to the edge of the hill. I had to find water before it got dark. I had about half a water bottle left, which I was planning to use to make myself a cup of very sweet tea once it cooled down. The energy I would get from it would hopefully get me down then back up the hill once I had collected water. With my mouth was parched and my lips were starting to crack. If I could not find water tonight I would have to ask one of my call-signs to bring me water or call a helicopter for resupply, neither of which was to my liking. Laying flat on my stomach, elbows spread wide, binoculars to my eyes, ignoring the ants and flies, I slowly swept the villages below. The valley was coming to life. The sun was going down and the heat was easing, and with that came movement of both animal and human. What I was looking for was a water party, or anything that would indicate the whereabouts of water. Ten minutes passed and I had still not seen anything. Giving the binoculars a rest, I gazed at the valley below with naked eyes. Binoculars are great for magnification, but they also restrict your view. I had no sooner put the binoculars down when I noticed a group of women heading for the base of the hill I was on. At this my spirits rose, my thirst seemed not so bad and the air even seemed cooler. Putting the binoculars back to my eyes, I had a closer look.

A water party it definitely was, but a traditional African water party it was not. It was nothing like it is often portrayed in the movies, with tall African women with the bearing of a queen, in traditional dress, carrying large, beautifully crafted painted clay pots on their heads, walking along a path which wove its way through gently rolling hills covered in green grass and numerous animals, all heading to the stunning, crystal-clear waterhole. Gone was the traditional dress and clay pots, replaced by colourful but cheap and gaudy Western dresses and plastic containers of various colours and shapes. There was nothing dignified about the group or their walk; they slouched down the path, their dragging feet raising clouds of red dust that seemed to hover in the still air before finally returning to the baked earth. I watched for as long as I could until they disappeared into the bush at the base of the hill. That was one problem solved: as soon as the light started to fade I would make my way down there and fill up my water bottles and one surviving black sandbag liner.

"Ye gods, get a grip of yourself my man. You are carrying on like a prima donna," I muttered to myself some time later. I had woken up again in a bad mood. My head ached, my eyes looked and felt like somebody had pissed in them, while my collection of cuts and bruises and the awful smell that rose from my filthy body added to my misery. Sweet tea or no sweet tea, the water collection had been a disaster. Suffice to say, I returned with only my four water bottles filled, my sole surviving sandbag liner having fallen prey to one of the many thorn bushes I had met on my way back. Adding to my world of self-pity was the fact that the meeting that was supposed to be between Corporal Clemence and a local resident group of terrorists had encountered some snags. The letters and questions had been flowing freely between the two groups since early in the morning, but for some reason they no longer wanted to meet with Clemence. They now wanted to know who he was, where he had trained, who was his instructor etc. etc. I wanted to call out the fire force, but Clemence wanted to carry on trying to organise a meeting. He was the man on the ground, not me, so I waited, getting more pissed off by the minute. I spent my time killing flies and ants and studying the villages below through my binoculars to see if I could pick up on any out-of-the-ordinary behaviour that would indicate terrorists in the area. Yet there was nothing but red sand. In the back of my mind I wondered what had brought about the sudden change of attitude by the terrorist group. The reason could be anything from not wearing two sets of clothes – as was the case in some areas – to Clemence having been seen talking on the radio.

The hours dragged by slowly, then at about 0900hrs I was asked by Corporal Clemence to put the fire force on standby. Things had gone from bad to worse and there was no chance of a meeting; in fact from what they could gather from the locals who supported them, the real group of terrorists was planning to attack them. (This incident gives the reader a good idea of the confusion that a pseudo-group of terrorists can cause in an area. The locals do not know who is who.) After much shouting and screaming, I realised I was not going to get the fire force, mainly because there wasn't one to get! However, I could have a Canberra bomber drop bouncing bombs in the area where the terrorists were situated. Bouncing bombs? I wanted to scream. What the fuck did I know about bouncing bombs? The only bouncing bombs I had heard about were used to blow up a dam wall during the Second World War. What was I going to tell Clemence when he asked about the fire force? "Do not worry my friend, we are going one better than the fire force, we are sending a Canberra bomber which is going to drop bouncing bombs; not ordinary bombs, oh no, these are special bombs: they bounce!" Throwing down the receiver of the TR28 radio I always carried and used to contact my HQ, my already bad mood worsened. Self-pity oozed out of every pore of my body, and like a spoilt child I started kicking the empty food tins. To my rescue, through the mist of my anger, came Andy: "And now arsehole, what's your problem, feeling sorry for yourself? Instead of trying to make a plan, you are walking around in the open kicking tins like a spoilt 4-year-old child. What's the matter with you? Nobody's going to drop bombs on you. You are safe here on the hill. What about Clemece and his call-sign, for God's sake, get it together." All the anger gone, I sat with my AK in my hands next to the A63 radio, waiting for Clemence to call.

The way I saw it we had two options: attack the terrorists ourselves or let the Canberra and the bouncing bombs do their thing. As there were no helicopters available for casevac, I figured the best was the Canberra. Approximately five hours later, at 1400hrs, the silence above my hill was broken by the gentle whistle of a low-flying Canberra, followed a few seconds later by what sounded like short bursts of fire from a machine gun, only a whole lot louder, sharper and quicker. How many bombs were dropped and how many short bursts of explosives I heard, I do not know. In the silence that followed, the sound of what I assumed to be the bouncing bombs exploding echoed over and again, slowly fading away in the distance. Upon checking the area, Clemence found no bodies, but saw blood in several places, plus bits of clothing and shoes spread over a large area. Was I disappointed? Yes I was; a lot of hard work had gone into the operation and no kills was disappointing. If I had the chance to use the Canberra and its bouncing bombs again, would I have used it? No, I would rather wait and buy time until the fire force became available.

Mortars, Mozambique – Helicopter Deployment, 1977/78

Dressed in a pair of green army shorts and camouflage shirt, with velies on my feet, a bit of 'black is beautiful' slapped around my face, arms and legs – old habits die hard – AK webbing on my chest, radio on my back, map and 81mm mortar range tables stuffed down the front of my shirt, my AKM clutched in my unfeeling hands, I was there, but I was not there. My bloodshot eyes stared unblinking, unseeing, at the ground flashing by a mere 10 or 20ft below the helicopter. My body, buffeted by the wind created by the rotor blades of the helicopter, was numb, as was my brain.

To me, the sense of excitement, the challenge, the thumbs-up to the mortar crew in the helicopter with me were a thing of the past. This was now business as usual, no smiles, no thumbs-up, no excitement, no challenge: just do what had to be done, quickly and efficiently, and try to survive and get out in one piece. Looking across the helicopter at the blank, unsmiling faces and staring eyes of the two-man mortar crew accompanying me, I could see they felt the same. Forcing myself to relax by shutting my eyes, taking deep breaths and staring at the trees as they flashed by just metres below the helicopter, I let the previous days flow through my mind.

Everything had been going so well. It had been more of a holiday than an operation, at least it seemed that way to me, especially as I normally operated alone .This time I had company aplenty. No longer confined to a fort (the name given by the Rhodesian armed forces to the tin Selous Scouts operational camps scattered around the country), my suntan had come along in leaps and bounds, regardless of all the sarcastic "you look like a freak ready for a sideshow at a circus, with that brown-almost-black face and bright blotchy red body, scraggly beard and long hair" comments from my so-called friends. I had to admit that after the continual use of 'black is beautiful', my face had taken on a greyish tint, and it did not take much sun to turn it a very dark brown. It was the first time in a long while that I had not gone on an operation covered from head to toe in foul-smelling camouflage cream, loaded down like a mule, dressed in long trousers, long-sleeved shirt and balaclava. This was great in itself, but the cherry on the top, as far as I was concerned, was that I could shower, bath, wash – whatever you wanted to call it – whenever I wanted to, could clean my teeth using toothpaste rather than salt, and just as importantly had no more foot rot. Coming a close second was decent food and drinkable water .No more half-cooked chicken and various other local 'delicacies' supplied by my call-signs. No more cow dung and urine-tasting water. In many cases the water I used came from a water point used by livestock, and you could taste them. Water had always been a problem for operators in the bush. Hampered by their white skin, which even when covered by 'black is beautiful' would never have passed close daytime scrutiny, they had to collect their water by night in most cases, thus making water a precious commodity. Climbing and crawling around in the dark with black plastic sandbag liners filled with water, trying your best not to puncture them, was not my idea of fun.

We had been deployed to provide support fire with the 81mm mortars to an operation taking place just across the border in Mozambique, and for a change I was not directly involved. After a long and tiring drive along some really terrible dirt roads, chased by large swarms of biting tsetse flies, which had a field day every time our vehicle stopped or slowed down, I figured I lost at least a half a cup of blood. How they managed to bite through the thick layer of dust we were all covered in, plus our clothing, lord only knows. After each successful bite, the victim would erupt, the swear words would flow like water and the slaps, though many, seldom made contact with the fast-flying tsetses; the score remained in favour of the attacker.

We had arrived at our destination, somewhere near the Mozambique border in the area where South Africa, the then Rhodesia and Mozambique met, late in the afternoon. It had taken a couple of days to settle in, after which it had been all beer and skittles as far as I was concerned. What was going on inside Mozambique I had no idea, but it seemed very quiet considering a major operation was taking place. Not being on the need-to-know list, I did not worry too much about it. For all I knew, the operation had not even started. The only thing I knew with any certainty was that Dennis Croukamp had been in, or was in, the area on a reconnaissance; I was told no details, only that I should keep an eye open as he might be along the road somewhere waiting for uplift by us or helicopter. All I can surmise is that maybe something did not go as planned.

One glorious day flowed into another. Each morning started with a glorious sunrise like only Africa can produce. The bright reds, brilliant oranges, equally shocking pinks and purples, all set against a rapidly lightening blue sky, the nearby hills slowly emerging from the darkness, the trees and huge boulders gradually taking shape as the sun's power increased. Throw in the bark of the baboons drinking at the nearby river with the cries of the Franklin and guinea fowl, and you have a welcome to the day second-to-none. The sunsets were equally breathtaking, the colours the same as the sunrise, brought vividly to life by the slowly setting ball of fire.

During these first few days all was quiet. Too quiet, considering we were operating in Mozambique and our base camp was just inside Rhodesia. This being FRELIMO country, I expected the odd mortar attack just to keep us on our toes. So far nothing, not that I was complaining as being attacked by mortars, day or night, was a nerve-racking experience. On day four or five – I'm not sure which – just as the sun had started clawing its way into the sky, was interrupted by the distant sound of gunfire. Everything seemed to freeze in anticipation of what was to come next. The volume of rifle fire slowly increased, the machine guns joining in and sending their message of death in short, angry, shuddering bursts. I sat there transfixed by the sound of the distant battle raging. My heart pounded, I started to sweat, my ears produced a strange singing noise, my muscles tensed and my hands clenched and unclenched. War does strange things to a person. It is easy to get addicted to the adrenalin rush provided by battle. Half of me wished I was there, while the other half was happy I was not. Wearing only my green army shorts, bare-footed, a hot cup of tea in one hand, letting the breeze cool my chest – complete with its countless mosquito bites, not that any part of my body had fared well against the nightly attacks by thousands of mosquitoes from the nearby river – it took all of 10 seconds for me to realise that I was not in a holiday camp; I was there to provide fire support to my fellow soldiers when they needed it. The fire controller with the attacking force was none other than Vancy Meyers, one of the more colourful members of Support Commando who had ended up in the Selous Scouts. (If the truth be told, he was a skelem – or villain – of note, well-known throughout the Rhodesian Light Infantry, Selous Scouts and most other units. In later years, when I was trying to get into Iraq to make a few Rand as I was unemployed at the time, my good and trusted friend Vancy Meyers stabbed me in the back. He told my would-be employers not to hire me as I was an epileptic. Shame on you Vance! I did not want *your* job, I just wanted *a* job.)

Jumping to my feet and trying to take a sip of hot tea at the same time resulted in me bellowing at the top of my voice "Stand to!" from a burnt set of lips. Why I shouted "Stand To" and not "Positions" I do not know. Maybe too many clearance patrols, something I last did when I was in the Rhodesian Light Infantry. I hated doing clearance patrols, for the duration of which I walked stiff-legged as if I had a carrot up my bum, my back muscles tense and throbbing in anticipation of being shot by one of my own after being mistaken for a terrorist in the poor light. I often wondered what would happen if we actually met a group of terrorists on one of these patrols. Would the clearance patrol deal with them, or would the rest of the section get involved with us ending up shooting each other to pieces?

The manning of the mortars took a whole lot longer than I had expected. I was not the only one who had frozen on the sound of the distant gunfire, nor the only one who was half-dressed thinking he was on holiday. After several minutes of chaos, order emerged. The mortars were manned, with ammunition of various types prepared. I had my plotting board and pencils at the ready, radio glued to my ear. I might have appeared cool, calm and collected, a picture of the highly trained professional soldier. Yet appearances are deceiving, as inside, my mind was running riot – what about this, what about that? – with each question lowering my morale so that by the end of my self-imposed cross-examination I was a nervous, incompetent wreck. My hands were shaking, my eyes were watering and I could not sit still, staring at the radio with the eyes of a condemned man. This was for real: if I fucked up, or Vancy fucked up, our own troops would die.

The minutes passed, nothing happened, and gradually the sound of battle faded away. Maybe I wouldn't have to supply fire-support after all. Sitting on the ground with my plotting board on my knees, I wondered what was happening. Had we attacked the camp and destroyed it or had we got our arses kicked? However, before I could follow this train of thought any further, two Hawker Hunter jets screamed in just above tree level, straight over our base camp. I got such a fright that I momentarily froze, before instinct and training took over and I ended up in a mortar pit with my head buried in my hands. The arrival of the two Hunters made me think that maybe we had underestimated the enemy and had got ourselves in the shit. Several minutes later I watched the two Hawker Hunters, in the far distance, do what appeared to be multiple rocket strikes. Like two great silver birds of prey, their wings flashing in the early morning light, they came out of the rising sun, striking again and again. I could only faintly hear the explosions, but on occasion see what appeared to be white flashes as the rockets left the wings of the diving Hunters. They left as fast as they came. One moment they were carrying out air strikes, the next they streaked just above our camp heading back to their base, job done. Or so I thought ...

I felt a great sense of relief as I watched a black cloud of dust rising from the area of the airstrikes. If the Hawker Hunters had done their jobs correctly, there should be no need for mortar-fire support. I was good at my job. I was the master of the mortar, and what I did not know about being a fire controller CPO (Control Post Operator), or a good-old number one, two or three on the mortar line itself, was not worth knowing. I had been taught by the best: mortar men like Frank Ricardo and Stan Van Breda, both great friends and awesome soldiers. Nevertheless, as good as I was I did not enjoy using the plotting board. It was big, clumsy and after a few minutes' use was covered in hundreds of little crosses. If you did not concentrate 100 percent the potential for major fuck-ups was great. I preferred a map, a good radio and a set of range tables.

In the distance, carried by the wind, I could hear the sound of sporadic gunfire. Nothing heavy, just short bursts or double taps, as if the troops were advancing in extended line to clear a terrorist camp. After a while, the sound of the gunfire no longer registered as our ears got used to hearing it. Life returned to normal on the mortar line; in other words, everyone lay around doing nothing, apart from smoking, trying to kill the ever-present mopani flies and the favourite pastime of all, bitching. I started making a cup of tea to replace the one that I had spilt. Sitting on a mortar ammunition box, thinking about nothing in particular, I waited for the water to boil. Suddenly my body tensed, my back straightened, my head swung towards the sound of distant gunfire and my eyes stared unblinking into the distance as I listened. Seconds passed, but there was no change as the sporadic bursts of gun fire continued. I started to relax – "Hearing things, Jim?" I had no sooner finished talking to myself when I heard the sound that my sub-conscience had perceived: the slow, thudding thump of a heavy machine gun. As far as I knew, our troops where not carrying any heavy machine guns. That being the case, the weapon I was hearing was being operated by the terrorists and in all likelihood was a 12.7mm Russian-made heavy machine gun. I also now knew what the Hunters had been having a go at, and that they had failed. With this knowledge of the failure of the Hawker Hunters to neutralise the terrorists' heavy machine gun came a cold shiver of fear and inevitability. I knew what was going to happen next; they were going to have a go at the heavy machine gun with a heliborne mortar team. How many heavy machines guns there were I had no idea. All I knew was that if the Hawker Hunters could not get to them, they must be well dug-in and could probably only be neutralised from above. It was the perfect job for an 81mm mortar.

As the saying goes, pre-warned is pre-armed, so I started organising all the necessary bits and pieces required for the successful deployment of a mortar by helicopter. Guessing that the target might be dug-in with overhead cover, I had half of the high-explosive bombs I intended to take with me set on fused delay, which would allow them to penetrate what cover there was above the machine guns before exploding and hopefully destroy the guns and their operators. The briefing when it came was short and sweet. There were 12.7mm heavy machine guns dug into the side of a cliff and they needed to be destroyed as they were giving our ground troops a hard time. Four or five minutes later we were airborne.

A punch on the arm brought me back to the present and reality. Jerking my eyes away from the flashing trees below, I looked across at the helicopter pilot. Helicopter pilots all seemed so cool and laid back. Even during a contact, their voice remained very calm and clear, whereas I shouted and screamed and acted like an idiot. How they managed to keep their cool was beyond me. Following the direction of the pilot's pointing hand, I noticed several white-painted buildings below. Roofless, with all the doors and windows removed, along with most of the white plaster, they looked as if they might have previously been part of the Portuguese border post or trading store. Pointing his finger at me and then again at the white buildings below, I got the message: he was going to drop me near the buildings. Giving him the thumbs-up, I looked again at my mortar crew. There was no change: the same faraway look in the eyes, the deadpan face, the overly relaxed slouching body, all put on to give the impression of indifference – "check me, I am cool and nothing bothers me. I can handle it." Nothing was further from the truth, as I knew they were shit-scared like I was. Their brains were clogged with fear, their muscles were frozen and stiff, their heads felt like they did not belong to them and their hearts pounded so loud that they could barley hear the sound of the rotors as they slashed through the air just above them. Young as they were, they were also veterans. They had done this before, and would do it again if needed.

The helicopter landed, or rather hit the ground, with a thud and a blinding cloud of dust. I noticed the pilot put us off to one side of the buildings, using the buildings to protect us from any incoming rounds fired from a nearby range of hills. I might have been shit-scared, but I did remember the briefing saying something about hills, cliffs and 12.7mm heavy machine guns. I just hoped the buildings could stop a heavy machine-gun round.

In a matter of seconds, with the help of the technician, the mortar barrel, base plate and bipods were offloaded, closely followed by the ammunition. I reckon that just 30 seconds later, the mortar – pointing in the direction indicated by the pilot – was up and ready to fire its first round. Standing to the rear of the mortar, range tables in one hand and radio receiver in the other, with AK47 laying in the dirt at my feet, I waited for instructions from the helicopter pilot. As the dust cleared, I looked around the spot where we had been dropped. It was devoid of any vegetation – no trees, no grass, no rocks, no anything. Only red sand. Talk about sticking out like a dog's ball: it could not get much worse than this. Looking at the nearby white buildings, all I could see was bullet holes – some big, some small. It looked like either it had been used for target practice or a major fight had taken place in and around it. The walls looked very thin, and I doubted very much if they could stop a standard AK47 round, never mind one from a heavy machine gun. The silence was eerie, broken only by the sound of the helicopter rotors. There was no sign of life – no birds or even a lizard – and no breeze to move the dust filled air. Yet as always when I was in Mozambique, I had the feeling I was being watched and that death was just around the corner. If there were any terrorists in the immediate area, then stuck out in the open we were dead meat.

I did not know what the problem was with the helicopter, and why I had received no instructions. All I knew was the longer I stood where I was in the open, the more chance I had of getting killed. I was already getting very nervous, the sweating had started and I was finding it difficult to concentrate. My head swung from left to right, eyes darting all over the place, as I stared imagining I could see terrorists in the buildings. I was no longer standing upright, but rather crouching with my AK clutched firmly in my sweaty hands. The problem was, I did not know which way to face. Looking at my two-man mortar crew, I could see they were also feeling the strain. Their weapons were no longer laying in the dirt at their feet, but instead were in their hands. The seconds dragged on, each one feeling like an hour. My shirt was by now soaking wet and my imagination was running wild. It was the first time that I had time to think about how exposed and vulnerable a heliborne mortar crew really was. We were alone in enemy territory, isolated, with the nearest help miles away. An unarmed helicopter was not much help.

I was so preoccupied with trying to face all directions at the same time, talking to myself and trying to remain calm, that I only managed to hear the tail end of the message that my radio received. Picking up the receiver with a shaky hand, I managed to croak out: "Say again." I was informed that the pilot had pointed out the wrong direction for the mortar to face, and he was going to fly over us to give us a new direction. With something to occupy my mind, all the demons of previous minutes were gone. "Shot bombs gone – time of flight?" I screamed into the radio. All my fears and uncertainties disappeared with the bomb leaving the barrel. My mind was now focussed on getting the bombs on target, and with a bit of luck destroying the 12.7mm. While I waited for corrections for line and range from the pilot, I could not stop looking to my left and right, eyes darting all over the place. The corrections were small and few, and it did not take long before the pilot reported "Target destroyed; prepare for uplift."

It sounds so simple: get into the helicopter with a mortar and ammunition, get out of the helicopter, set up the mortar, fire a few bombs, destroy the target, get back into the helicopter with the mortar and return to base. All so straightforward, almost mundane, a walk in the park. Yet nothing could be further from the truth. It was dangerous; in fact it was extremely dangerous. From the moment you are told you are going on a heliborne mortar mission, the tension, the pressure and the uncertainty immediately start to take their toll. The smiles disappear, replaced by deadpan faces. The laughing eyes go dead and have a faraway look, tempers are short and movements are abrupt and jerky. Talking is almost non-existent, while laughs become high-pitched and shrill.

The mortar team consists of only three men, and each has his own job to perform. To perform his job efficiently, each has to put his own life at risk. There was nobody to watch your back while you concentrated on the job in hand. Always dropped in the open because of the high trajectory of the mortar, the crew were a sitting duck for anybody to have a go at. You went in alone without protection; all you had going for you was speed. No matter how you looked at it, it was definitely not boring or mundane. It was dangerous, and it took brave men to operate the mortar.

The trip home was more relaxing, with the odd smile and thumbs-up. Why the Hawker Hunters could not destroy the machine gun I do not know, and I did not ask. I just wanted to get back to base and put something on my blistered lip.

Cheredzi, North of Nygena Tribal Trust Land, 1977-78

I couldn't believe my ears. Only one kill. Anger, unstoppable and blinding, surged through my body. "Confirm only one kill!" I shouted into the radio handset, trying to confirm with the K-Car commander that despite the fixed-wing aircraft napalm strike, there were was only one kill. Three weeks of hard work down the drain. "Confirm only one kill!" I repeated into my radio. No answer. My hand holding the handset started to shake as all the anger and frustration of the past months came bursting out. Staggering to my feet, AK in one hand, handset in the other, all aches and pains of the previous weeks forgotten, I started screaming at the K-Car in the distance: "What is the matter with you fucking people? Are you fucking blind?" It was no longer about my country or my unit, it was all about me, I, yours truly, Andrew James Balaam. Did they know who I was? How dare they only manage to kill one terrorist after all my hard work? For God's sake, do they want me to mark the position of each individual terrorist with red Day-Glo panels. Slowly, the anger departed and I slumped to the ground, head bowed in shame.

"Ye gods, Jim," I muttered to myself in a hushed, dry, embarrassed voice. "Get a grip of yourself, arsehole. You are not a one-man army. If it was not for your pseudo-team feeding you the intelligence they gathered, you would never have found the terrorist camp anyway. So shut the fuck up and stop bitching. If you think you are better than the fire force, then get off your fat arse and go down there and show them how it is done. It is not about you; it is about protecting your country, it is about destroying the enemy, so be happy that you are alive and that you have got the fire force to call on, and do not have to take on the terrorists yourself."

One was better than none, but it was not what I had expected, especially after all the hard work my troop and I had put into the operation. I had a troop of about 25 men, which I normally split into three groups of eight or so. The size of the groups would change depending on the number of terrorists operating in the area I was sent to. If they operated in groups of six, we operated in groups of six. If they carried an RPD light machine gun per group, we carried an RPD per group. If the political commissar carried an AKM assault rifle, then our political commissar carried an AKM. If they attacked police stations, we attacked police stations. We tried to find out where they were trained – Mozambique or elsewhere – who their instructors were, who the camp commander was, what he looked like and whether he had a nickname. Who was the head nurse at the camp, and was she the camp commander's girlfriend? (Believe it or not, in a lot of cases she was.) We dressed as close as possible to the way they dressed, right down to the type of shoes. All this effort was not so much to fool the terrorists themselves, but rather the locals. The terrorists – real or pseudo – depended on the locals for survival. No local support for a real terrorist group, for whatever reason, spelt disaster. A pseudo-group of Selous Scouts terrorists could be blown or compromised by a simple thing like how they walked. Too much time on the parade ground resulted in them marching around the bush, not walking; the heels digging in and the swinging arms were a dead giveaway. Many a pseudo-group was comprised because of this simple little detail.

Hence nothing was a 'no, no' in the effort to get local support, be it the cutting-off of lips of so-called sell-outs, the bayoneting of pregnant women or the murdering of local tribesmen on the orders of the village headman. All of these murders ordered by the headman revolved around women, grazing rights and of course cattle, and had nothing to do with the victims being informants to the security forces. Even today in rural areas of Africa, cattle are regarded as the only real sign of wealth. As I explained in *Bush War Operator*, sometimes pseudo-groups had to use the same tactics to be accepted by locals, but only as a last resort.

In my troop I had four or five 'tame' terrorists (real terrorists who had been captured and had changed sides), who were highly thought-of and trusted. These, because of their intimate knowledge of the ins and outs of terrorist operational procedures, did in many cases act as group commander or group political commissars, where they could put to good use this knowledge. In an effort to make these 'tame' terrorists feel part of the Selous Scouts, their families were removed from rural areas and given accommodation at the new Scouts barracks at Nkomo, just outside of Salisbury. They also received food and a salary, and as an extra incentive were given a bonus for each terrorist killed by the group. The bonus system worked as follows: one to five terrorists killed or captured, 50 Rhodesian Dollars; six and above, 100 Rhodesian Dollars. In due course, because of the ill-feeling it caused amongst the regular Selous Scouts operators, the bonus was paid to all members of the group involved in the contact. The monies were, to the best of my knowledge, supplied by the South African Government to the Selous Scouts special branch, who then paid out the required bonus per kills. Life is very cheap, especially in times of war. The monies I talk about are small, but to recipients – especially the tame terrorist – it was a sign of appreciation and gave a bit of value to their life. Whilst on operations, I often wondered what they felt like working for the enemy. Did they join the fight for freedom because they believed it was the right thing to do and believed in their cause? And were they prepared to lay down their lives for the cause? Were they forced to join under the threat of death to themselves and their families? I do not know, but the ones I spoke to said they were promised training as doctors, pilots, etc., provided they joined the cause .What happened to the 'tame' terrorists in the Scouts I do not know. I just hope that they did not fall into the hands of their former comrades-in-arms.

Many people think the life of the terrorists in Rhodesia was hard and involved fighting the struggle with little help from anybody, dressed in rags, their weak and frail bodies covered in cuts and bruises, lack of food meaning they were always on the brink of starvation, poorly armed, forever running out of ammunition, spending day and night living in thick bush that was alive with dangerous wild animals, all alone, with only their burning desire for freedom keeping them warm in the freezing cold nights. Nothing could be further from the truth. All the terrorists I saw in the field looked fit, fat and healthy, courtesy of the locals. As far as the cuts and bruises went, many of the mission stations members were more than willing to sort that problem out. As for the dangerous animals and freezing cold, I never saw or heard anything about it. What I can tell you is that the terrorists' nightlife was far from the thick bush full of dangerous animals; it was around the villages. Their nightlife really hummed: the wine, women and song were something to be seen. The speeches might have been long and boring, and their methods of ensuring the message was received and appreciated might have been a bit barbaric, but what's a couple of missing lips, the odd missing arm and a bit of bayonet practice between friends? The singing and dancing were second-to-none, while the local beer flowed like water. To top it off, sex was readily available. As to the inferior weaponry story, the AK47 could hold its own against most weapons.

꘏

I struck the ground with my filthy camouflaged fist in frustration. A low moan of pain escaped my lips – I had forgotten about my badly damaged fingers, the result of trying to open a tin of baked beans with a rock and a coin. The result was a win for the tin of baked beans, which I had failed to open and was now back in my pack – a bit bent and buckled, but still intact – while I had a couple of damaged fingers to show for my efforts.

"God, what a waste of time," I muttered to myself. Three or four weeks' effort down the drain. Tired and frustrated, I leant back against the large rock that had provided me with a home for the last three days. Ignoring the countless thousands of ants and baby ticks crawling all over me, I tried to figure out what had gone wrong. I would have bet my life that the small group of terrorists my call-sign and I had been following were based at the grid reference I had supplied to the fire force. As I sat there scratching the exposed white skin of my lower leg, my mind drifted back to the beginning of the deployment.

We had started on the dreaded infiltration route close to the Mozambique border and headed into Rhodesia. One of the tribal trust lands we had to pass through to our target area was the fully subverted Nygena one. Once again, the move through the area was extremely difficult. We struggled to convince the locals we were the real deal, and thus food and information were slow in coming. On one of my previous visits to the area, one of my operators had a curse put on him by the local witch (I use the word because that is what the woman who put the curse on him was, a witch, a doer of evil things, not to be confused with the traditional healers or medicine men). In my troop I had a Corporal Elton, a fully trained *Songoma* (a traditional healer), who tried to lift the spell. It was not to be; no matter what he tried, all seemed to fail. According to the information I was receiving from the call-sign, Maxwell, the operator who had been cursed, was going from bad to worse He no longer talked, did not eat and was having great difficulty standing up. His walk had been reduced to a shuffle, like that of a very old man. His weapon webbing and other items had been split up amongst the rest of the call-sign, as he was no longer capable of carrying them. Two days later, in the evening, I met with the call-sign concerned, with the intention of taking Maxwell off their hands and sending him back to Fort Cheredzi, where maybe somebody could help him.

Crouched in a clump of thickly wooded rocks at the beginning of a small ravine, nerves stretched to breaking point, I waited for my call-sign. The long wait had been bad for my already stretched-to-breaking-point nerves. Being alone, loaded down like a donkey, I had nobody to watch my back. Every sound I heard was instantly converted into a threat to my life by my wild imagination and instinct for survival. Any sound to my rear I could only check by turning around, which was not easy considering how loaded down I was. Why I bothered, I do not know, as any turn to check my rear was slow, clumsy and very noisy: all it did was give my position away. The huffing and puffing, the bitching as I struggled to free my big pack and AK47 from the thick undergrowth, would have any terrorists who might have seen me while I was on the move to the rendezvous think they were on the wrong path. There was no way a human could make all that noise; maybe the buffalo were back after a hundred years of absence! To anybody watching, the continual jerking as my eyes and head swung from one potential threat to my life to another would make it appear I had lost my mind and was best left alone. Mad people, in African tradition, are not to be harmed.

I had been very tempted to call my groups of operators together, organise a supply of food from my controller and move through the area, ignoring the locals. It sounded like a good idea, but I knew from experience it would not work; it would only make matters worse. No matter how fast I moved through the area onto the next tribal trust land, the word of my coming would precede me, as would the fact that I was a SKU-ZAPU. The villages would empty of all able-bodied men, women and children, leaving only the frail and sick behind as I approached them. So I had decided to push on and at the same time uplift Maxwell.

The uplift had not gone exactly as planned. Maxwell had been so weak I had to take one of the call-sign members to help me get him to the road so he could be picked up by vehicle. With one look into Maxwell's eyes, coupled with the smell of his body, I knew he was a dead man walking. His eyes, sunk deep into their sockets,, blu- grey and unblinking, stared straight ahead. His body was all skin and bone, and smelt like a corpse. Two days later he was dead: cause of death unknown.

We had struggled on through Nygena, taking the good with the bad. One thing was for sure: nobody got fat. Once we got into the adjoining tribal trust land, things had slowly improved. The locals were a lot more accommodating, food and water were freely available and it was not long before a meeting was held, and with the meeting came information. The pseudo-groups were doing fine, but I, on the other hand, was taking a beating. The area I was operating in was densely populated. There was no cover, every hill for miles around was devoid of trees, every blade of grass had been eaten by the thousands of goats and cattle. There was nowhere for me to hide, as the few trees scattered around were all close to the villages and I knew from past experience that these would be used as toilets by the locals and my chances of remaining undiscovered were nil. My only option was to hide in the adjoining farmland.

Crouched behind a small anthill, just inside the farmland, alone as usual, dressed in my favourite black trousers and green long-sleeved shirt, balaclava pulled down over my ears, hands welded to my AK47, back bent under the weight of my big pack, I waited. I had been carefully moving up the fence line dividing the farm from the tribal trust land, looking for a place to lay up for the day, when I thought I heard voices and the sound of a large vehicle. I was in an unfrozen area (where any Rhodesian forces could enter) dressed like a terrorist, so was fair game to every farmer and security force member. I was not present when Andre Rabie, a founder member of the Selous Scouts, was killed by Support Commando of the Rhodesian Light Infantry, but what stuck in my mind was that he had been trying to pull off his shirt to show he was white when he was killed. As I was using the farmland to hide and I could walk into a farmer or security force patrol at any time, I had not blackened my face. It just might make the difference in getting killed or not.

Minutes passed, but nothing happened. The sweat stopped running down my back and my hands slowly released their death grip on the AK. I stopped trying to second-guess myself about whether I had left signs of my passing as I moved up along the fence. My breathing slowed down, my heart stopped thumping like a bongo drum and returned to almost normal, my muscles relaxed, my vision cleared and my brain started to function normally. "Man," I muttered to myself, "you are hearing things again." The sense of relief I felt after convincing myself that I was hearing things was difficult to describe. A smile spread across my face, and I felt lightheaded for several seconds as the tension left my body. Plonking from my crouching position onto my bum, I felt like laughing out loud and screaming "Fuck you all!", such was the feeling of relief. Unfortunately it was short-lived. Leaning against my big pack, using what little shade there was, I was busy congratulating myself on I don't remember what – maybe it was about just being alive – when my ears again picked up what I had thought was a figment of my imagination. There were voices and the sound of a large truck, only this they were a lot closer.

Fear hit me light a bolt of lightning. What was I to do? Get up off my arse and hide behind the anthill, which was about 30 metres from the fence line and the road the truck was following, and hope I did not end up being killed? Stand up and move into the open with my hands up? Try and get to the road before the truck, stand in the road with my hands up and hope for the best? The problem with all these options, apart from the chances of them working being nil, was that I was too shit-scared to move. I was petrified. As I lay there, pressing my body into the soil below me, hoping it would swallow me, flashes of what had happened to Andre Rabie raced through my mind. Head buried in my arms, my body as stiff as a board but somehow managing to shake at the same time, I awaited my fate. I did not hear the truck go past. I do not know, even to this day, what type of truck it was and whether there were soldiers on the back or it was only the farmer and his workers. How long I lay there, unmoving and unhearing, I do not know, but eventually the great roaring in my ears subsided and I lifted my head, forced open my tightly shut eyes and looked around. I was not surrounded by soldiers trying to kill me, and all my ears could hear was the peaceful, natural sounds of the bush. Instead of feeling relief and happiness at still being alive, I felt nothing: neither happy nor sad. As I lay there, my mind blank, a great wave of exhaustion swept over me. Not bothering to move, I lowered my head onto my arms and slept like the dead.

That night I left the farmlands and moved into the treeless, grassless waterless tribal trust lands. If I had to try to hide where there was nowhere to hide and urinate where I was laying, struggle to get water and only contact my HQ at night, so be it. If I had to lay, slowly boiling in the hot sun, tormented by millions of mopani flies and other biting insects, and eat only at night, so be it. Never again would I venture into an area that was not frozen. Being alive and covered from head-to-foot in 'black is beautiful', smelly though it was, was a whole lot better than being dead.

The days that followed were long, hard and thirsty. On several occasions I had close encounters with the locals. When I say 'close', I mean around 20-30 metres. They stared at me; I stared back. They waved and I waved back, they went their way and I went my way. Dressed as I was, everything being original terrorist except for my big pack, there was not much chance of being recognised as a white man. Yet this did not stop my heart pounding, my hands gripping my AK47 like there was no tomorrow, bucketloads of sweat running down my back or my mind churning through thousands of 'what ifs' on each close encounter. One hot summer's night melted into one hot summer's day, and after a while I lost all sense of time. As the days and nights passed, I hardly even noticed the flies, mosquitoes and other biting insects. I forgot all about how bad my body smelled and about the runny septic sores. My whole world revolved around survival. Days were spent laying in or under whatever cover I could find and trying not to fall asleep. Sleep was always a major problem when operating in areas with no cover. Sleep by day in the open could and would lead to your untimely death/ Nights were spent gathering water, which in most cases tasted like cow dung and smelt like piss. To keep awake I would try to pinpoint the water hole in the area and a route to it, avoiding all the villages I could because, as usual, the dogs were a big problem. A lot of the time the only cover available was the furrows in the ploughed land. The fact that I had to keep my A63 radio open 24 hours a day in case my call-sign needed me did not help. I have seen locals try to track me after I had visited their water hole at night and caused the dogs to bark. I did not need any locals trying to track me in the area I was now operating in, what with its lack of cover. I was therefore extremely careful on my nightly visits to the water holes.

As we had moved further north, the population decreased, the bush thickened, water became more plentiful and – more importantly – information became more up-to-date. The previous three or so weeks hiding where there was nowhere to hide, drinking water that stank and tasted disgusting, laying in the boiling hot sun, unable to sleep, being attacked continually by a horde of bloodthirsty insects, living three days off one tin of bully beef and rock hard, tasteless dog biscuit – unable to eat my biltong and salami due to the lack of water – were now behind me. Christmas had arrived, as far as I was concerned. I managed to get in a good couple of nights' sleep, regardless of the efforts put in by the mosquitoes and other nasties of the night. I managed to wash my face and get rid of the thick layer of baked-on camouflage cream, letting my skin breath for a few minutes before applying a fresh layer of the same black-green evil-smelling cream.

I had been reluctant to leave the flatlands and the ready water supply and move up into the highland areas, but information suggested there was a small group off terrorists operating in my immediate area. Being no hero – never figuring I was bulletproof – I moved up into the hills. I found myself a large rock on the side of a hill and decided to call it home for the next couple of days. It provided me with cover from view, as well as from fire, and water was not too far away. It gave me a chance to carry out some running repairs on myself. The next morning rose clear and beautiful, a multitude of colour, and the surrounding bush was alive with the sounds of birds. Opening my eyes with my fingers (on occasion I had to use my fingers to prise open eyelids that had become glued together by the camouflage cream), I looked around. Ignoring all my aches and pains, my vile-smelling body and burning eyes, I decided to forgo my normal cup of sweet tea or water and instead check out my surroundings. Armed with my binoculars, AK47 and radio, I moved cautiously around the summit of the hill, trying to find a place that offered me a view of the villages below. Barely 10 minutes later, I had called in the fire force onto a visual group of terrorists. They were sitting under some trees about 500 metres below me, having their breakfast.

Later, sitting head bowed, drowning in a world of self-pity, I could not understand why only one terrorist had been killed. In the back of my mind I could hear the K-car circling; I could hear it but I was not listening. I was too busy feeling sorry for myself. It was all about me. Cutting through my melancholy like a hot knife through butter came a voice over the radio: "K-Car, we have found another four dead terrorists; they were hiding in a hole but unfortunately for them the 'framtan' [napalm] bomb landed on top them. They are all dead and all pink."

Hearing thisa, my spirits soared. Leaping to my feet, head tilted back, eyes staring at the K-Car circling in the distance, I screamed at the top of my voice: "Yes! Yes, I told you they were there. I am Andrew James Balaam and I am the best. I do not make mistakes." The words had no sooner left my mouth when a great wave of remorse washed over my body. I felt bad – ashamed in fact. I did not know what to say. Minutes before I had been running everybody down, including the men on the ground. It had all been me, I, and nobody else. Stretching out my shaking, battered hand, I picked up the radio handset from where I had thrown it. "Thank you K-Car for a job well done," I muttered in a dry, croaking voice. Thoughts flashed through my mind: "One day is one day Jim. Steady on the mouth, my friend, steady on the mouth."

Lieutenant General John Hickman, 16 May 1977
Wisdom in Hindsight. Selous Scouts Round Bar, INKOMO Barracks

General Peter Walls had just been made Supreme Commander of the Rhodesian Armed Forces and Lieutenan General John Hickman made Army Commander. A bad day for the Rhodesian Army, as far as I was concerned. General Walls had that little something – call it man-management, call it charisma, there was just something about him that instilled confidence, a feeling that he would always do what was best for you, for the country, no matter what. He was a man you would follow to the end. His replacement was a disaster, a man hell-bent on his own path to glory and fuck anybody else. A real 'I, I, I; me, me, me' man. (My opinion, of course. I am sure history and a whole lot of people will disagree with me.)

"Gary Glitter, Gary Glitter; go for it oh Gary Glitter!" The voice of my friend Pete Mac shattered the awkward, smoke-laden *chibuku*-smelling silence that had enveloped the Round Bar after newly promoted army chief General Hickman's speech revolving around how lucky we were to be fighting for Rhodesia and all it stood for. He ended off with the line: "If you get killed you will be buried in 6 feet of Rhodesian soil that nobody can take away from you." Looking at him standing there in his full-dress uniform, with glossy medals, gleaming black jodhpur boots, shiny buttons, mutton chop moustache, moist red eyes, legs spread and firmly planted, chest and head thrust forward aggressively, small in stature, he had a small man's aggressive look and attitude. All aggression; all mouth; all arsehole!

A cold shiver ran down my spine as I moved uncomfortably from one foot to the other, my once-cold beer clutched in my sweating hand forgotten as I struggled to dispel the feeling of unease that had settled over me. Why in God's name he had to appear at what was basically a piss- up dressed in full uniform was beyond me. We all knew he had been promoted, and as far as I knew nobody in the rank and file gave a shit either way. He looked exactly like pictures of British officers I had seen in a book about the Boer War. The same arrogant look, the thrusting chest and chin, the spread-eagle legs, the bushy moustache. It was a look that said loud and clear: "I am the boss and I will do whatever it takes to remain the boss. Whatever I say goes. If you cross me you are dead."

In the months and years to come, I would realise how accurate was that feeling of unease I had felt, as he surrounded himself with a bunch of 'would be, should be but never were' officers and started to get rid of those he felt were a threat to him. On the hit list was one Lieutenant Colonel Ron Reid-Daly. The reasons for getting rid of Ron Reid-Daly were, in my opinion, many and varied. His power in the Rhodesian Army was probably second only to General Walls, whose backing he had. He was easily the most popular and well-known officer in the Rhodesian Armed Forces, and like General Walls he had that something extra that men trusted. They would follow him to the ends of the earth. I was to hear rumours towards the end of the war to the effect that there was a fear amongst certain high-ranking officers that because of his popularity amongst the rank and file, he had the power to upset the apple cart when it came to negotiations with Britain. (Here I will put my neck on a block and say loud and clear, without hesitation, that most, if not all, senior officers in the Rhodesian Security Forces were guaranteed some sort of reward, payment if you will, apart from their pensions, not to cause any problems with the return to British rule. Who made the payment? South Africa? Britian? Who knows. All I know is that I never saw one senior officer struggling after the war.)

To put it bluntly, many high-ranking officers were afraid Ron Reid-Daly would call for a military coup. Far fetched? I think so, but not out of the realms of possibility. The man's reputation and popularity were incredible. I do know that the whole of the Selous Scouts – to a man – which he had founded and commanded, would have followed him, as I am sure would a lot of the Rhodesian Light Infantry. The Rhodesian African Rifles, I doubt very much, and the same applies to the Rhodesian Air Force. Lieutenant Colonel Ron Reid-Daly might not have been on officers' courses, but neither was he stupid: he would know that without the full backing of the whole of the Rhodesian Security Forces, plus that of the backing of the South African government, a military takeover was a nonstarter.

These were dark and scary days in Rhodesia. All the senior officers in all the branches of the Rhodesian Security Forces would be sharpening their knives to stab each other in the hope of getting a better deal for themselves from the returning masters in England. And anybody who they thought could throw a spanner in the works needed to be got rid of as soon as possible. Chaos and stupidity were the order of the day. Like Rhodesia's Prime Minister Ian Smith said: "When times got bad, the blacks stuck together; the whites, on the other hand, turned on each other and it was a case of dog eat dog." So sad, but so true.

I can remember receiving a visit from the CO of the Rhodesian SAS, Major Brian Robertson (known as Barney Rubble, of *The Flintstones* fame, to the rank and file in the Rhodesian Army), who had come with the sole reason of shitting on Reid-Daly and the Selous Scouts for carrying out operations that Robertson considered the sole domain of the SAS. Short like Lieutenant General Hickman, he had the same aggressive nature. The outcome was a foregone conclusion. Reid-Daly was at the height of his power and success; there was no way he was going to take any shit from Major Robertson, so he had him removed from our camp and banned, and issued orders to that effect. There followed a series of bizarre stories. First the SAS were keeping our camp under surveillance, then they were going to raid our operations room. One story followed the next. We had our horse unit patrolling the fence line of our barracks for an extra security measure. After a couple of weeks of stressing, much screaming and shouting and a full dose of overreaction, things slowly returned to normal. Whatever normal was!

The feeling of isolation started to grow. Here we were, camped about 40km outside Salisbury, led by an 'over-promoted corporal' (which was how many officers at Army HQ referred to Reid-Daly) who seemed hell-bent on isolating us from the rest of the Army. These were very confusing times. We, the rank and file, did not know what was happening. We were supposed to be in the same Army, fighting the same enemy. It is difficult to describe the feeling of uncertainty, anger and helplessness that was taking a hold of the Selous Scouts as the senior officers fought it out.

As always with uncertainty, there were the rumours. It was said that a monitoring force from England was due to arrive, and that the South Africans were pulling out and were no longer prepared to supply us with weapons, ammunition and fuel. Into this murky world of uncertainty and lies, where dog ate dog, where officers spent more time watching their arse and stabbing each other in the back rather than fighting the war, came the scandal of all scandals: the telephone tapping. This phone monitoring was organised by none other than the Army Commander himself, the king of the 'fuck you Jack, I'm alright' brigade, General Hickman. The writing was on the wall. We were being sold down the river by all and sundry, and what does our dearly beloved, fearless Army Commander do? Nothing! He is too busy looking after himself – to hell with the country and the safety of its people, nothing matters but himself. Fate now presented him with an opportunity to get rid of the man he feared and detested most in the Rhodesian Army.

What followed was a circus, with accusations and counter-accusations. Poaching hit the rumour circuit. Elephant ivory, Rhino horn ... nothing, it was said, was safe from Reid-Daly and his fellow poachers. Then came the big kicker: not only was Reid-Daly poaching, he was using Rhodesian Armed Forces equipment to do so, including helicopters. The knives flashed silver in the dark world of betrayal; the blood – deep purple – ran like a river. The telephone lines hummed between the Scouts HQ and Army HQ. The roads melted under the procession of cars visiting both HQ. All the over-promoted corporal's 'friends' at Army HQ, all wearing cheek-to-cheek smiles of satisfaction, must have been rubbing their hands in anticipation of his fall.

What was been an efficient, highly disciplined army disintegrated into a leaderless, listless rabble of many factions. With morale at rock bottom, kept in the dark and fed on shit, a sense of inevitability settled over the Army. The writing was on the wall: the end was near.

In this self-centred, chaotic world in which the Rhodesian Army now found itself, there was still, believe it or not, time for officers' balls. It was at one of these balls that Reid-Daly accused Hickman of having tapped his phone. Hickman replied by putting Reid-Daly on a disciplinary charge. Reid-Daly was found innocent, which must have distressed many at Army HQ, but they need not have worried as he subsequently resigned.

While all this crap was taking place between two of the most powerful men in the Rhodesian Army, the Army itself wallowed in a state of self-induced inanimation. The British, who I do not doubt knew exactly what was happening, must have been laughing themselves silly. United we stand, divided we fall. All the rumours of attacking the terrorist assembly areas, and getting rid of the evil once and for all, faded away to nothing as dog ate dog and the country rolled over and gave up.

❊

I was dragged back to the real world from the sea of self-pity in which I found myself by a "Hey Andy, wake up my friend, there is a customer on the front counter looking for bamboo boards."

Part 3

After the Rhodesian Army

Hillbrow, Johannesburg, South Africa, 1987

After a short but illustrious money-filled (which I spent like there was no tomorrow) career with my previous employers, whom I had met at the Indaba Hotel in Sandton, I was once again unemployed.

I was sitting in a dark, dirty, urinal-smelling, fly and cockroach-infested bar-cum-restaurant, complete with cracked floor tiles, in Hillbrow, a drugs and drink-ridden prostitute haven suburb of Johannesburg, not far from the equally rundown hotel I was hiding in. I was really feeling sorry for myself, hiding out in insalubrious parts of the city in sleazy hotel rooms. There was nothing exciting about; it was dull, boring, played hell with your nerves, and each day seemed like a lifetime.

Every time somebody looked at you, you broke out into a cold sweat and your imagination went wild. Questions like "who was that?", "are they looking for me?", "did they recognise me?", "what should I do – play it cool, or run?" and "my God, what am I going to say if they start asking me questions?" all popped up in rapid succession in your mind.

Moving around uncomfortably in my still damp clothes, ignoring the urge to scratch my extremely itchy skin – the result of my wearing damp clothes – I tried to get comfortable on the old bar stool I was sitting on, which was not easy, considering it was in a state of near collapse, badly cracked, with the nails attempting to keep it in one piece digging into my backside. I needed to concentrate on my future. My past was a mess, but my future was not looking too rosy either.

The impending free elections and the certain change from a white minority government to a free and fairly elected black government was good news to countless oppressed blacks. But for me, and people like me who had worked for the present government, the writing was on the wall. The end of the good times had arrived.

Times had been hard of late. The hotel I was staying in did not allow the washing of clothes in the rooms, and I had no money to take my clothing to a laundry, so I washed by night and tried to dry by day. Nothing really got a chance to dry, and I had been wearing damp clothes for nearly a month. Looking down at my once-cold Castle beer, which was now warm and flat, I knew time was running out. Most of the little money I had, I had used to pay for the hotel room I had been staying in for the last month. It was not that I hadn't been offered jobs. Going to the same bar every day at the same time, sitting on the same bar stool, ordering the same beer, day in and day out, looking as I did – with long hair, scraggly beard, sunken eyes surrounded by dark puffy rings, with a vacant grin and slightly unsteady hands, dressed in patched denims, old colourless t-shirts and a pair of veldscheons on my feet that had seen better days – it wasn't long before I was approached by various seedy-looking individuals, all of Portuguese origin, and offered various jobs, ranging from bodyguard to cattle rustling. Unfortunately, all of these jobs were in Mozambique, and at that stage I'd had enough of Mozambique to last me a lifetime. However, money was the key. For the right price I would give anything a go. After a series of meetings with some very hard-looking characters in smoked-filled, evil-smelling bachelor flats, where everything was discussed except a decent salary, I was still unemployed. There was no way I was going to lock horns with my old friends and comrades in the FRELIMO for nothing. However, beggars can't be choosers, and unless my luck changed soon I would have no choice but to accept one of the jobs offered, like it or not.

Growing tired of watching the barman trying to kill the numerous cockroaches and flies that frequented the bar, I looked around at my fellow drinkers. A cold shiver ran down my spine: it was like looking into a mirror. That was what I would become unless I got a job, and sooner rather than later. They were men, old long before their time, with dirty, torn, unwashed clothing; thin, anaemic rundown bodies; tangled hair; mouths devoid of teeth; thin, hunched shoulders; and, most frightening of all, eyes that had given up hope, that stared aimlessly into space, seeing everything but seeing nothing.

Lurching to my feet, knocking over the bar stool, I pushed my warm, flat beer to one side and almost ran out of the bar. Standing in the hot sun on the busy street outside, sweaty and shaking, I knew I had just looked at my future self unless I got a job soon – real soon. Stumbling down the road, I headed for my hotel thinking "Please God, let there be a message for me."

Sometimes it is better to be careful for what you wish in case it comes true.

Bodyguarding, Transkei
Independence Day Celebrations, Umtata, Transkei Homeland, 1985-86.

The song's lines "He'd fly through the air with the greatest of ease, that daring young man on the flying trapeze" might have flashed through the mind of any spectators watching as I left the front seat of the Unimog I was travelling in. The front right-hand wheel of the truck had dethatched itself from the axle, which resulted in the right side of the vehicle digging into the tar road and catapulting everyone out.

"There you go, arsehole!" screeched my brain. "This time you are going to see your ass, my friend, your big mouth, all the years of surviving against what at times seemed impossible odds, all the ducking and diving, all the bullshitting, the overcoming of brain-numbing, morale-destroying fear, all means nothing now as it's all down to luck. And a lucky person you are not."

The day had started early and the night had ended late, with the result that I was suffering a huge and unforgiving han over. My throat was raw from puking, my stomach muscles aching from continual heaving and bringing up nothing but green bile. I had tried all the supposed quick ways to cure a hangover, from cold showers to eating something oily and hot, but nothing had worked. I was still going hot and cold, my whole body shook, and bright white lights flashed in front of my eyes. Sitting on my bed, dressed in full camouflage uniform complete with shiny black boots, eyes firmly closed in an attempt to cut out the flashing lights and spinning room, I concentrated on breathing deeply. In and out, in and out; the seconds turned into minutes and slowly I started feeling better. My heartbeat returned to normal, the hot and cold flushes disappeared, and with them the sweating also stopped. Sitting hunched over on my unmade bed, I summoned all my remaining willpower, drive and ambition, and opened my eyes. The room was no longer spinning, the floor looked like a floor should – flat, and still no longer heaving, twisting and turning. All things being equal, I might even make it through the day. But the more I thought of the day ahead, the more uncomfortable, ashamed and embarrassed I felt.

The highlight of the Independence celebrations which were to take place in the stadium in Umtata was a mortar display by 1 Battalion, Transkei Defence Force. The display was a watered down version of that put on at Salisbury showgrounds by Support Commando of the Rhodesian Light Infantry. It was very basic in concept, yet at the same time very realistic. The demonstration started with two vehicles, complete with 81mm mortars and crew, speeding into the stadium and stopping in a cloud of dust. The crews would then dismount and assemble the mortars (at a pre-determined elevation and deflection) as quickly as possible, and then commence firing. The ammunition used was drill rounds, which were solid steel and did not explode upon hitting the ground. To make everything appear more realistic, explosives were buried around the area in which the drill rounds would land. Hidden in a bunker overlooking the area of hidden explosives was yours truly, whose job it was to use a ripple box to detonate saidexplosives as the drill rounds hit the ground. It should have been very simple and very effective.

However, for the upcoming demonstration we had no drill rounds or explosives to imitate the bombs exploding, so it was decided that we would use smoke rounds minus the smoke but have live nose fuses to create the bang. It took a while to drain the liquid from the smoke bombs, but in due course all was ready.

My head pounded, my legs felt weak and rubbery, and I struggled to stop myself from puking. Even on the back of the bouncing vehicle, the heat was incredible. Never in my life have I felt so embarrassed, so humiliated. I was approaching 40 years old, a professional soldier, and here I was hanging onto the canopy railing of a speeding truck, about to perform like a clown in a circus, staring straight ahead – hearing nothing, seeing nothing, feeling nothing – my body shaking in anger as I prepared myself to do what I had to do. A job was a job.

All the anger, frustration and self-pity faded into the background as my eyes took in the rapidly approaching ground and the barbed wire fence. My brain slipped into survival mode. As I hit the ground, I closed my eyes, hoping that all the training and experience I had gathered through the years would get me through in one piece.

Clothes became hooked, flesh bled, head pounded and hands shook as I desperately tried to free myself from the barbed wire that had somehow wrapped itself around my body. The harder I tried, the less progress I seemed to make. I pulled and I turned, almost crying in frustration as I tried to get clear of the barbed wire, all the while keeping my eyes firmly shut. Nothing seemed to help: the more I pulled, kicked and turned, the tighter the barbed wire seemed to get. Frustration was slowly turning to panic. "Steady Jim, steady! Take your time and relax; you are alive. It might even be a plan to open your eyes," came the advice from my never-far-away, ever-steady other self.

Forcing my body to relax, I opened my eyes. The sky above was blue – spinning a bit, but nevertheless blue. There were no billowing clouds of smoke, no cries of agony, no roaring fire, no unbearable heat. Maybe I had made it; maybe I had not died and gone to hell. To confirm my good luck, I decided to sit up and do a double-check. Shock can do amazing things. Getting to sit up was a major mission, but eventually I managed. Looking around, I could see the other occupants. Everyone seemed alive and none the worse for wear. The trees looked nice and green, as did the grass, the sun was shining and everything looked great. Lucky me: I had indeed managed to stay in one piece (or so I thought – shock does strange things to you).

My spirits climbed and I started congratulating myself on my escape from what seemed an impossible situation. My morale improved even further when, looking down at what had seemed like multiple strands of barbed wire around my body, it proved to be only one. It'sx amazing what a difference opening your eyes can make. Several minutes later I was on my feet, free from the barbed wire. Chest puffed out, head held high, bursting at the seams with pride and arrogance, I sang my praises to not only myself but to anybody else who would listen. I must have looked a sight: torn trousers and combat jacket, blood-streaked face, hair and beard full of grass and big mouth going 10 to the dozen. Old habits die hard.

⁂

It was dark, the occasional bare lightbulb hanging from the ceiling doing little to brighten up the room. The air was thick with the smell of overcooked cabbage, urine, unwashed bodies and bed pans. Welcome to the dirty, dark, survival-of-the-fittest world of Umtata Hospital. All my bragging and strutting around, all my self-congratulation, had been premature. I had in fact broken my left arm at the elbow.

Moaning softly under my breath, I looked around in the semi-darkness, hoping to see a nurse. The pain was intense: the operation on my elbow had left my whole arm feeling like it was on fire, and I was hoping to try to get some form of painkiller. Like I have said before, shock does strange things. I did not realise it at the time, but I stood more chance of going to the moon than finding a nurse and getting some painkillers. As I lay there trying my best to ignore the raging fire my left arm had become, I let my mind drift back to the altogether less stressful, laid-back stint as a bodyguard to Kaiser ('K.D.') and George Matanzima, the President and Prime Minister respectively of the Transkei.

⁂

It was grey with a greenish-blue tinge, and was so raw that the blood ran out in a steady stream. Actually, to say it was raw was an understatement: to be any rawer it would still have to be in the goat it had come from, alive and running around. Thirty minutes previously, I had been standing outside a crudely made mud hut, next to the poorly dressed, shoeless local villager when he had cut the throat of the goat whose charred, bleeding liver was now lying on my blue and white, badly chipped and cracked china plate.

The trip to arrive at the hut had been long and hard, slow and sweaty.

The old blue, long-wheel-base Land Rover that my friend Pete Mac had, for the want of a better word, stolen from the Selous Scouts on the disbandment of the unit, huffed, puffed, grunted, groaned and smoked its way down the well-used, potholed dirt road. We were on our way to secure an old deserted store and broken-down church in preparation for an upcoming political rally to be addressed by the Prime Minister of Transkei, George Matanzima. The fact that we were running hours late due to a breakdown did not worry us. This was, after all, Africa, where time meant nothing.

Myself and Pete Mac had the dubious honour of being personal bodyguards to George Matanzima, although whether he knew or cared about the fact that we were his bodyguards was highly debatable. He had his own bodyguards supplied by the Transkei security forces, so exactly where we fitted in I do not know. One thing I did know was that they all had fast, luxurious, reliable cars, while our mode of transport was neither fast, luxurious nor reliable, hence we were invariably late. Our weapons, like our transport, were old and unreliable: I carried a misused, very dubious looking and wobbly .38 revolver, and Pete Mac a 9mm pistol. What we were supposed to with the rubbish we carried if our principal came under fire, only the gods knew. Being a bodyguard in Africa to African leaders who were normally dictators, and generally hated by the locals, was a dirty, deadly and dangerous job. There were no fast cars, beautiful women and luxurious casinos for us in Africa; instead wse had dirt, violence, death and poverty. Africa: the land of the strong.

There was a red sun, red soil, red derelict church building, red grass and red trees – all painted by huge billowing clouds of red dust. In to this red, dead world arrived myself and Pete Mac. This unobtrusive piece of land was, according to our calculations, the site of the upcoming political meeting organised by George Matanzima. Peering through the howling wind, I could see no gathering crowd; in fact, apart from the derelict buildings, the odd leafless tree and howling red dust clouds, it was just Pete and I. After a bit of a discussion we decided to have a look around and then proceed to the nearest village to see if we could find out anything about the meeting. I thought it had been hot in the Land Rover, but now as I stood in the open, drenched in sweat, hoping the wind would cool me down, I realised the Land Rover was not half bad compared to the wall of heat that engulfed me. My lungs burned, my throat dried out in an instant, my eyes turned red and felt as if sand had been poured into them, and my damp hair and beard were coated with a layer of red dust, blow-dried by the hot wind..

The wheels spun, the engine screamed and the bodywork creaked and groaned as the Land Rover clawed its way up the seemingly endless potholed dirt road. Wherever you looked, all you could see was red. The over-grazed rolling countryside, deprived of all forms of grass – including the roots – thanks to the many goats kept by the locals, had nothing to protect it from the elements, and soil erosion ran rampant. There were red mini-Grand Canyons, red mini-deserts, red dust storms and, in the rainy seasons, raging red rivers that ripped up the topsoil, leaving nothing in which any plant form could put down roots. The country was bleeding to death. As we climbed higher, the wind seemed to die down, as did the dust storms, but the one constant was the heat.

An hour later, 10lb lighter, soaking-wet reddish shirts clinging to our chests, faces covered in streaky sweat paths, beards and hair cardboard-hard, we arrived at our first village. Luck was on our side, as there before us, red-covered from top to bottom, arrayed in all its splendour was George Matanzima's official motorcade. Now that we had found our principal, we did not know what to do. Once again embarrassment, anger and frustration came to the fore. We had never formally or otherwise been introduced to either George or K.D. – we just sort of followed around, uninvited and unwanted, an embarrassment not only to ourselves but to our principal too.

After much soul-searching, it was decided we should go and join a small group of men gathered around a bleating, kicking, very unhappy goat. We huffed, we puffed, we straightened our damp, dust-streaked clothing and tried in vain to do something with our dusty hair and beards. We looked at our feet, we looked up into the sky, we stared into the distance, we looked at each other, we smiled, we shuffled our feet. Moving forward was no easy task, especially to join a group of people you were pretty sure did not want you around.

The meeting was awkward and strained, to say the least. All conversation died as we approached – no introductions, no hellos, no smiles, just a silence that could he heard a thousand miles away. Standing in a semicircle around the goat-killer-to-be, we all stared at the struggling, bleating animal as if our lives depended upon it. The goat was then slaughtered and the liver was cooking in the coals, the blood oozing out, sending the sweet, nauseating smell of burning blood into the air.Still the silence held us in its grip: unseen, unbreakable. The wind blew, the dust swirled, the sun beat down, the liver burned, and we stared transfixed at nothing. "Sir, sir! The Prime Minister wants you to join him." The silence was shattered, its grip broken, only to be replaced by our own uncertainty. In the end, after much debate, nervous laughter, smiling and dusting of beyond-local-repair clothing, it was decided that I would grace the upcoming lunch with my presence while Pete sacrificed and did guard outside. Lucky bastard!

My back was hunched, my shoulder muscles throbbed, my eyes watered and my head pounded to a beat all of its own. The speeches were finished, the praise singer had done his bit, and it was now time to eat the star of the show, the bleeding, greenish-blue, charred liver. With shaking hands, sweaty brow and heaving stomach, I picked up my knife and fork – the moment of truth had arrived. "Shit, Jim," I muttered to myself, "you have eaten all sorts of inedible things – from rotting, half-cooked chicken to baboon – so a piece of raw liver is a walk in the park."

Fork clutched in one sweaty hand, knife in the other, with a faraway look in my eyes and the smile of a condemned man, I lowered my hands. The fork sunk into multi-coloured liver, blood oozing down its sides and slowly filling the chipped plate, while the knife with no edge struggled to cut through it. Cut, hack, push, pull – I was having a hard time as the liver was not giving up without a fight. The blood oozed over the sides of the plate onto the unstable table, then started to make its way towards the guest sitting directly opposite me.

I panicked. I had to do something to stop the slow-moving stream of blood's progress. My head jerked to the right and left, looking for something – anything – that I could use to stop the blood, but there was nothing. I was losing it: the room was turning, twisting, the voices receding, and I was falling.

"Hey Jim, you OK?" The question and a shaking had brought me back to reality, and with reality came the pain of my broken arm and the dark, dingy hospital room of the Umtata General Hospital.

Squinting through the darkness, aware of the thick cigarette smoke and overpowering smell of cabbage, I could make out several faces of my friends who had come to visit me. Putting on my 'devil may care, hard as nails, pain means nothing to me' smile, I assured everybody I was fine. Like most soldiers, they did not like to be in the presence of pain and injury, and within 10 minutes they had gone.

With their departure the pain returned, all-consuming, turning me into a whimpering wreck. My mind once again drifted away.

Port St Johns, Transkei, 1982

The sky was a an array of blues, pinks, reds and yellows, the sea a murmuring, gentle, rolling symphony of greens and blues. The breeze was soft and cooling, barely moving the thick undergrowth on the banks of the Umzimvubu River. Clutching my swollen injured right hand, a result of a disagreement in the pub the night before, my bare feet planted knee-deep in the cool sea water – which brought some relief to my throbbing head – I looked around. I still could not, even after three or four years in Port St Johns, get over the beauty of the town and its surrounding countryside. The clean, golden beaches, the abundant birdlife, the excellent fishing and the clear sea and massive sheer cliffs – between which a battle as old as time raged on stormy nights, the roaring clash of these two Titans keeping the whole town awake.

I had spent the previous night at the Cape Hermes Hotel, much against the advice of all the deep sea fishing professionals. Go deep sea fishing with a hangover and you will regret it, they told me. Take advice, me? I could handle it: what was one more hangover after all the hundreds I had already handled? Bring it on! Little did I know what was waiting for me. As the saying goes – ignorance is bliss.

Now, standing in the early-morning sun, body going hot and cold, my eyes bloodshot and weeping, head feeling like a maniac was playing a drum solo inside it, I wondered if perhaps the professionals were not right after all, and that going deep sea fishing with a hangover was not the brightest thing to do. I stood there deciding what to do next, and realised I had two options. I could either take a plunge into the cool, inviting waters of the Umzimvubu and hope for a miracle, or call it a day and head home; I could always use my injured hand as an excuse. Before my alcohol-soaked brain could sort out the options, never mind come to a decision, I heard my name being called. Turning away from the sea, I looked upstream: about 300 metres from where I was standing, the rest of the crew were getting ready to launch the boat .My heart sunk to my feet. This was it; there was no escape; time had run out. I knew my fellow fishermen. They were all ex-Selous Scouts, and they would put me on the boat whether I liked it or not. It was time to put my money where my mouth was.

A bare hour had passed since the boat, expertly piloted by skipper John Costello, had exited the river mouth, and already I was laying in the bottom of the boat, pale-faced, weak as a kitten, curled up in the dirty warm sea water, diesel and pieces of bait sardine, my injured hand now forgotten. My 'I can handle it' smile and bullshit confidence didn't last 20 minutes as I rapidly turned into a whining, sick-as-a-dog cry baby.

I had spent about 10 minutes puking up all the beer and curried chicken I had consumed the night before, after which I had spent a further 10 minutes destroying my stomach muscles and puking up vast amounts of green bile, and with it the last of my strength and willpower. I had turned from a steely-eyed killer into a quivering lump of flesh engulfed by self-pity.

Up and down, up and down went the boat; thump, thump, roll to the left, roll to the right. 'Burn, burn', went the sun; 'puke, do not puke', went the overpowering smell of diesel from the motor. What should I do? Lay down, no sit up, no lay down; jump into the cool waters of the sea, no lay down, no sit up! I was feeling so bad I could not make up my mind, and all the while a low moan of anguish escaped through my lips. I felt death was knocking at the door, and I wished it would take me and end this hell on earth. There was no way I could feel so sick, and suffer like I was suffering, and not die.

My body shook as if I had malaria, my stomach muscles ached like I had done a million sit-ups, my throat was dry and felt like it had just been cleaned by sandpaper, my head was one mass of pain, and out of my weeping eyes poured all the blood in my body. Death was surely close at hand. So much for 'live by the gun, die by the gun' – I was going to die from a hangover, and the sooner the better! As far as I was concerned, death could only be an improvement over my current predicament.

The beautiful view of the monster white-capped waves smashing against the defiant, sheer granite cliffs of the wild coast, the awesome crack and deep roar that followed each clash of rock and salt water, was lost on me as I struggled to survive what I was convinced was a fate worse than death: a hangover on a deep sea fishing boat. The long hot trips with a hangover I had endured in the back of closed-in trucks belching exhaust fumes whilst in the Rhodesian Army, even the hangover I had suffered with in the Dakota while on a parachute course in South Africa, paled into insignificance. They were a walk in the park. This was the real deal, the real McCoy. If I survived this, then I truly could wear the t-shirt: I would be a veteran!

Just as I thought I was going to die and finally get some relief from the ordeal I was enduring, the constant desire to puke started to weaken, the blood stopped pouring out of my burning eyes and the evil-smelling diesel no longer smell so bad. Even the up, down, thump, thump, left-right motion of the boat seemed soothing. I could finally make sense of the barrage of words hurled at me by the leering faces that surrounded me. I was alive; I was going to make it and I was not going to die. Little did I know it at the time, but this mother of all hangovers and the consequent pain and suffering were going to be an inspiration to me when, years later, I was to suffer another awesome hangover in Maputo, Mozambique.

Johannesburg, South Africa. Riot-torn Black Townships of the Early 1990s.

"And you, white man, that gun you have is for shooting birds. You cannot kill people with it. Be careful or we will cook you. There are no policemen here to help you." Oh God, a weapons expert, I thought. Looking down into the sea of black sneering faces and flashing white teeth of the locals surrounding the Coca-Cola truck I was standing in, a cold shiver of fear ran down my back. It was not the threats that did this – talk is cheap, and while they were still threatening me I figured they were trying to build up the energy to do something about me. So according to my fear-frozen brain, I was still in there with a chance of survival. It was the eyes – glazed, red and staring, unblinking seeing everything and yet seeing nothing – coupled with a low, almost painful undulating moan that sent the shiver down my back. I had seen the look before and had heard moan; I knew that time was running out. The talking was finished, the party was about to start and I was the guest of honour! I was back in the shit, courtesy once again of my big mouth and small brain.

I was a white man – a symbol of the hated apartheid government – in a black man's area. I was up the creek with no paddle. Crouched on the back of the open Coca-Cola truck I was escorting, armed with a .410 gauge shotgun and four shells in the riot-torn East Rand townships of Johannesburg, South Africa, a bad day had just got a whole lot worse. Dressed in an old pair of blue jeans, t-shirt and a black wind breaker, clutching my basically useless shotgun in trembling, sweaty hands, my back against the red and white driver's cab, I looked down into the face of the man who appeared to be the leader of the large group of black township residents now surrounding the truck. He looked like something out of a horror movie. His eyes were a watery yellow and bloodshot, as if he had spent the night drinking the local homemade brew which had many ingredients, including shoe polish, and smoking dagga. He had spittle running down his chin from a mouth full of rotten teeth as he screamed abuse at me. I could see the hate, anger and frustration in his twisted face, but also lurking in the back of his eyes were fear and uncertainty.

These were chaotic times in South Africa. Mr Mandela was about to be released from prison, and a wave of optimism and hope had swept over the country. The future looked bright; but that was the future. The present was a different kettle of fish. The South African Security apparatus was still a force to be reckoned with – very little happened without their knowing about it, and their reaction to any anti-apartheid protests was swift and brutal.

It had been raining on and off for the last couple of days, and the clouds hung heavy, grey and sullen in an overcast sky. The makeshift dirt roads running through the countless thousands of tin huts and small brick buildings scattered about in the over-populated township were ankle-deep in dirty brown rainwater and raw sewage, and were littered with rocks and still-smouldering car tyres The rainwater and sewage were courtesy of bad town planning, the rocks and burning tyres a gift from the protesting locals.

I forced a sickly, devil-may-care grin on my face and swallowed hard, my mouth dry as a bone compliments of a healthy dose of fear and too much smoking. I slowly stood up in an effort to get the blood flowing to my cramped legs. Lighting up another cigarette, keeping an eye on the rowdy crowd and their hate-spewing spokesman, ignoring the cold, foul-smelling sweat of fear running down my back, I looked around.

Everything was wet, grey and depressing. The smell of raw sewage hung thick and heavy in the air, held down by the brooding, slowly darkening, rain-laden clouds. The only colour in this grey picture of depressing waterlogged poverty, apart from the clouds of oily black smoke rising from the vehicles set alight by the strikers, was the numerous different-coloured pieces of plastic which had been thrown on the leaking roofs of tin hut and brick building alike, and the occasional 'Free Mandela Now', scrawled in reds and blues on whatever flat surface that could be found.

The feelings of isolation, fear, and loneliness, the trembling hands, the smell of rancid sweat and the jerky head movements were not new; they were old forgotten friends returning: "Hello darkness my old friend", as Simon and Garfunkel sang.

I had been hired by the security company appointed by Coca-Cola to guard their trucks on their deliveries into the volatile black South African townships. My job was simple: I was to train the security company's personnel in the use of the Browning pump-action shotgun. Train them in the use of the shotgun, my brain reminded me, not do their job and escort the vehicles. Especially not with a single-shot .410 shotgun.

Now, cringing, knee-deep in the shit, with a stupid smile on my face on the back of an open delivery truck, I wondered if I had done the right thing in answering the message that was waiting for me at the hotel when I returned from the pub. At the time it seemed a godsend – but now I was not so sure. Almost in a trance, staring down at the hate-filled faces, my mind – in an effort to escape from the fear and uncertainty in which it now found itself – drifted to what it considered better times.

Maputo, Mozambique – Kadosa Hotel, 1992/93

"Alua Continue – the war continues. Viva FRELIMO, Viva Samora Machel!"

They were everywhere, the old enemy and his slogans – the cause of nightmares I still suffer to this day – and this time I was alone, unarmed and isolated. I had no friends, no support, no place to hide, no fire-force to get me out of the shit; only my overactive imagination for company. My hands automatically tightened on a weapon that wasn't there, while my eyes darted left and right looking for non-existent cover to use in case I came under fire. The chances of coming under fire were virtually nil, but old habits die hard. I was in a big, busy city with people and cars everywhere, but unfortunately my overactive imagination was having none of it. I was in Mozambique – the slogans were there, as were the FRELIMO, so I must be in the shit. My mouth was dry, sweat poured off my body, my ears rang and my back muscles throbbed. All the old feelings came rushing back. Twelve years of training and a survival instinct honed in the heat of the Rhodesian Bush War do not disappear overnight.

Pulling myself back to the present from the violent past and the brink of disastrous panic, with a shaking hand, I lowered my suitcase to the ground. I breathed deeply, pushing back the fear and anxiety, and dug around in the pocket of my brightly coloured shirt trying to locate a cigarette, all the while attempting to look like an unperturbed tourist as I slowly and carefully looked around. Jesus wept – everywhere I looked I saw FRELIMO soldiers and slogans. Gathered in small groups, dressed in Portuguese camouflage, wearing black boots and chest webbing, carrying AK47s, they were everywhere, from the filthy, dilapidated, fly-ridden old restaurants to every street corner. Filth, noise and decay reigned supreme. The streets were overrun with chickens, goats, pigs, packs of dogs, plastic bags, cardboard boxes, old car tyres and – to top it off, the cream on the cake as it were – piles of maggot-filled dog and human excrement, humming with countless flies. Each foul-smelling, breath-snatching, eye-watering mass of excrement seemed alive, appearing to move and change shape under the constant assault of the thousands of big blue-green flies. It was the height of summer and the smell of raw sewage and rotting food and vegetables literally took my breath away, leaving me panting open-mouthed as I tried to get oxygen into my lungs.

"Welcome to Africa run by the Africans," I thought to myself. The Portuguese may have been lazy, but at least they were clean, unlike the new owners of the country, who were both lazy and dirty.

Sweat – some of it a result of the damp, moist heat, some of it from fear – was running down my face, chest and back by the bucketload, drenching my shirt and the waistband of my denims. The feeling of wellbeing I had built up on the short flight from Johannesburg to Maputo in Mozambique, compliments of several cold beers, disappeared by the time my taxi reached the hotel where I intended to spend the next week. I was a dry-mouthed bundle of raw nerve ends.

The four just-below-boiling-point frothy Manica beers I had drunk while sitting on a bent and buckled steel chair next to the green-watered, foul-smelling, palm tree and plastic chair-filled swimming pool while I had waited for my room to be prepared had not helped. I was still wound up as tight as a coiled spring, plus I was now feeling as sick as a dog compliments of the warm beers. Everything had seemed so simple and clear-cut over a couple of cool beers in the safety of a beer garden in South Africa. But that was then, and this was now.

I had seen numerous adventure/war movies in my time; movies where the hero, undaunted by an unseen turn of events, remained cool, calm and collected throughout. However, this was not the movies, and in my overworked imagination every unseen turn of events had panic stations written all over it in huge red letters.

My body was still tense, my legs stiff and unbending, as the strange, sickly smell of fear-induced sweat filled the dark passageway. Stumbling along like a drunk, dressed in short trousers and a colourful cotton shirt, with several cameras hanging around my neck, I followed the bell boy, who had my suitcase in one hand and a candle in the other. I tried desperately to pull myself together. This was day one, and already I was falling to pieces. My task was simple: I was to set up an informer network in Maputo. However, this was easier said than done. Unable to speak Portuguese, I would have to proceed slowly and carefully. The cover story for my latest venture into the dark, murky and dangerous world of espionage was that I was a rich, eccentric South African/Zambian wanting to open up a tour company in South Africa and introduce Mozambique to the South African market All the cameras, the long hair, the scraggly beard, the brightly coloured clothing and the handing out of money like it was water – plus the fact that I acted as if Mozambique and South .Africa were long-lost friends rather than enemies – all added to the image I was trying to create of an eccentric middle-aged white man who was out of touch with reality.

It gave me a reason to talk to many people and to ask numerous questions, visit nightclubs, take pictures, and say and do stupid things. Once I had hired several people under the pretext of them being tourist guides, it would not be too hard to get them to tell me not only about the hotels, nightclubs and beaches in the area, but also to include the disposition and strength of any FRELIMO or South African dissidents who happened to be in the same area.

Two weeks previously, sitting in a beer garden in a sleazy hotel in Hillbrow, receiving my briefing from my new employers, everything looked good. The money was flowing like water. I had spent a month or two sitting on my arse doing nothing, and now it was payback time. Not that I minded finally having something to do – I was getting tired of just eating, drinking and sleeping, and waking up every morning with a hangover.

In the flickering light of the huge candle the bell boy was holding, the room looked like something out of a *Dracula* movie. It had heavy red satin curtains which hung limp at the windows, a massive mahogany four-poster bed – the mattress of which was covered in a gold-trimmed red satin bedspread – and on the floor lay a threadbare red carpet. There was an old, dark, cigarette-burned dresser, with an equally old and misused red lounge suite, all of which were scattered haphazardly around the huge room. The overwhelming smell of decay was enough to get my imagination churning. And churn it did.

I was hungry, I was thirsty and I was dead-tired, but overriding all these was fear: an overwhelming, brain-numbing fear. I was all alone. If I fucked up I was dead; there was no fire-force, no friend, to get me out of the shit. An overwhelming feeling of helplessness, anger, self-pity and at the same time acceptance descended over me. I was here of my own free will. The time for bitching was long-gone; it was now time to pull myself together and do the job I was being paid for.

Lying as stiff as a board on the four-poster bed, wearing only my denims and sweating from fear and the heat, I tried to get some sleep, hoping that my anxieties would disappear in the coming morning light. As far as I knew I was the only guest in the hotel. I had tried to get into the nearby Palarno Hotel, but unfortunately it was fully booked. Now, lying sleepless, I tried to kick-start my brain and get a grip of my imagination.

Every sound seemed like footsteps coming down the passageway, heading straight for my door. Every word and every voice, even though they were in Portuguese – which I did not understand – seemed to spell impending doom. An hour-and-a-half later, muscles throbbing, tired of lying uncomfortably on the hard mattress in the decaying room and fighting a losing battle with the mosquitoes, I gathered together what was left of my courage, put on my colourful cotton tourist shirt, filled my pockets with money and headed for the dilapidated bar. As I walked down the poorly lit corridor, I hoped I was not about to make a major mistake. The last thing I needed was get drunk and start running off at the mouth.

My entrance into the pool bar was a total disaster. As I stepped through the doorway, one of my brightly coloured flip flops got caught on an old sliding door rail. The calm, casual, happy-go-lucky stupid tourist entrance I had hoped to achieve went out of the window and was replaced by an undignified hands-and-knees arrival. On all fours, my face burning red from embarrassment and sweat running down my body, I looked up. My throat went dry and a ripple of fear ran down my back. There were no amused looks on the faces of bar patrons, no understanding smiles, only silence.

A thick, menacing silence enveloped the bar and its many customers. Through the thick cigarette and dagga smoke, I could see at least 20 people, both men and women, all staring at me with blank, emotionless eyes. The mask-like faces were totally African and totally frightening. It was like stepping into a room of zombies.

As I struggled to my feet, ignoring my burning hands and throbbing knees, an uncontrollable shiver made the hairs on the back of my neck stand up and I broke into a cold sweat. I had seen that look many times before whilst in the Selous Scouts. It was a look, a mindset if you like, devoid of pity and any feeling of compassion. I had seen it settle over many of the Scouts' black members when questioning captured terrorists. The interrogation session would invariably be short and extremely brutal. There was a saying that nobody is as cruel to a black man as another black man.

Straightening up and regaining my balance with a bit of help from the door frame, I headed for the bar. I tried to put a bit of a swagger and devil-may-care confidence into my walk. I failed dismally. My legs, which had become stiff and unwieldy, would not co-operate, my back muscles throbbed and my eyes were wide and dry, staring into the foul thick blue smoke that filled the bar.

God, I hated the way my body reacted whenever I found myself in big-time shit, be it a contact with the enemy or, as now, caught unprepared by the hostile reception of the patrons in the bar. Thankfully my brain seemed to function regardless of my body's inability to handle the shock of the unexpected. Yet everything seemed to be in slow motion; it seemed to take forever before my awkward walk finally got me to the bar. "One *Chevez*," I croaked, my throat bone dry, whether from thirst or fear I was not sure, but most probably the latter.

Like most Rhodesian Army members – in fact most Rhodesians – I had been into Mozambique before, and one of the first words I learnt was '*Chevez*', Portuguese for beer. As well as my dry throat, I felt dizzy and light-headed. I had not eaten for a while, and the beers on an empty stomach – plus the realisation that I was all alone, coupled with a healthy dose of fear – was beginning to take its toll. God, all I needed to do now was to collapse and the whole show would be over.

I gave myself a stern internal lecture: "Get it together man, for fuck's sake! Pull yourself together, you're carrying on like a pregnant 60-year-old woman. This is day one, and already you're falling apart. Nobody forced you to take the job; you are doing it of your own free will. Get it together man, get it together."

Staring back at the massive, black, sullen-faced barman, who was dressed in an old, badly repaired red velvet jacket with the faded words 'Kadosa Hotel' embroidered on the pocket – he actually seemed more of a bouncer than a barman – I gripped the bar with one sweaty hand to keep myself from falling down. I dug into my pocket with the other hand and removed a fat wad of South African Rand. The change amongst the sullen patrons of the bar was instant and amazing. A huge smile lit up the barman's face as he bent down and dug into a huge tin bath full of ice and beer; the bar fridges had obliviously broken down like the swimming pool pump, and like the swimming pool pump, had not been repaired. Grabbing a beer, he opened it and with a flourish set it down in front of me.

"A glass, sir, or would you prefer to drink out of the bottle? By the way, my name is Maxwell," he said in amazingly good English. Looking at the array of chipped glasses on the filthy shelves behind the now-beaming Maxwell, I indicated that the bottle would be fine. A few seconds ago the bar had been as silent as a tomb – you could have heard a pin drop – but now the music was blaring and the room was full of voices, some loud, others low, some high and shrill. As my eyes adjusted to the bad light and smoke, I noticed most of the drinkers were women. Some were old, others young, mostly black with a sprinkling of coloureds. The common denominator with all the ladies were the bright dresses of varying lengths and equally bright make-up, shoes and wigs.

The once high-powered Kadosa Hotel was now a rundown, 'ladies of the night' haunt. And like most ladies of the night the world over, I reckoned that the ladies of the night of Maputo would have an incredible amount of knowledge stored in their heads, gleaned from their many clients, the vast majority of whom were most likely to be soldiers and police. They were ideal candidates for my new venture into the dark and mysterious world of espionage and counter-espionage. The thought had no sooner hit me than it disappeared back into the smoke from where it had come. Hopefully it would stay there.

God, how stupid, I thought. After just a couple of beers I was already losing my ability to think clearly and logically. I was already imagining myself as South Africa's answer to James Bond and 'M' combined. Pushing thoughts of my upcoming task to one side, I concentrated on trying to strike up a conversation with Maxwell the barman and attempted to get to know my fellow-drinkers. To say I was popular would be an understatement. I was treated like a long-lost brother, manna from heaven, courtesy of the large amount of South African Rand I was carrying. I was being looked on as a mobile exchange-rate dispenser!

When I went oujt the next day, a large number of the shops in Maputo were closed. Those that managed to stay open were starved of goods. The majority of the items they had on display came from South Africa, which they needed Rand to buy, which were in short supply. The only options open were to approach the Indian moneylenders, with their ridiculously high interest rates, or wait for a stupid tourist with more money than brains. My colourful cotton shirt, somewhat creased from my sleeping in it, clung to my soaking wet back, while my face, arms and legs felt on fire and I looked like I had a bad dose of chicken pox, the result of the mosquito onslaught at the bar and my subsequent scratching. My head pounded, my hands shook and my eyes were red from the sweat that ran down my forehead. I had a grade A hangover, which in itself was bad enough, but added to this I had a really bad case of diarrhoea, most likely from the dodgy bar snacks I had eaten the previous night with my new-found friends. I felt like I was going to die, which I figured wouldn't be so bad, as anything would be an improvement on my present condition.

The cement veranda was old, dirty and cracked, and like the dilapidated old restaurant of which it was part, had seen better days. Sitting on an old plastic chair overlooking the sea, I waited for my friends from the previous night's drinking to join me. Why I had arranged a meeting, the Lord only knows. At the time, drunk as a skunk, it had seemed like a good idea. Now, in the clear, hot, breezeless light of the morning, sick as a dog and racked by severe stomach cramps, I was definitely having my doubts. The curse of the drink had struck again: one too many always led to a big mouth and a small brain!

Try as I might, for the life of me I couldn't remember much of what I had said or done last night. Had I invited the whole bar or just a select few? God, I could not even remember if I had given a time and place or not. If not, then what the fuck was I doing sitting here? Looking around frantically, I tried to get my brain working: "Think man, think; panicking is not going to help." The more I thought about the previous evening, the more nervous, unsure and uneasy I became. Had I reached the bigmouth bragging stage before staggering off to bed? Had I blown my cover on the very first night?

Moving around uncomfortably on the plastic chair, I tried to concentrate. However, this was easier said than done. I had a pounding head, a feeling of wanting to puke, I could see flashing lights and had a painful rumbling in my stomach, all of which made the simple task of thinking virtually impossible. Every person sitting in the decrepit, filthy restaurant, to my eyes, now had all the hallmarks of being a member of the Mozambican secret police. What I had initially taken as friendly smiles and whispers about my hangover and loud, colourful dress code, had been converted by my wild imagination into sinister and undeniable signs that as far I was concerned, I was under police surveillance. Like a cornered animal, my eyes darted from one face to the next, trying to identify from which of the people in my immediate area the threat was likely to come. My breathing was fast and shallow, my body was shaking and I was starting to panic. Why in hell had I got so drunk?

Gently, I lowered my throbbing head onto the cool plastic cloth which covered the rickety table. Dirty and sticky it might be, but it was also cool. I had to calm down and somehow get my alcohol-soaked brain going again. Managing to breathe more deeply and slowly, I cleared my mind of all thoughts of disaster and death, and instead concentrated on getting to the inviting nearby sea in an attempt to avert the fit I knew was just around the corner. I felt myself starting to come round. A sense of wellbeing settled over me, the headache seemed not as bad, the sweating was beginning to come under control and my tightly clenched eyes almost felt normal again.

"You are going to make it; you are to make it my man. You are going to survive after all – no jail for you," I muttered to myself, a smile of self-congratulation spreading across my dry lips. While I sat there congratulating myself on my new-found powers of self-healing, my stomach decided enough was enough – I had to go.

My first trip to the foul-smelling, faeces-covered toilet was a disaster. I spent all my time trying to stop myself from puking and fighting the big green flies that descended on. Upon returning to my table – sweating, pale-faced and shaking like a leaf – I was determined not to return to the 'black hole of Maputo', no matter what. The toilet and I would never meet again; if necessary I would do a

'Greek tourist' and use the sea! However, there was no way in this lifetime or the next that I was going to make it to the sea in time. Using the table for support, I struggled to my feet. I knew I had a matter of seconds and no more before the ultimate humiliation happened. I gave one despairing look at the oh-so-close, yet oh-so-far sea and bent over double from the pain in my stomach. I then headed, amid all the sniggers and outright laughter of the now nearly full restaurant, to the toilet I had sworn never to enter again. Several minutes later, still racked by stomach pains, weak and pale, I staggered back to the table, and for the want of a better phrase collapsed in a heap of shit.

Breathing like a pensioner who had just finished running a marathon, shirt sopping wet from sweat, hands waving in a vain attempt to keep the numberless flies that had followed me from the toilet at bay, I tried to piece together the highlights of the previous night's drinking. It was a waste of time and energy – all I could think of was my current condition. Abandoning all thoughts of the previous evening, I now just concentrated on keeping alive and getting out of the mess I found myself in, hopefully in one piece. The first thing I had to do was to pull myself together and get my alcohol-soaked brain working again. With this in mind, I decided it was now or never: the time had come for a swim in the cool-looking waters of the nearby Indian Ocean. Taking a deep breath, I struggled unsteadily to my feet, eyes tightly shut, fighting the sudden overwhelming feeling of wanting to pass out. Swaying like a palm tree in a breeze, hands clutching the table for support, I concentrated on not falling over. Lights flashed in front of my eyes, my breathing was short and shallow, and my head felt like it was going to burst. I am an epileptic and I had broken my own cardinal rules: never, no matter what, get drunk when you are by yourself. Stay away from the booze if there is going to be nobody to look after you the following morning, because as sure as shit, the next morning you will have a fit. Here I was in a strange country, amongst strange people, about to pay the consequences for breaking my own rules. In a hot and cold sweat, my shirt clinging to my body like a second skin, a strange high-pitched whine filled my ears and flashes of blinding light obscured my vision. I could feel the strength leaving my body. I was going to have a fit. In the next couple of minutes I was going to end up in more trouble than I had ever been in. I had to get to the sea and cool down; it was my only chance.

Several minutes and many deep breaths later, a plastic bag containing six beers in one hand, a packet of brown Portuguese cigarettes in the other, I stumbled down the broken steps of the restaurant and headed for the sea. The beers were to try and numb my brain, the cigarettes to calm me down. My forthcoming meeting was forgotten. All thoughts of what I was going to say at it disappeared; it was now all about survival. I had to get to the sea and cool down or I was dead meat.

Moments later, as sea water slowly cooled down my overheating body and the soothing murmur of gently breaking waves cleared my mind, I drifted away to another time, another place and another hangover. A place where the sea, unlike the dirty brown water I was laying in, was crystal clear, not gentle but a roaring mass of water that constantly attacked defiant cliffs that stood in it way. A time when stress and fear were just words, when life was good and my biggest problem was deciding how to spend my weekend. Should I play golf, go deep sea fishing, do a bit of diving and grab a couple of rock lobsters for lunch, or just hit the pub, relax and handle the hangover the next morning? Some of the hangovers I suffered were so bad that I used to go to our medic, Sammy Moll, who would on occasion put me on a drip to speed up my recovery. Somehow I had always managed to survive, just as I was hoping to survive the hangover I was now battling.

This time, however, there was no Sammy Moll, no drip, no friends; just me in a strange country up to no good. As the memories of my hangover at sea in a fishing boat off the coast of Port St Johns slowly penetrated my confused mind, I started to relax – hell, I had survived worse. The hang over I had suffered on the fishing boat made this one seem very minor in comparison. My brain managed to neatly package all my worries and problems – real or imagined – and hide them deep in the recesses of my mind. Before I knew it I was drinking the beer like water, smoking the cigarettes like there was no tomorrow. Man, life was good. A fuzzy feeling of wellbeing descended upon and enveloped me, and I relaxed totally. Here I was, laying in the warm seas of the Indian Ocean, with now not a trouble in the world, and the huge plus that I was getting paid to boot. Man oh man, this was the life. An hour or so later, my back burnt a bright red from the sun but feeling on top of the world, I dragged myself out of the sea and, on somewhat unsteady legs, headed for my meeting with my future employees. The cooling sea, the beers and cigarettes had worked miracles as far as my memory was concerned: I not only knew where the meeting was taking place, I even knew how many people were going to attend and their sexes. Their names were another story, but it was a whole lot more than I knew a couple of hours ago.

⁂

"Would you like something to drink, sir?" the air hostess enquired softly. "A beer please. Any kind will do so long as it is cold," I replied. Stretching out in the seat of the aircraft taking me back to South Africa, completely relaxed, I thought back to the previous day's meeting with my soon-to-be co-workers. The main concern was the money: how much, what currency and how often? The feeling I got was that they would do anything if the money was right. Which was both a good thing and a bad thing, and was something I would definitely keep in mind at all times when dealing with these people in the future. But who was I to criticise? I was doing what I was doing for the money, not for any other reason.

Lurking in the back of my mind, however, was a question that would not go away. Whether I was drunk, sober, tired, relaxed or stressed, the question remained: "Why?" There was no time left to set up any form of informer network. I was pretty sure the South Africans already had plenty of networks in place, so why was another one needed? The writing was on the wall, the end of apartheid was near, so why was I doing this?

Portuguese Islands, 1992/93

The sound of the screaming fishing rod reel pieced my alcohol-pickled brain, and my bleary eyes shot open. Thus began the longest 15 seconds of my life, or so it seemed to me. A sense of panic and heart-stopping fear hit me as my eyes took in the piercing, white-hot sun, the gently rolling turquoise blue sea, the worse-for-wear leaking fishing boat, the equally worse-for-wear fishing rods and reels, and – most frightening of all and not looking too worse-for-wear – the two black men dressed in an assortment of FRELIMO uniforms. The AKs they were holding seemed in pretty good shape too. Both men were in their mid-30s, of medium build, and one appeared to be coloured – not unusual for this part of the world – and the other African. Both looked like they knew what they were doing, faces expressionless as they stared at me.

My drunken brain struggled to deal with what my eyes were seeing: Two Frelimo, the old enemy, sitting less than a metre from me. My God, what was happening? Was I finally losing my mind? Through the fog of fear came my ever-present second voice: "Relax my man, relax. It is just a bad dream. You will wake up and all will be well." To which I answered to myself: "What do you mean 'all will be well'? Are you fucking crazy? Those are Frelimo sitting in the boat. 'All will be well' my arse!" My body soaked in my old friend the sweat of fear, head pounding, I tried to get my addled brain working. Nothing made sense as my darting red eyes once again went over my surroundings: the leaking boat, the beautiful green-blue sea, the worse-for-wear rods and reels, the spluttering boat motors and their puke-inducing smell, and, most confusing of all, my armed lookalike Frelimo guards. The more I looked around, the more I panicked. My body started shaking, going hot and cold, my brain darting around like a cornered rat as it tried to come to terms with what my eyes were seeing. I was losing control, so taking deep breaths I forced myself to relax.

Eyes closed, I concentrated on my hands. I forced them to release their painful, white-knuckled grip on the arms of the chair I was sitting in. As I opened my eyes, they were assaulted by bright reds, yellows and greens. Closing my eyes and shaking my head, I opened them and looked again. The colours took shape: they belonged to my gaudy tourist-type shirt and shorts. The sense of relief was palpable as my brain slowly made sense of what was happening. My racing pulse dropped back to almost normal and the sweating ceased, as did the shaking of my body. A smile of relief hesitantly appeared on my chalk-white face as I realised why I was where I was. I was in Mozambique on a fishing trip off the island of Magaruque. The two Frelimo types were actually Frelimo and were my captain, my guides, bodyguards and keepers, making sure I did not do anything I should not do. I was the businessman who claimed to be exploring the potential of Mozambique's islands as a tourist destination for South Africans. When I had got onto the fishing boat earlier that morning, I was still very drunk but could vaguely remember being loaded onto it by my Frelimo escorts, after which I had obviously passed out.

I needed something to try to sort myself out: headache tablets, food, coke, anything. My eyes darted around the boat, looking for my black medic kit bag in which I had put a box or 10 of headache tablets. I come to Mozambique to enjoy myself, not suffer unnecessary discomfort and hardship. I looked and looked again, but failed to locate the magic black bag. Deep inside, I knew I did not bring it. Shit! I was drunk – I would not have made the boat myself without the help of my two guides – and it was really clutching at straws to think I might have remembered the black bag. But my mind refused to accept the fact: the thought of spending the entire day at sea was too much for it to accept. Even in my drunk, disorientated state of mind, I could still remember my hell-on-earth experience with a hangover in a fishing boat off the coast of Port St Johns, and it was not something I wanted to handle again.

After desperately searching for something I knew was not there (why I refused to accept the fact that I had not brought any headache tablets with me I do not know – maybe the thought of having to handle the incredible headache and feeling of nausea I was suffering from for the foreseeable future was too much for my feverish brain to accept), I had to admit defeat. There were no tablets. Worse still, my mouth was slowly filling up with last night's beer and crawfish. Pulling myself out of, or rather falling off, the canvas chair, I dropped to my hands and knees and crawled to the side of the rolling boat, stuck my head over and started puking like my life depended on it. Sweating, my mouth tasting like the inside of a parrot's cage, feeling as weak as a baby, I managed to pull my self back into my chair. Huffing, puffing, moaning and groaning, trying my best not to fall onto the deck, which was no easy task considering my condition and the rough sea, I moved about uncomfortably as I tried to get my thoughts together.

I was beginning to have some serious doubts about one of the sayings I really believed in: bad beginning, good ending. This whole venture had started off badly and had only got worse, mostly brought on by myself. If only I had drunk a few beers less and ate only one or two crayfish instead of four or five, I would not be in the position I was now. "Yeah Jim, you and your 'ifs'. You do not want to learn, so grin and bear it," I muttered to myself. "In time it will disappear."

Five or six hours later, the bow of the fish-laden boat I had spent the morning on fishing and puking rammed into the golden beach just metres from the bungalow I was staying in. A sigh of relief escaped through my cracked and badly burned lips. As we were on *terra firma* now, maybe I would get a bit of relief from the pain and discomfort I had suffered. Standing up and getting off the boat was the first obstacle to clear. My first attempt was a dismal failure. My legs struggled to hold my weight as I swayed back and forward, left and right, all the while clinging desperately to my fishing chair. To make matters worse, my eyes were assaulted by an array of colourful, blindingly bright lights. My mind, my body, my inner self, call it what you will, could not handle the pressure and I started going hot and cold and felt as if I would faint. Desperately trying to ignore the urge to puke my heart out, I had an overwhelming desire to lie down and sleep forever. I had already made a complete fool of my self in front of my Frelimo guards during the day's fishing. What they thought of me, I would hate to know. I was determined not to make their day and confirm what they thought of me by collapsing in front of them.

Grasping onto the arm rests of my fishing chair as if my life (or what remained of my dignity) depended upon it, I tried to bring my shaking legs under control. My first effort to disembark from what I considered a floating torture chamber with a bit of class and dignity, i.e. not falling flat on my face, failed miserably. My legs were having none of my mind-over-matter crap and simply gave way .Somehow, in a desperate effort to save face and avert a minor disaster, I managed to pull the chair under my rapidly descending behind. Several seconds later, arse firmly in the fishing chair, I opened my eyes and looked at my guides, who were by this time seated on a nearby rock, staring pointedly out to sea. I was not fooled for a minute; I knew that they had watched the whole incident with great interest and would be telling all and sundry about the drunk South African they took on a fishing trip. My misfortunes would be the talk of the island for months to come. Even if it was the last thing I ever did, I had to get off this fishing boat with a bit of class.

Eyes closed, breathing deeply, trying to put the sniggering and laughter of my guides – which had restarted as soon as I looked away – out my mind, I prepared for my second attempt at disembarking. It is all in the mind, I kept telling myself; all you've got to do is stand up, walk two paces to the side of the boat and jump down to the sand 2ft below, then walk the 20-odd metres to my bungalow. There were five bungalows close together along the beach front. They all looked exactly the same: which was mine I hadn't a clue. That was another problem I would have to deal with later. First things first: get off the fishing boat without tripping and falling flat on my face, losing what little dignity I had left. "A piece of piss, a walk in the park, nothing to it; you can do it no problem," I told myself in an effort to build up a bit of confidence. But as the saying goes, 'Bullshit baffles brains', and what little bit of brains I still had, soaked in alcohol, was not working, so the continual bullshitting seemed to work. Slowly my breathing steadied, my legs stopped shaking, the hot and cold flushes subsided, the flashing lights in front of my eyes disappeared and I actually started to feel human. Sick, yes, but human. Forcing the last of the tension out of my body, I looked around at what was to be my home for the next four or five days.

What my red swollen eyes beheld was truly stunning; a piece of paradise. The beach sand was almost white, with not a cigarette butt, Coke can, broken beer bottle or plastic bag in sight. No need for graders here every morning to remove the dirty sand and rubbish from the previous day, as was the case in the beaches around Durban. The water was a bluish-green and crystal clear, turning into patches of liquid golds and reds as the setting sun caught the incoming swells. With a visibility of at least 20ft, I was to spend many happy hours snorkelling among the rocks in the days to come. To top it off, palm trees, but no beautiful dancing girls in grass skirts; there was no need, the palm trees completed the picture of a piece of paradise .

As my eyes wandered up the gentle green, densely vegetated slope leading towards the hotel and bar (the cause of my present condition – there was no ways

I was going to accept responsibility; if I did it would mean admitting that when it came to receiving brains I was at the back of the queue!), I could not help but notice several large, sprawling, derelict buildings. Obviously homes that were now uninhabited, their owners long gone, the once whitewashed walls now a dirty grey, they stood alone and roofless, reminders of the island's colonial past.

Before my vivid imagination could take me down the road of what it would have been like living here in colonial times, I was brought back to earth by a persistent "Hello my friend". Looking down to where the voice was coming from, I saw the barman-cum-manager-cumcook – and owner, for all I knew, of the hotel and maybe even the island – smiling up at me. Small, fat, round and happy would be the best way of describing him. Dressed in whiter-than-white long trousers, jacket and shirt topped off with a yellow bow tie, and a huge, flashing, whiter-than-any-Colgate smile across his black face, his feet clad in white tennis shoes, he looked like a cross between an Al Capone gangster and a modern-day African dictator. All that was missing was the machine gun. All things being equal, I am sure he also had an AK or two stashed away somewhere.

This, I assumed, was the gentleman I had spent the past evening getting drunk with. I use the word 'assumed' because then, and even to this day, I can remember very little of the evening. The only thing that stuck in my mind, apart from the beautiful sunset, was a tour of a massive, dark and smelly cold-room, which he insisted on showing me and assuring me repeatedly that the fish I was going to catch by the hundreds would not go rotten as he had a generator which he used to keep the cold-room cold when he had guests, which from what I gathered was not too often.

Looking down into his smiling face, my morale started to rise, which was not hard as it had been rock-bottom the whole day, dragging through the shark shit on the ocean floor. Could this happy little man be my saviour? With his help there was a good chance I might manage to get off this floating hell hole.

Forcing a smile on my face, trying to ignore the pain this caused to my cracked, salt-covered lips, I managed a very hoarse and painful "I am well, my friend, how are you?" His answer, a mixture of Portuguese and English, was lost on me, but looking at the wildly gesturing hands and broad smile I figured all was well. In an effort to delay the inevitable disembarking, I pointed to the pile of large fish laying in a pool of warm, oil-laced water at the bottom of the boat. How fresh they were after lying there for several hours in the sun was anybody's guess. I was to learn later that they were King Mackerel.

His face lit up. Business at last, and with the business came money. He could start up the generator, get his pride and joy – the massive cold-room – going and charge me a small fortune to keep my catch of oil-soaked King Mackerel, most of which were caught by my guides, frozen. Turning around, he beckoned to a group of women and children (whom I had not noticed, being too busy feeling sorry for myself) standing at the bottom of the crumbling, moss-covered concrete stairs leading up to the hotel. Half the children were coloured, which was not unusual in Mozambique. I had visited many Portuguese Army camps and *Eldomentos* (protected villages) on my trips into Mozambique, and at each and every one at least half the children were coloured.

At first I thought they might be hotel staff, but as they got closer and their clothing became more visible I realised this could not be the case. Broad smiles across their faces, laughing and joking, dressed in a mixture of civilian clothing and Portuguese Army uniforms, most with bands tied across their foreheads Rambo-style, they looked more like a bunch of beachcombers than hotel staff Happy and smiling they might have been, but they were quick and efficient when it came to unloading the boat. Barely 15 minutes later I was back in the same bar, sitting in the same seat, drinking the same beer that had turned my day into a nightmare. 'Once bitten, twice shy' and 'there's no fool like an old fool' meant nothing to me – all I can say in my defence is I am not a quick learner.

The offloading of the fish and myself had been accomplished with the minimum of fuss. I had, with the help of my friend the barman, managed to disembark without any major mishap and had even retained what little I had left of my dignity. The walk from the beach up the crumbling concrete stairs had been a bit of a mission; it still felt as if I was on the boat and I found it difficult to keep my balance. After many rests, much huffing and puffing and plenty of encouragement from the barman, I finally made it to the top. Now, sitting in the bar, cold beer in hand, staring out across the golden-yellow beaches and gently rolling blue-green sea, I tried to relax. My head still throbbed, my eyes – in the semi-darkness of the bar – seemed to have stopped bleeding, and my cracked, sore lips would after a couple of beers become numb. Hopefully the beer would also work a miracle on my mouth, which tasted like a burst sewage pipe. I had not yet managed to get to my bungalow and grab a few headache tablets – my barman friend had assured me tablets were not the answer to my problem, and more beer would cure all my ailments a whole lot quicker.

Putting all my aches and pains to one side, I focused on my reason for being on the islands off the coast of Mozambique, a reason which had played second fiddle to all my self-inflicted injuries. I was here to buy an island; any one of the group of islands situated off the east coast of Mozambique. Money was not a problem and the choice was mine to make. If I thought it was a good place to retire to, I was to buy it. As I was to learn later, the looking was the easy part; the buying would prove to be long and hard going.

The next three days passed in a blur. My bungalow was a small thatched rondaval, 2 or 3 metres above the high-tide water mark. There was no electricity, so I was provided with candles for light and in the place of air-conditioning I was supplied with a large tin bath filled with ice, courtesy of the deep-freeze which was keeping the fish I had caught on my best-forgotten deep-sea fishing trip. All in all, I loved it. I would not have changed anything for the world.

Under blue skies and hot sun, in warm blue-green water with hardly a wave, I spent my free time diving in the crystal-clear seas surrounding the island, getting a tan and exploring the island and nearby fishing village. (I had fleetingly toyed with the idea of doing a bit more deep-sea fishing, but the suffering I had endured on my first trip was too fresh in my mind so I gave it a miss). I could easily spend my old age and die happy in these surroundings, not that a bit of 'wine, women and song' wouldn't go amiss. The only blot on the page was the small FRELIMO section of four men who followed me every time I left the hotel or my bungalow. Whether they were told to keep an eye on me or were following me because they had nothing else to do I do not know, but their presence made sure I never relaxed completely. And forever in the back of my mind was my upcoming flight in the same aircraft that had brought me here, and flown by the same pilot, to the nearby island of Santa Carolina. The barman assured me it was not worth the visit. Not only was the hotel crumbling into the sea, but they had no deep-freeze as he did, the airstrip was even smaller than his, running water was non-existent and, sin of sins, they cooked in dirty pots over an open fire. The last pilot who had tried to land on Santa Carolina had failed, and had returned to the mainland with his passengers. How the barman knew about the incident I did not ask: this was Africa and there was the good-old bush telegraph, which seemed to be able travel across vast plains, huge mountain ranges and roaring rivers with the greatest of ease, so a couple of miles of open sea would present no problem at all.

Day four found me standing, overnight bag in hand, on the edge of the clearing that was supposed to be an airstrip. I was going to spend the night on Santa Carolina. It was about nine in the morning and already it was hot. I was nervous, to say the least. I could not stand still: a pace to the front, a pace to the rear, a pace to the left, a pace to the right, crouching, then standing up. The hangover was not helping, and I had long-since run out of headache tablets. The more I moved, the more I sweated, and it was not long before my gaudy, bright-coloured shirt was clinging to my back.

When I landed here the first time, I was so happy to be alive. I had not paid any attention to the condition of the so-called landing strip and had avoided it like the plague since. Now, with time on my hands, and also to keep my doom-and-gloom imagination under control, I gave the airstrip a closer look. It was a stupid move: I should have left well alone. I should have had a smoke, taken a walk, anything but have a closer look at the airstrip. The more I looked, the more I realised how lucky I was to have survived the previous landing! The airstrip was really only two strips of cleared ground, just wide enough to accommodate the aircraft's landing wheels, running parallel to each other. The clearing was a patch of bush in which all the large trees had been chopped down, but there were still plenty of other trees just below wing-height. Hidden in the grass, at places almost knee-high, were rocks and dead tree stumps, all capable of seriously damaging or even destroying any small aircraft straying off the beaten path.

What had before been a slight feeling of unease and anticipation, with a touch of excitement, now turned into a full-blown case of fear. Collapsing on a nearby stump, I dug out a cigarette, stuck it in my dry mouth with a not-too-steady hand and tried to light it. Half a box of matches later, I succeeded. Where I was and what I was supposed to be doing disappeared from my mind, and my entire being swung into survival mode. Somehow I had to get out of boarding that plane – to do so would result in my death, of that I was convinced. My brain failed me, although it came up with wild, irrational ideas – from trying to cancel the flight (I had no communications with the pilot, so that was a non-starter) to something going wrong with the plane or the pilot having landed somewhere else and never being found.

An hour and 40 cigarettes later, mouth dry and tasting like the proverbial bird's cage, I was seated in the small aircraft that had brought me to Magaruque, ready to take off for Santa Carolina. Sure, I was sweaty, nervous and more than a bit scared, but at the same time I was more relaxed and confident. I had watched in amazement as the pilot had skilfully landed the small aircraft on the excuse for an airstrip with, from what I could see, no problem at all. Sure, the tiny aircraft bounced all over the place and the wings seemed ready to break off at any moment, but somehow, in a huge thick red cloud of dust, leaves and grass, the pilot managed to stop the aircraft just short of the trees at the end of the clearing. The angle of approach was a bit too nose-down for my liking, but it definitely was not the nose dive it had appeared to be to me when we had landed here a couple of days earlier.

Somehow the pilot also managed to get us off the ground before smashing into the trees at the end of the clearing. How, I do not know. When we started our run for take-off amid a cloud of dust and leaves, with screaming engine, I had manfully kept my eyes open and had even managed a sickly smile, complete with a thumbs-up to the pilot and the interested spectators lining the runway. When I started to fear we were not going to make it, were going to smash into the trees at the end of the clearing and meet a fiery death, my eyes closed, my hands gripped the arm rests of my seat with all their strength, my feet did their best to push through the floor and do a Fred Flintstone-style stop, and my mouth opened in a silent scream of fear and anger. All I can basically remember of the take-off is what my tautly stretched muscles and straining ears told me. My ears told me the engine was at full revs; even wearing a headset given to me by the pilot, I could hear the engine screaming as it strained to deliver every ounce of power it had as quickly as possible. I was sure that due to the shortness of the clearing-cum-runway, it was not going to be fast enough. My muscles told me there were bumps – way too many bumps for the aircraft to get to the required speed for take-off. All this information was fed to my fear-frozen brain, which came to the conclusion that we were not going to make it. As I sat there waiting for what I was sure was a fiery death, the engine note changed, the screaming subsided and all but disappeared, to be replaced by a steady 'thump, thump'; the bumps were no more, it was as if we were floating on air. My ears started to pop. I opened my eyes: lo and behold, we were off the ground; not very high, but high enough to miss the trees at the end of the clearing. We were up and flying. I was going to make it. I was going to survive another day in my new-found role as a living-by-the-skin-of-my-teeth, cool, casual, big-time drinking secrete agent. I needed to get a grip of myself in the fear department, and of course my dress, before I could compare myself to James Bond and company, but hey, you've got to start somewhere. The main thing was, the fiery death I had imagined was not going to happen.

The view from the aircraft was awesome, and after what I considered my close brush with death everything seemed brighter, clearer. The white sands of the beaches seemed almost transparent, the sea below so clear I could see the dark shapes of what I assumed to be sharks cruising along the edge of the clearly visible reef. The smell of the sea that rushed in through the small open side window of the aircraft seemed fresher, cleaner, the clear blue stretching-forever sky seemed clearer, bluer and never ending. It was indeed great to be alive. Ten minutes later, everything was looking black and gloomy, with a fiery slash of red; my newly found feeling of well-being had disappeared a lot more quickly than it had arrived. My career as a supposedly fearless, badly dressed, cool, non-stressing secret agent was about to come to an end. Stress and fear would be in, cool and fearless would be out; the only thing that would stay the same was my bad dress.

I was looking out of the side window of the banking aircraft as it slowly circled the island of Santa Carolina. The beaches were a glimmering white, the topaz waters crystal clear, the vegetation greener than green, all in all a small piece of paradise – the key word being 'small'. No matter how hard I looked, I could not see anything that resembled an airstrip, no clearing that I thought could handle the aircraft we were travelling in. Nothing. The longer I looked, the more apprehensive I became. Things were not looking good, to say the least. Before the apprehension could turn into fear and my imagination turn the beautiful island below us into a fiery funeral pyre, my earphones crackled into life: "Hey Andy, look just to the left of the hotel. There is somebody in a clearing waving something red, maybe a shirt or towel." The island was small and there was only one hotel, so it did not take long to locate the figure waving the red shirt. "Got him," I replied. "Maybe he is telling us to get the hell out of here as it is too dangerous to land," I added half-jokingly through a rapidly drying throat, mouth and lips. "No, I do not think so, where he is standing seems to the airstrip," came the casual reply from the pilot. "Airstrip?" I thought to myself. "Airstrip? You must be joking. I do not know what you have been smoking, my friend, but it must be potent, because as far as I can see it is a clearing – and a small one at that. I would not like to try and land a helicopter in there, never mind a fixed-wing aircraft." Unfortunately I was not the pilot, who seemed quite happy to land the aircraft in the clearing indicated by the figure waving the red shirt or towel. I could pull rank, as it were; I was the payer of the bills, which gave me the final call.

I might have been shit-scared, shaking like a leaf and covered in sweat, and every fibre in my body screamed out loud and clear "do not do it – give it a miss, you are going to see your arse", but there was a little voice in the dark, misty recesses of my mind that I could not shut out. Like a stuck record, it kept repeating itself: "Pull yourself together, what is the matter with you? You took the money, now do what you have been paid to do and stop bitching and complaining."

My body went as stiff as a board, my head throbbed, my throat was so dry I could not swallow, my lips were dry and parched as if I had not drunk anything for days, my red eyes stared unblinkingly ahead, and even my runaway imagination had called it a day. This was it; do or die. I was there in the aircraft as it shot across the sea, what seemed to me merely centimetres above the waves, and then I felt

I was not in the aircraft; it was as if I was outside, looking down on proceedings. This was not the first time I had experienced this strange feeling of being on the outside, watching what was happening to me. After the failed coup attempt in the Ciskei, I found myself sitting alone at a garage in King Williams Town awaiting pickup by a vehicle that I had arranged with my friend over the phone. With the pressure, the uncertainty and the lack of control over the situation I found myself in, my brain decided enough is enough, it's time to leave and get a break from all the pressures, and somehow seemed to float away, taking me with it. Sounds strange, I know, but that is what happens to me. Maybe it is just my fearful, rampant imagination that makes it feel like I leave my body.

"The trees – dear God, the trees. We are too high and we are going to hit the trees." My brain was back and working, and my mouth opened in a silent scream of agreement. We were about to see the world from the other side, from a fireball. I was back in my body, of that there was no doubt. We were basically wave-hopping, like the Dam Busters. I do not think the pilot was any keener on the wave-hopping bit than I was, but he, like me, was paid to do a job. And unfortunately, due to the positioning of the airstrip, you had to come in very low over the sea to avoid hitting the trees at the beginning of the strip-cum-clearing.

My brain was still issuing a long list of silent "go left, go right, higher, lower" when we hit the ground in a cloud of sea, sand, palm tree leaves and the inevitable plastic bags. At least on this runway we could see where we were going, unlike at Magaruque, where everything disappeared in a cloud of red dust. Now, as I watched the rapidly approaching trees situated at the end of the clearing and a few meters beyond the sea, and hence the end of the island, I wondered if the blinding red cloud of dust was not a better option. At least you could think everything was going to be alright.

Now, with engine in reverse – or was the pitch of the propeller just changed? Either way, the noise was deafening as, with flaps down, brakes screeching in protest, bouncing along at what seemed to me a hundred miles an hour, we headed for the trees and beyond them the sea. The landing had been a real touch-and-go affair, but somehow the pilot had managed to keep everything under control. With a combination of skill and luck, he had managed to stop the aircraft just short of the trees. Several long seconds passed after the engine was killed before there was any movement from me or the pilot; then, as if a pressure valve was opened, there was much shaking of hands, patting on the back and high, shrill, nervous laughter.

Walking on weak, shaking legs, my overnight bag clutched in my trembling, sweaty hand, the pilot and myself followed our red-shirted guide to the nearby Santa Carolina Hotel. The hotel appeared in reasonable condition from a distance, but the closer you got the more apparent the neglect became. Most of the front of the hotel was slowly being swallowed by the ever-restless and hungry sea, eroded to the point of collapse . The inside of the hotel would have to wait: first a beer to calm the nerves.

"Chefez, chefez, beer, cold Castle, my friend!" I was speaking to the man in the red shirt, who turned out to be the hotel manager. Whether he spoke English or not I did not know, but I hoped to get my message across with plenty of smiling and sign language. Tall and thin, with an 'I am the boss, here this is my island' expression slapped across his face, he looked on with cold, unblinking eyes as I went through my 'I would like a beer' routine. Once I had smilingly used every word I knew for beer, I stopped and looked at him, at least expecting a smile for my efforts. Nothing: not a thing. His face remained expressionless, reminding me of a couple of Zanu/Zapu political commissars I had spoken to whilst in the Scouts in Rhodesia. The same deadpan face and expressionless eyes as the organizers of the cutting off of lips, hacking off of arms with choppers or pangas, bayoneting in the stomach of pregnant women – real animals and really full of themselves. Like all men of that kind, they were open to bribery and were often used by different members of the same village to settle old scores. I had also seen that 'I love and am full of myself' look change into one of total lip-trembling, blabbering fear.

My troop had managed to capture one of these so-called hard-arsed political commissars in Motoko Tribal Trust land. He really loved himself – arrogant and full of shit – and would not answer any questions.

We gave him the old one-two. Half an hour later, stripped naked ,sitting on his behind on a rock, legs spread-eagled, hands tied behind his back, the little blue gas burner was alight and edging ever closer to his pride and joy, his baby-maker. All the loudmouth propaganda and arrogance was replaced by mind-blowing fear. The hardened so-called liberation fighter, the leader of the masses, was no more, replaced by a crying, jabbering, ready-to-spill-his-guts animal. An animal that had hurt, maimed and killed countless innocents was now begging for mercy. A mercy he expected to be granted even though he showed none to his victims.

One would think a head man would be a man of stature with an air of command about him, not the head-bowed, cringing, whining, hand-wringing individual we seemed to meet every time we entered a village. Each one gave the self-same answer when questioned about terrorists in the area. "Terrorists? What are terrorists? Never heard of such a thing." If any strangers arrived in the area he would report them to the nearest police station or District Commissioner straight away, he said. All the questions were answered, with every second word being 'boss'.

As the war progressed and I learnt more and more about how the terrorists and their supporters operated, and I thought back on my time in the Rhodesian Light Infantry, I would on occasion break out in a cold sweat, my face would turn red and I would get up and pace around as I realised how I had been played for a fool by basically uneducated headmen using their natural talent for acting and lying. Maybe I was also being a bit harsh (there we go, the good old Christian upbringing already trying to forgive somebody who was a sellout); after all, the head man was there to look after the villages and do what he thought was best for everybody. We, as security forces, would come and go, never staying in one area for any length of time; our army was just too small to hold ground, and because of this the winning of the hearts and minds of the local rural population was doomed to failure. We also did some amazingly stupid things. When I say 'we' I mean those fine, upstanding officials in Home Affairs, most of whom I am convinced did not even go into the rural areas. (That's my opinion, and I am sure somebody will prove me wrong.) One thing that really sticks in my mind is the issuing of passes to the local black population. Instead of going for something official-looking – maybe we could not afford it – they used old cattle-breeding name cards. Talk about a major blunder! The terrorists could not have asked for anything better to use as propaganda. In my mind's eye, I could imagine them all gathered around a small smoky fire, blankets over their shoulders, in the dead of night, the flames flickering and dancing, softening and hardening their faces in turn, most looking down, wishing they were somewhere else. At centre stage stood the political commissar, a cattle pass in one hand, AK47 in the other, who said: "See, I told you. These whites consider us black people the same as cattle, the same as animals." There was nothing anybody could say; the proof was before their eyes.

The terrorists, on the other hand, once having moved in would stay. They did not worry too much about the winning of the hearts and minds of the local population. They employed the principle of "grab them by the balls and the hearts and mind will follow". Say what you like, you cannot argue against success: it was a winning principle. We – the whites, the security forces – were so busy not wanting to offend or upset the international community that we lost the war.

✄

Back now to the present, and Santa Carolina Island.

Forcing the smile on my face to remain in place, I tried a new approach, changing from the happy-go-lucky tack to the bowing-and-scraping, we-are-all-friends approach. "Hello sir," I said. "We are looking for the manager of the hotel." As soon as the 'sir' left my mouth, I could see the change. A slow smile curved his lips; this was more to his liking. Having the hated white man call him 'sir' was music to his ears. All of a sudden he could speak English. "I am the manager and owner," he snapped back. "What do you want?" No name, no smile, no handshake, nothing: just a big dose of 'I love myself and I hate all white people'. The time had come to see if he was a man of principle, or was it a case of 'talk is cheap, money buys the whisky'? "I want to buy this island for my retirement," I answered. He looked at me in stunned silence. I could imagine his thought process as he did a quick recap on what he said and how he had treated me since I had arrived on the island. He obviously did not like what he saw, so in an attempt to salvage the situation and his dreams of living the high life in Maputo, he brought out the big beaming smile, the wringing hands act. "Buy the island: you want to buy the island?" he repeated, all the while shaking his head and rubbing his hands together. "Yes," I replied. "I want to buy this island if the price is right and I like what I see."

It took a few seconds for what I had said to sink in. Once it had, we were like long-lost buddies. After much handshaking, beaming smiles and head shaking, we started a non-stop talking tour of the island and the hotel. Less than an hour later I was sitting strapped in my seat of the tiny aircraft waiting for take-off. The island was too small; the hotel was falling into the sea and would take countless millions to sort out.

As the engine built up revs and the aircraft started to shake violently, my mind automatically went into its 'doom and gloom' predictions of a fiery or watery death. I even managed to give the pilot a thumbs-up, followed by a smile. Sure, not a 'bright and breezy, I will handle whatever comes my way' smile. Nevertheless, a smile. After several landings and take-offs on impossibly small so-called runways, my confidence in the pilot had grown in leaps and bounds.

That evening, as I sat at the bar on Magaruque with a cold beer in my hand watching the sun go down, relaxed and happy, I knew which island I wanted to buy. I also knew my time on the islands was coming to an end, and I thought back to my arrival at Maputo airport just over a week ago.

Maputo Airport (the previous week)

I felt like a weary, losing boxer on his last legs, in the ninth round of a 10-round fight, lungs burning, head battered and bleeding, eyes puffed closed, struggling to stand upright, receiving a blow to the solar plexus.

Standing on the top of the stairs of the South African Airways Boeing 707, the air went out of my lungs with a gentle, long-drawn-out sigh, my shoulders hunched and my head dropped as if expecting a blow. All I could see from the top of the aircraft stairs were FRELIMO. Dressed in Portuguese Army camouflage and armed with AK47s, they were everywhere.

My thoughts of palm trees, golden beaches, ice-cold cocktails with brightly coloured miniature umbrellas stuck in crushed ice, and the inevitable grass-skirted dancing girls disappeared under a barrage of emotions. Feelings of fear and frustration, of almost overpowering isolation, raced through my mind as I struggled to get myself under control. I wanted to run and hide, like a trapped animal darting this way and that as it struggled to find a way out of its predicament.

"Easy Jim, easy, steady in the butts. Count to 10, my friend, and relax." (I had never managed to kick the habit of talking to myself when under pressure.) "There is nothing you can do about the FRELIMO, so slap a smile on your face and go with the flow. Remember, you are a tourist guide operator trying to open up Mozambique to South African tourists. You are legitimate; you even look the part. Believe, my man, believe; if you don't believe your story, how the hell do you expect anybody else to believe it? Pull yourself together and do a bit of positive thinking for a change."

If anybody looked like a tourist-cum-businessman it was me. I had cameras hanging around my neck, skinny white legs sticking out of the bottom of a multicoloured pair of three-quarter length shorts, dark glasses, flip flops, a stupid hat, long hair and a scraggly beard, topped off by a shocking red, yellow and green collarless cotton shirt. I was a somewhat shit-scared sweaty tourist-cum-businessman, but a tourist-cum-businessman nevertheless. Under the gentle prodding of the air hostess, I started my stiff-legged walk down the stairs. God, how I hated the fear and the pounding heart, the foul-smelling sweat running down my back, the shaking hands, the dry mouth and never-resting, vivid imagination – an imagination that forever predicted doom and gloom.

Clinging onto the stair rail for dear life, and willing my legs to relax, I slowly made my way down the steps. My shirt was soaking wet and clung to my body, my legs refused to obey my brain, remaining stiff and awkward, and my intended slow, dignified walk to the tarmac below turned into a stumbling, rail-clutching embarrassment, more like a condemned man heading for the gallows than a tourist out to have a good time.

Several hours later, or so it seemed to me, I finally reached the bottom step and the runway. Standing in the blazing sun, blinded by its piercing light, breathing as if I had just run a marathon, my pounding heart sounding like a bongo drum in my ears, drowning out all other sounds, I looked around through squinted eyes. Everything looked peaceful and quiet; there were no FRELIMO running towards me, shouting and screaming, with weapons pointed. I began to relax and my spirits lifted. Maybe, just maybe, I would survive the airport and all its potential pitfalls and manage to get to the small single-seater aircraft I had hired to fly me to the islands just off the coast of Mozambique. I still felt isolated and very nervous as I shuffled along, trying to blend into the small group of people heading for the airport terminal. The last time I had felt so alone and powerless was when I had been arrested in the Transkei and thrown into solitary confinement in the newly built detention barracks in Port St Johns after our failed attempt at overthrowing the Ciskei Government.

It may have seemed peaceful and quiet, but on closer inspection it looked more like an army camp than an international airport. Camouflaged armoured cars were on each end of the runway, with machine-gun nests scattered all along the perimeter fence, some occupied and others deserted. Groups of FRELIMO dressed in Portuguese camouflage, wearing brown canvas chest webbing and carrying AK47s, were leaning on anything and everything. I don't know what had happened in the month or so since I had last visited the airport, but the change was huge. Previously, it had not exactly been a fun place, but there had been the odd friendly smile and handshake, plus it had been a whole lot cleaner and most of the slogans of the war of independence had been removed or painted over. As I made my way towards the main terminal, I could see all that had changed. The slogans were back, bigger and brighter than before, as was the dirt – the place was littered with everything from plastic bags to empty beer bottles – and the atmosphere had changed from fairly friendly to openly hostile. It was now like a high security prison: there were no handshakes or friendly smiles, just blank, sullen stares and an air of hostility thick enough to cut with a knife. There again, Mozambique was no friend of South Africa, and the diplomatic relations between the two at the time would dictate the warmth of your welcome. Obviously things had taken a turn for the worse.

I was sweating like the proverbial stuffed pig as I stood in line with the other four or five people who had disembarked from the flight from Johannesburg and were waiting to be cleared by Mozambican customs. It was a slow, nerve-racking, dry-mouthed experience. In Africa there is a saying that time means nothing, and the big fat black female immigration official, dressed in a blue uniform and wearing a huge black wig, checking our travel documents proved beyond doubt that the maxim was true. There was no smile or welcoming words, no conversation at all, just an arrogant, aggressive 'I am the boss here, white man' attitude and an 'I will do things my way, right or wrong' glare.

An hour or so later, alone, and leaning against one of the filthy yellow-brown walls in the arrival lounge, luggage at my feet and sipping a warm Coke, I was starting to get worried. The other passengers had long-since departed for what I can only assume was Maputo; some with waiting friends, others via taxi. All Portuguese, they appeared to be returning residents, from where I did not know. Soberly dressed, subdued, heads bent, speaking in whispers, eyes darting from place to place, they gave the impression this was the last place they wanted to be and wished they were invisible. There were no colourful shirts, flip-flops and three-quarter shorts for them, and there was no laughter; it was all about survival. I was trying my best to act like a tourist – casual, but at the same time excited. I walked from one window to the next, waving and smiling at the many FRELIMO and the odds and sods lounging around. I don't know why I bothered; nobody returned my smiles or the waves. Time passed slowly, and my holiday tourist feeling was fading quickly. I was beginning to feel trapped and isolated. Midday was rapidly approaching, and time was running out. Where the hell was the small aircraft I had chartered to fly me to the Portuguese islands? I knew from previous conversations with the charter company providing the aircraft that the islands, situated just off the east coast of Mozambique, were at least two to three hours' flying time away.

My brain was churning and my body slowly tensing up. My free-and-easy walk was turning more into a stiff-legged gait. To say I was worried was an understatement. My imagination started to run wild as I began to lose control. Sitting on an old wooden, cigarette-scarred, name-engraved bench, I reverted to my never-failing last line of defence against panic: I started talking to myself.

"Your name Andy?" asked a friendly Rhodesian sounding voice. Looking up, I stared blankly into a smiling set of brown eyes. I had been so busy talking to myself in an attempt to get my brain working and ignore my wild imagination that I hadn't noticed the approach of the man now standing in front of me.

About 6ft tall, dressed in khaki shirt and shorts, brown boots with khaki socks and deeply tanned, he looked exactly like I imagined a bush pilot would.

This, then, was the pilot who had been hired to fly me to the different islands off the coast of Mozambique. The feeling of relief was instantaneous. It was as if a tightening band round my chest had been broken, like a great weight had been lifted off my sagging shoulders. My breathing steadied and my shoulders straightened. Another white man, and by the sound of his voice a fellow Rhodesian: things were looking a whole lot better.

It was beautiful – the multicoloured blues and purples of the sea lapping up onto golden, almost white deserted beaches. Topping off the idyllic picture, situated a couple of hundred metres from what could only be the hotel was a small fishing village, complete with nets drying in the sun and wooden fishing boats. Some boats were out at sea with their square Arab dhow-type sail billowing in the wind, others laying haphazard on the superb clean beach. All in all, a place to relax and enjoy life, in stark contrast to the harsh, brutal, endless miles of yellow-sanded, flat as a billiard table, seemingly lifeless stunted mopani tree plains we had just flown over. 'Lifeless' was the correct word: not an animal, not a bird, not a path nor a road no water and villages, just thousands of kilometres of vast, awesome nothingness

It was a sea and beaches that I would not get a chance to explore unless we could get the aircraft down safely, which appeared to be touch and go at this stage as I stared down, with eyes straining, at the airstrip below. God, it looked small. How we were going to land the little single-engine aircraft we were in on the small clearing below us which some mentally retarded idiot had laughingly referred to as an airstrip was beyond me. It had no beginning, no end, no left or right: it was basically just an oblong clearing in the bush. The pilot pulled up and banked the tiny aircraft for the fourth or fifth time, its engine screaming as it tried to claw its way back into the clear blue sky. I was not counting just how many times the pilot had made the attempt – I was too busy trying to control my fear and my imagination's prediction of certain death if we attempted to land. Once again we lined up with the airstrip and headed downwards.

To say I was nervous would be a massive understatement. I had passed the nervous laugh, sweaty hands and unable to sit still stage several landing attempts ago. I was now in the stiff as a board with fear stage; my mouth was dry, my head was on the brink of bursting and my heart sounded like it was trying to escape from my chest. I had landed in many very small airstrips while serving in the Rhodesian Army, the difference being the pilots were among the best in the world and if anything did go wrong help was at hand. This ordeal was taking place in a fixed-wing, single-engine aircraft flown by a pilot I knew nothing about, apart from the fact that he was Rhodesian – which I had to admit was a comfort – in a strange country I had only previously visited with evil intentions in mind – not that my intensions were any more noble this time round – and where help was several days away.

The beauty of the shimmering sea lapping up against stunning beaches was lost on me as I fought to control my fear and mounting urge to throw up. I had thought the stress and fear that had enveloped me at Maputo Airport was as bad as it could get, but that was a walk in the park compared to what I was going through now. Looking across at the pilot in the expectation of getting a thumbs-up or a confident smile, my hopes that every thing was alright were dashed. The look on his face told me as clear as day he was also under immense pressure and the landing of the aircraft safely was going to be difficult and dangerous.

I was sure we were going to crash. The ground and the trees were rushing up to meet us, we were coming in to land too steep – it was as if we were in a nose dive. This was it: after all the shit I had been through, I was going to die in a plane crash on an island off the coast of Mozambique. My mouth open in a silent scream of fear, feet pushing a hole through the bottom of the aircraft, hands gripping the armrests in a vain attempt to pull the aircraft up and out of its nose dive, I watched – eyes wide and unblinking – my rapidly approaching death.

Fortunately, the fiery death I had imagined did not come to pass, and after several landings and take-offs from similar-sized runways my confidence grew in my pilot's ability. I would never relax completely in such a small aircraft – I would always imagine death was around the corner just waiting for me. But at least I could give a thumbs-up accompanied by a somewhat sickly smile.

Beira, Mozambique, 1994/95, Prawn Buying

It was back, like a long-lost friend. The foul-smelling, cold, rancid sweat of fear had returned, as had the straining, taut back muscles, the shaking hands, the pounding heart, the jerky head movements, the all-seeing telescopic eyes, the all-hearing radar ears and the frozen brain struggling to beat back the enveloping mists of fear.

Surrounded by huge hessian bags crammed full of Mozambican bank notes, crouched in a corner in the Banco de Mozambique behind a badly marked and cracking concrete pillar in the Mozambican central bank in Beira, I tried to make sense of what was happening.

The gunshots – some single, others long shuddering bursts – the screaming, the nerve-racking moments of complete silence, the whining of ricocheting rounds, the revving of vehicle engines, the shattering glass and now, more ominously the cries of pain from what could only be the wounded. This was Mozambique in the late 1980s: the war was supposed to be finished, Rhodesia was a distant memory, South Africa was a history story and all was supposed to peaceful in this part of Africa, and it was apart from the odd skirmish the FRELIMO Government troops had with a splinter freedom fighter group going by the name of RENAMO.

We had arrived at the bank scarcely an hour ago, complete with an evil, death-has-arrived hangover compliments of Club Nortica and a touch of the runs compliments of the local grilled chicken. I was new to Beira and had spent the 20 minutes we had to wait for the bank to open looking around trying to take in the sights, sounds and smells. Everywhere I looked in the busy square I saw AK47s, chairs, tables and piles of rubbish. The tables and chairs – some wood, some steel, others a combination of both – were all brightly coloured, and all situated under badly worn, torn canvas umbrellas on the pavements which gave the square an almost continental feel. From what I could see, most of the restaurants-cum-coffee shops appeared to be owned by Portuguese who had stayed behind and taken their chances with the Frelimo rather than go back home to Portugal and face the poverty that was surely awaiting them.

It seemed as if every second or third black person was dressed in some sort of a uniform, consisting of green-grey trousers and shirt. Head wear ranged from gaudy baseball caps covered with a replica of the USA flag to the all-too-familiar green camouflaged bush cap of the Portuguese Army, while the foot wear was equally diverse – anything from barefoot to broken old black army boots and Nike running shoes seemed acceptable.

The once brightly coloured walls surrounding the square were in a bad state of repair, and in places were falling down. Unlike Maputo, where every square inch of every wall was covered in Frelimo propaganda, here the walls were strangely devoid of any political slogans, apart from the odd 'Viva Samora Machel'. Then again, this was RENAMO country so it was maybe not so strange.

RENAMO, from what I understand, was a group of pro-Western fighters – or anti-Frelimo fighters, depending on how you look at it – formed and supported by the South African government to keep the Frelimo busy and thus not have time to support and assist the ANC and the various Rhodesian liberation movements. It was not a huge success, to say the least, but had enough support to claim Manica province as it own.

Finally, my eyes settled on a massive old building that could have come straight out of a *Beau Geste* movie; the only thing that was missing was the French Foreign Legion guards with bolt-action rifles at the shoulder, wearing their funny little hats, and the endless desert stretching away to the horizon, broken only by the odd lonely date palm, all under a burning unforgiving sun. Situated on one corner of the square was the Beira Central Prison. Built like a fort of old, out of blocks of what appeared to be sandstone, complete with watch towers, I could not take my eyes off it. I had thought buildings like this no longer existed. Standing alone, isolated from other buildings by high thick walls, framed against the clear blue sky it was a sight to behold, a reminder of the brutal colonial days. Hanging out of every barred window I could see were prisoners' heads, one on top of the next, four high in some cases, depending on the size of the window. On the early-morning breeze came a strange sound, almost a wail of despair of defeat, accompanied by the stench of untreated sewage and unwashed bodies.

It was still fairly early in the morning, but already the sun was beating down and I was sweating, partly from the heat and humidity and partly from a combination of uncertainty and fear. Fear of saying something wrong, of being in the wrong place at the wrong time and ending up in this beautiful old building, which to me would be like a death sentence Once inside, the chances of survival were nil. If I lasted an hour it would be a long time, and it would be an hour of hell on earth.

The previous evening, I had heard stories about how unhappy the old Frelimo soldiers were with the present Mozambique Government, the main complaints being the pay and accommodation. Beira at this time was a city in crisis. Much of the sewage system had been filled with concrete by the departing Portuguese, with a result that many of the streets had raw sewage flowing down them. The smell – heavy and cloying – made breathing a nauseating affair as you tried short and shallow breaths in an effort to stop yourself puking, while the accompanying dark blue clouds of millions of flies had to be seen and experienced to be believed. It was an ideal setting for cholera and dysentery, both of which flourished, causing untold suffering and countless deaths. Doctors were far and few between, and were mostly Cuban. Add to this the fact that water was in very short supply, and that on the odd occasion when it did come out of the taps it was too salty to drink. The only drinking water, apart from bought bottled water, was from people who owned boreholes. Realising they were sitting on a goldmine, they charged exorbitant prices for this water, which led to constant violent flare-ups between the supplier and his customers, often resulting in death and property being destroyed.

The shops were basically empty, and dairy products were non-existent, the national dairy herd having been slaughtered and eaten as the quest for red meat intensified. The only food readily available was fish, cashew nuts and coconuts. There was no tourism: all the hotels that had once housed thousand of visitors from South Africa and Rhodesia had been taken over by the retired Frelimo and turned into filthy eyesores. Unpainted for many years, they stood gaunt, grey and silent against the Beira skyline, a shell of their former selves; it was difficult to make out the original colour. Out of each and every window, and on each and every balcony, was hung clothes and blankets.

My wandering mind was brought back to the present by the sound of more gunshots and shattering glass, followed by screams from the wounded. What was I to do? I had never been in such a situation before. This was different: I was no longer in charge, I had no weapon, there were no friends nearby to help and likewise no fire-force. Even my frantic mind in full survival mode could not come up with a solution. So, discretion being the better part of valour, I lay, dry-mouthed and sweaty, cowering behind the bags of money we had been given in exchange for our Rands. The Portuguese gentleman we were buying the prawns from insisted on being paid in the local currency, saying he had no intention of ending up in prison for being in possession of foreign currency. And now having seen the prison, I did not blame him.

The screams died away, the revving truck motors faded into the distance and a deathly silence descended over the square, broken only by the squeak of the sole working overhead fan in the bank that blocked your thoughts. If your brain concentrated on that sound you did not have to deal with reality. It was as if time stood still – nothing was happening, as you mind, like a coward, did not want to deal with what had happened outside. But like the saying goes, you can run but you cannot hide, and slowly the wails of the wounded and the subdued questioning voices of the survivors penetrated the protective screen thrown up by my brain and reality came rushing back, ugly and deadly. With reality came the usual throbbing headache, the sweat-covered body, the taut back muscles and the burning red eyes caused by the river of sweat flowing into them.

Several minutes passed before I finally managed to beat back the fear that encased my brain and found the courage to at least raise my head above the level of the bulging sacks of money. I need not have felt so bad, as all of the customers whom I could see were still laying flat on the floor, their personal possessions – ranging from handbags to plastic bags – scattered all around, an indication on how quickly they took cover. My eyes moved slowly over the badly painted and cracked walls of the bank and the shattered windows, finally settling on the large, open main entrance, through which I could see a portion of the square. Ignoring my instinct for self-preservation, which screamed "keep your head down you arsehole, there are no medals to be won here; this is all about keeping alive!", I crawled leopard-like to a nearby mosaic-covered pillar. Once there, mustering all my strength and willpower, and using the pillar for support, I stood up. It sounds easy enough, but it took me several attempts to get it right, stop my knees from collapsing and convince my white-knuckled hands they were not holding a weapon and would be more usefully utilised clutching on to the pillar to help me gain my feet.

Keeping the pillar between me and the gaping main entrance to the bank, I cautiously stuck my head around the corner and had a quick look to see if it was safe. I do not know what I thought I was going to see: the speed at which I put my head around the corner and pulled it back again was mindboggling – talk about the speed of light! The instinct for survival combined with a healthy dose of fear was a hard thing to beat. My next effort was a great improvement, and after keeping my head around the corner of the pillar for at least three seconds and having had no pot shots taken at it, I relaxed and opened my eyes. I do not know what is was expecting to see, but after all the shooting that had taken place maybe a body or two on the stairs leading up to the bank's main door, maybe a burning truck, its tyres sending dark plumes of smoke into the sky. People are funny, or maybe it is just me, but when I did not see any bodies or burning trucks I felt disappointed, indeed robbed. "Man, after all that shooting somebody has got to have died," I muttered to myself. Looking across the square towards the coffee shops on the other side, all I could see was overturned tables, chairs and umbrellas. Glancing across at the prison, I noticed that the once crowded windows were now empty, while parked on the street running next to the prison wall were four or five Frelimo troop-carrying vehicles, some with canopies and some without. They appeared empty, apart from the drivers sitting in the front. These then must be the vehicles used by the new Frelimo (for the want of a better word) to sort out the striking old Frelimo.

As I lay there watching, the square slowly came back to life. The tables and chairs were righted, the gaudy umbrellas put into place and the broken crockery swept up and disposed of by very nervous waiters and business owners. At the same time, the laughing and joking new Frelimo returned to their vehicles, boarded them, fired off a couple of bursts of rounds and then drove back to their barracks. Upon the departure of the Frelimo, the patrons of the coffee houses-cum-restaurants reappeared, the prison windows filled up with inmates again and things went back to normal; or as normal as can be with the odd dead body lying around and the occasional burning car thrown in for effect. We loaded our car as quickly as possible with the money we had changed at the bank, and drove away from the area. This, then, was my introduction into what I had thought would be the nice quiet job of prawn-buying in Mozambique. But this was Africa, the land of the strong, where violence was the answer to most problems.

I do not know what I was bitching about. My brief career as a weapons instructor-cumtruck escorter in the security industry had come to an end. My services were no longer required as the townships had returned to normal, and it was no longer necessary for the delivery trucks to be escorted in and out. I cannot say I was sorry: the hours were long, the work dangerous and the pay ridiculously low. After a year or so of sitting on my fat bum, I had been approached by an old friend of mine who needed someone to help him with the buying of prawns in Beira, which was in, of all places, Mozambique. After 12 months of doing nothing, I was willing to try anything. A career change was supposed to be good for you, or was it that a change is as good as a holiday? Whatever, I now embarked on my new career of a prawn and fresh fish-buyer with great enthusiasm, hope in my heart and a bounce in my step.

My new career had both a downside and an upside. The upside was the pay; the downside was that I had no choice but to ply my new trade in my home from home – Mozambique. At least this time I was visiting not to kill and burn, but as a legitimate businessman. I wouldn't have to worry about what I did or said this time, as everything would be legitimate and above board. Or so I hoped. But this being Africa, only time would tell.

The truck, an old blue and white Mercedes Benz once used for furniture removal, had been converted into a 10-ton refrigerated prawn carrier, and like me, the truck had also seen better days. Nevertheless, I was really looking forward to my first trip to Beira. The sea, the sand, the seafood and the cold beers – man, it really sounded good. But as the saying goes, 'there is no fool like an old fool'.

After two days of body-numbing, skinless-bum-bouncing in the old and very, very slow Mercedes Benz truck, I finally arrived in Harare. I was about to be introduced to bribery and corruption on a vast scale. Whatever permits I needed to travel through Zimbabwe and on into Mozambique – and there were many of them – I had to pay for in either American dollars or British pounds. All other currency was frowned upon, especially at government institutions.

Four days later, early in the morning, I arrived at the Mozambique/Zimbabwe border post just outside the small Zimbabwean town of Mutare. The truck was empty, so the crossing over into Mozambique went pretty smoothly, but very, very slowly. By around midday, all had been sorted out and we were on our way to Beira, onwards to riches, fame and fortune. Or so I thought! Little did I know that in a couple of days I would be laying petrified on a bank floor, surrounded by bags of money.

The Opening of Parliament, Umtata, the Transkei, 1984/85

Dressed in a pair of blue denims and a t-shirt, my feet encased in a trusty pair of worn vellies, I was uncomfortable, I could not keep still and I found it difficult to stop muttering under my breath "what the fuck are you doing?". To make matters worse, I was sweating like a pig. Sure it was hot, but not that hot, the main cause of my sweating being embarrassment. Embarrassment at myself for having accepted the job as an adviser to the small army of the Transkei homeland and in my spare time bodyguard to the President and Prime Minister.

Where a small, impoverished homeland government like the Transkei got the money to hire us, and why they wanted or needed a highly trained army, was beyond me. Like an ostrich, I buried my head in the sand and refused to let my thoughts wander down that much-booby-trapped road.

"A job is a job," I kept telling myself. "The whys and wherefores are not your problem. Stop bitching; whether you like to admit it or not, it is the best job you have ever had. You have got a free house in the little piece of paradise that is Port St Johns, and you are doing a job you know like the back of your hand. It is money for jam so shut up and enjoy it!" Little did I know it at the time, but a couple of years down the line the money for jam would be a thing of the past and I would be knee-deep in shit as I tried to evade capture in the small town of King Williams after a failed attack on the Presidential Palace in Ciskei, another South African homeland.

The nagging feeling of not being wanted or needed, but being forced on the Transkei Government by the then-apartheid government of South Africa, was one that would stay with me until I was eventually arrested by the same people I was advising and thrown out of the homeland. Even today, 20-odd years later, I still feel uncomfortable when I think about the charade that was the Transkei.

Pete Mac and I had arrived earlier in Pete's trusty, but oh-so-slow, blue long-wheel-base Land Rover. We had stopped outside the public works building, the flat roof of which we intended to use as our observation post as it overlooked the main entrance to the parliament of the Transkei. This would be the entrance used by the President of the Transkei, K.D. Matanzima, when entering and leaving the parliamentary buildings in the forthcoming independence celebrations.

Pete, dressed much like I was in blue jeans and t-shirt, was armed with a .222 rifle with a scope borrowed from the South African Security Police. He was going to do the shooting if any was required. As for myself, I was holding a 9mm pistol in one trembling, sweaty hand, and in the other a pair of binoculars, with a security forces radio on my back, as I was going to be the spotter. Hopefully we could handle any threat posed to the life of K.D. and George Matanzima. What I was supposed to do with the 9mm pistol I do not know, and the same applies to the radio. We had drawn some strange looks from onlookers as we entered the lift to take us to the flat roof.

Now, crouched behind a small, metre-high retaining wall that ran along the top of the roof, I looked down at the sea of humanity jammed between the building myself and Pete Mac were on and the houses of parliament where the President would give his address to the nation on this, their independence day.

Our task, ridiculous as it may seem, was to ensure that no harm came to either George or K.D. Matanzima. (If the truth be known, I doubted very much if I would have been able to recognise either of the persons whose lives we were supposed to be protecting, even if I fell over them!) The former was the Prime Minister, the latter the President, of the Transkei, one of the South African Government-created, supposedly independent nations. Unfortunately unrecognized by the rest of the world, such nations became known as the homelands. Financed and controlled by the South African Government, they were doomed to failure, but that again is another story.

How the hell we were supposed to carry out any protection sitting on a roof about 100 metres away was a mystery then, and is still a mystery now. The only times we would see the two men we were supposed to protect would be when they arrived and entered the Parliament and when they left after their speeches. Who was protecting the pair while they were inside the Parliament I had no idea. I knew, or rather I had heard, that both the President and the Prime Minster had personal bodyguards made up from close personal friends-cumhangers-on.

This task was the same as many that followed – unorganised, unprofessional, sloppy and extremely dangerous. Whether the Transkei Police or the Transkei Internal Security knew about myself and Pete Mac, armed and hiding across the road on top of a building overlooking the Parliament, I doubt. So, ever-present and lurking in the back of my mind was a possible encounter with the Transkei Police. However, 'ours is not to reason why, ours is but to do and die'. Obviously, that saying was written by some sarcastic, long-serving and long-suffering soldier.

The hours passed slowly, the heat beat down relentlessly, the sweat ran like a river, the flies attacked continuously, and the dignitaries came and went. We scratched, we stood up, we sat down, we bitched, we complained, and we eventually fell silent.

Staring with eyes that did not see into the heaving crowd below, listening with ears that did not hear for the slightest sound that would alert us to any danger, trying to focus a mind that had been abused and battered by sights, deeds and pressures it was not designed to cope with, we sat each in our own little world, each battling our own demons. Forgotten and lost products of a bygone war, we waited for the charade to end.

FIN